PENGUIN BOOKS

Walking and Eating in Tuscany and Umbria

James Lasdun is the author of two collections of short stories and two books of poetry. His work has appeared in the *New Yorker*, *Paris Review* and *The Times Literary Supplement*. Pia Davis's fiction has appeared in *Pequod* and other publications, and she recently completed a novel. They live in Woodstock, New York.

Short hikes to consider
Radda to ?— 1st part.
p 66 —

Walking and Eating in Tuscany and Umbria

JAMES LASDUN AND PIA DAVIS

PENGUIN BOOKS

PENGUIN BOOKS

Published by the Penguin Group
Penguin Books Ltd, 27 Wrights Lane, London W8 5TZ, England
Penguin Putnam Inc., 375 Hudson Street, New York, New York 10014, USA
Penguin Books Australia Ltd, Ringwood, Victoria, Australia
Penguin Books Canada Ltd, 10 Alcorn Avenue, Toronto, Ontario, Canada M4V 3B2
Penguin Books (NZ) Ltd, Private Bag 102902, NSMC, Auckland, New Zealand

Penguin Books Ltd, Registered Offices: Harmondsworth, Middlesex, England

First published 1997
10 9 8 7 6

Set in 10.5/12.75 pt Monotype Bembo
Typeset by Rowland Phototypesetting Ltd, Bury St Edmunds, Suffolk
Printed in England by Clays Ltd, St Ives plc

Contents

The Walks

TUSCANY

Contents

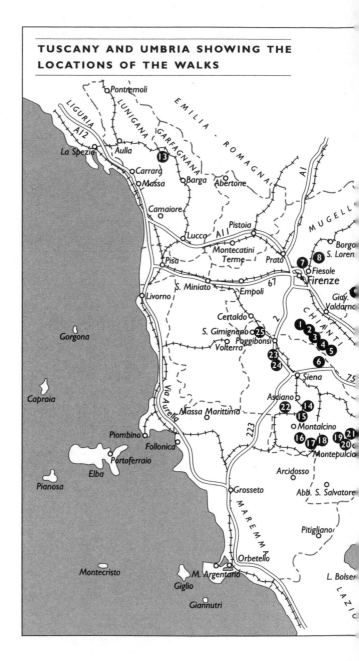

TUSCANY AND UMBRIA SHOWING THE LOCATIONS OF THE WALKS

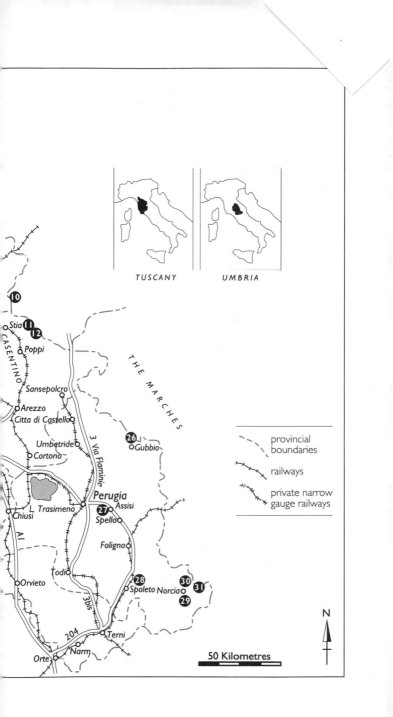

TUSCANY

UMBRIA

10

Stia **11**
12

○ Poppi

CASENTINO

Sansepolcro

○ Arezzo

Citta di Castello ○

THE MARCHES

Umbetride ○ **26**
○ Gubbio

○ Cortona

3 Via Flaminia

Perugia
27 ○ Assisi

L. Trasimeno
Spello ○

Chiusi ○

Foligno ○

Todi ○

28
30
Spoleto Norcia ○ **31**
○ Orvieto
29

3bis

204

Terni

Orte ○ Narni

N

	provincial boundaries
	railways
	private narrow gauge railways

50 Kilometres

Acknowledgments

Our warmest thanks to the following for their help in the research and production of this book: Ron Davis for his photographs, Susan Lasdun for her drawings, Alfina Colarusso, William Lasdun, Lorenzo Pezzatini, Caterina Poccianti, Ladislas Rice and Chris Shaw for their logistical support, and all at Penguin, especially Eleo Gordon, Robert Dreesen and Peter Mayer.

NON-LIABILITY

The authors and the publishers have taken great care to point out potential hazards that may confront walkers in certain places described in this book. Under no circumstances can they accept any liability for any mishap, loss or injury sustained by any person venturing into any of the places described in this book.

Introduction

On a clear day in the spring of 1993, we were looking out over the walls of the hill town of Montepulciano at a panorama of vineyards, olive groves and tiny hamlets that encircled the town and spread as far as the mountains on the horizon. We had been sightseeing in southern Tuscany for the previous week – the monastery at Monte Oliveto, on through the walled town of Buonconvento, Montalcino, the Abbey of Sant'Antimo, the little spa town of Bagno Vignoni, Pius II's unfinished Utopian town of Pienza – and a certain monotony had begun to creep into our daily routine. We both enjoy taking walks, and the countryside flashing by the windows of our buses and trains was beginning to seem at least as beguiling as the towns, museums and churches that were then our destination. Once or twice we had wandered off down promising-looking lanes, but these had a habit of either leading to the town dump or turning into busy roads or else just giving out. How to get out into those hills with their astonishingly beautiful old farmhouses and dovetailing fields and woods? Was it even possible? Was the land all private? Were there rights-of-way, farm tracks, dirt roads you could walk along? And if so, how could you find out where they were?

The answers proved somewhat tantalizing at first. Yes, the entire countryside turns out to be criss-crossed with mule tracks, old cart roads, woodland paths, even remnants of Roman roads and medieval trade routes. Yes, even on private land the paths are generally open to the public. Furthermore a large number of them, particularly in the hillier regions, have been waymarked by the CAI (the Club Alpino Italiano), an indefatigable if also infuriatingly unsystematic organization dedicated to keeping the countryside open to walkers. On the other hand, aside from Curzio Casoli's useful but slim pamphlet about walking in Chianti, there isn't a single detailed walking guide in English. Nor is much of the region covered by walking maps on a useful (i.e., 1:25,000) scale. The Kompass series, allegedly for walkers, is 1:50,000 and only works well for the major mountain routes where the trails are usually well marked. The military maps are the right scale, but they are expensive, hard to get hold of and hopelessly out of date. And even the walking guidebooks written for Italians, though they were invaluable to us in our research, can be unreliable.

What we discovered, however, after a great deal of trial and error, is that there are plenty of walks out there, and that they are often spectacular, combining natural beauty, historical interest, physical exertion and the ubiquitously accessible amenities of good food, wine, coffee and sun. Forest trails connect great Benedictine monasteries of the medieval period; old trade routes call at abbeys and hermitages tucked along wild ridges of the Apennines. Footpaths wind through the high slopes of Umbria to remote farms with pitched-roof haystacks and bundles of kindling still tied together with strips of bark. Vineyards on the cutting edge of modern oenological methods give way to ancient fig orchards and olive groves where nothing appears to have changed since Roman times. From the austere Sibillini mountains to the green hills above Florence where Leonardo conducted his experiments with human flight, from spring-fed pools to Etruscan ruins, splendid walks await the visitor curious to explore the landscape framed by their car or bus window.

When we returned to Italy to research this book, we were able to repeat our entire itinerary of the previous year, from the monastery at Monte Oliveto to Montepulciano, this time *on foot*. Needless to say, the difference in the quality of our experience – not only of the countryside, but also of the towns themselves when we reached them – was immeasurable. It's one thing to hop on a bus, say, from Montalcino to the Abbey of Sant'Antimo; quite another to arrive there on foot, having left Montalcino early in the morning, walked through the Brunello vineyards surrounding it, the rolling farmland beyond with its quiet little villages, and then crossed the wooded ridge overlooking the Starcia valley to find the lovely Romanesque abbey directly below you in its setting of olive groves and pastures full of white heifers. The difference, as every walker knows, is something like that between a spectator and a participant. The abbey, just like almost every human artefact here, stands in a peculiarly delicate relationship with the landscape. Walking brings you into this relationship more intimately and pleasurably than a bus ride can begin to do. It is our hope that the walks in this book will enable you to experience this enormous pleasure as vividly as we did.

This is emphatically a *walking* book, rather than a 'hiking' or 'trekking' book. There are single-day or half-day walks, as well as sequential itineraries that stretch over several days, any part of which can be done on its own. With a few exceptions, we've concentrated on walks that offer maximum scenic beauty while remaining close enough to civilization to ensure a bed for the night and a restaurant meal at the end of the day. Since the satisfactions of walking are, for us at least, closely bound up with those of eating and drinking, we've tried to build as many of the walks as possible around the best restaurants we could find in every region. Bear in mind that neither Tuscany nor Umbria represents the most sophisticated side of Italian cooking. A simple style prevails, based in the old peasant traditions of *cucina povera*: pastas, plain grilled meats, seasonal vegetables, bread-based vegetarian dishes such as *ribollita* and *panzanella*. All of these are, of course, superb when done well, and

on the whole they are. It's the places that offer a more elaborate menu that tend to be the most disappointing (with notable exceptions), and in general we recommend sticking to the simpler establishments. We also list places where you can buy prepared food for picnics, often the best way of sampling local dishes and *prodotti tipici*.

Finally, this is by no means a comprehensive guide. Omissions include not only most of the higher mountain trekking routes, but also whole areas in each province where for one reason or another we were unable to find walks that fit satisfactorily into the parameters of the book. Large parts of Umbria in particular proved especially difficult. Though ravishingly beautiful, the landscape has been poorly served by lax zoning laws that in recent years have allowed development to sprawl unchecked. All around Perugia and Assisi small ugly houses dot the countryside as though sprinkled from a giant salt-cellar, often as far as the eye can see. It isn't particularly conducive to walking. That said, much still remains unspoiled, not just around Gubbio and the area between Spoleto and the Sibillini mountains in the south-east, where we found most of our Umbrian walks, but also around Todi and Orvieto, and our failure to come up with walks near these stunning towns remains a source of real regret. Perhaps in a future edition . . .

Climate and When to Go

In our own view it is almost always better to be in Italy, whatever the time of year, than not to be there. As far as walking goes, much depends on the kind of weather in which you most enjoy doing it.

Because of the relatively small geographical area we're dealing with, the main variation of climate within the region is less a question of north to south than of high to low.

The lowland hikes which comprise the bulk of the book can be done year round. You might occasionally encounter snow during the winter, but there is no serious snow under 1000 metres. The higher Apennine trails can be walked from May to October. But in either case, we would recommend avoiding the hottest weeks of summer. The climate during July and August is hot and dry. If you do your walking early in the day, you should be fine. Alternatively, you can choose areas that are cooler: near to Florence you have Vallombrosa or, for a longer walk, the routes in the Casentino section of the book. Further afield, to the south the Sibillini is a possible option for summer walking, and to the north the Garfagnana offers a cool summer respite.

Spring is perhaps the best time of year all round, especially for the gentler Tuscany walks: mid-April until late May (or late May to June for the higher-altitude walks, those in south-east Umbria and the Casentino, for example) is best for orchids, wild flowers and comfortable walking weather. But September is also a fine time of year, and later in the autumn you can enjoy the *vendemmia*, the grape harvest.

It seldom rains day after day, and you can often wait out a shower, either in bed or at a café. If it looks like you're in for a day of it, there are always the churches and museums; other than the 'Casentino Excursion' and the walks in south-east Umbria, none of our itineraries is so far removed that you couldn't reach a cultural centre, even if only for a day visit.

What to Take and What to Wear

One of the reasons why walking is so easily incorporated into any kind of trip is that you don't need to bring a lot of special equipment. Most of what you need for walking you would probably bring with you anyway, with the possible exception of footwear.

A pair of sturdy and comfortable walking shoes is the most important item you can have for successful walking, wherever you are. This kind of shoe is becoming increasingly popular and makes a good choice for city sightseeing too. While some of the walks (most of the lowland routes) can be done with ordinary shoes – sneakers or whatever – a good, lightweight boot is always preferable, if for no other reason than the extra ankle support it provides. The stronger soles on these shoes are also an asset, providing more shock absorption and better grip than the soles on street shoes. Look for a boot that seems robust, flexible and, above all, comfortable. There seems to be an inherent dilemma in the trade-off between waterproofing and the ability of the shoe to 'breathe'. We have always managed with non-waterproof boots. (True, our feet have had a few soakings, but not too many, and the boots usually dry out overnight.) If you are already a walker, you probably have such a pair of boots, and whatever you use at home for woodland walking is fine for any of the walks in this book. But if you need to buy, there are many models available at any sporting goods store. Just make sure they're comfortable, *before* you leave on your trip.

A single pair of 'hiking' socks is usually adequate, though you might want to carry an extra pair in case you get a soaking at some point. The socks that 'wick' perspiration away from your feet seem to work well. Again, ask the salesperson in a good sports store for advice; don't be surprised if the recommended socks – even for summer walking – are fairly thick. If possible, give them a few trial runs with your boots before you leave on your trip.

Any trousers that permit a wide range of movement are fine. Jeans, cotton Chinos, anything along those lines. In summer you may be more comfortable in shorts, even if that means the occasional run-in with scratchy undergrowth. A cotton T-shirt, and a light sweater or long-sleeved shirt in case of chill or prolonged exposure to sun are also essential. In cold weather, several layers are more effective than one heavy garment. Naturally you would also want gloves and hat if it's cold, and perhaps some thermal underwear.

A lightweight, hooded windcheater or anorak is essential for high-altitude walking. It doesn't have to be waterproof, although the light Gore-Tex models do have that advantage.

A small backpack, or day pack, is also necessary, to carry your water bottle (filled), a pair of sunglasses, a hat, a multi-use pocket knife or Swiss Army knife (you may want to ensure that your model has a corkscrew), perhaps a small flashlight, and, depending on the weather, a lightweight windcheater or an umbrella. Two other non-essential but useful items are a miniature pocket dictionary and a compass (*bussola* in Italian). NEVER set out without water and a hat. Sunscreen and lip protection can also be useful in the summer. The well-prepared walker will carry Band-aids or 'moleskin' (available at sport stores and most pharmacies) for blisters, a small roll of toilet paper, and, depending on your level of concern about the matter, a snake-bite kit, or *succhia veleno*, for viper bites.

Packing Suggestions for Overnight Walks

Everything you need for a walk of more than one day can fit easily into your day pack. (For suggestions for leaving your main luggage behind, see the 'How to Use This Book' section.)

You'll want to carry the least weight possible; one way to do this is to make clothes serve dual functions if you can. So, for example, the clean T-shirt you change into on your arrival after your first day's walk becomes your walking T-shirt on the second day. The same with underwear. Your walking trousers or shorts remain the same every day (as can your socks), but you'll need something to change into when the day is done, either a clean pair of trousers or a skirt. Many silk skirts or pants have the advantage of being both lightweight and virtually crease-proof, so you may want to consider something along those lines.

Sandals can also be lightweight. We each shopped for the lightest pair of cheap sandals we could find, knowing we would only be wearing them for the limited walking we would do in the evening.

Your lightweight windcheater or sweater completes the evening-wear picture, though if it is cold, you may need to add something warmer – silk thermal underwear, for example.

The only other things you need to pack are your minimum toiletry requirements – do you really need any more than a toothbrush, toothpaste and comb? Hotels always provide soap, and very often shampoo and other amenities as well; on the other hand, you may be staying in other types of accommodation, so try to gauge accordingly – a book in case it rains, and your passport; in Italy you will be asked for your passport every time you check into a hotel.

Transport

With a couple of minor exceptions, which are duly noted in the text, all the walks in this book are accessible without a car. Public transport in Italy is very good and you should have little trouble getting around. The larger cities have maps and/or brochures detailing the railway and bus systems, usually available in English. The best place to find these is at the local tourist office or information bureau. The local tourist office is a very useful resource; you will nearly always find a person who speaks English there, and they will look up schedules, make calls to bus or train stations for you, etc. (Keep in mind that tourist offices, like most other places of commerce, close down from midday to late afternoon.)

Many of the locations at which our walks begin or end are small towns, and bus services are infrequent (and on Sundays usually non-existent), so it pays to check the schedule before the day you're planning to go, as you cannot assume there will be a bus ready to go exactly when you are. Occasionally we have given schedules in the text: this is meant only to give some idea of frequency. Actual schedules change all the time, so ALWAYS check the current schedule. Once you know when a bus departs, make sure to arrive a little early, because the buses often do – and they don't wait around. And in the smallest places there may be no other bus that day.

Finally, always check the return schedule for your trip before you leave, unless you are planning to hitchhike back.

On that subject, if you do miss the bus, you can always hitch, but you may have to wait quite a while for someone to stop. Chances are that when the time comes, you're going to be on a little-travelled road; while this limits the traffic, it does seem to incline those few drivers more in your favour. Hitching is not the ideal way to travel, but in a pinch it may be your best option.

Using the Bus System

The bus system in this part of Italy is very efficient; here are a few particulars you should know ahead of time.

- Schedules are given in terms of:
  giornaliero – every day
  feriale – workdays (includes Saturday, unless it says *escluso sabato*)
  festivo – Sundays and holidays
- Tickets (*biglietti*) are, of course, sold at bus stations. But they are also sold at bars or 'Sale e Tabacchi', the tobacconist/newsagent shops displaying the T sign outside. (Bear in mind that these shops, like most other businesses, may close for the midday break.)
- Tickets are not sold on the bus. You buy your ticket ahead of time, and when you get on the bus you'll find a little machine at the front or back of it into which you insert your ticket to be stamped. That's it.
- If you are out of town, you can catch a bus along the road wherever there is a '*fermata*' or '*fermata a richiesta*' (request stop) sign. Sometimes the sign will just say 'SITA', or whatever the name of the bus company servicing the route is. Often the schedule for the route

is posted at these signs. If you don't have a ticket, you can purchase your ticket at the end of the ride – just nip into the bar or *tabacchi* where the bus stops, buy your ticket, and then return to the bus to have it stamped.

Using the Trains

Trains are a useful and pleasant option between the larger hubs. There isn't anything particular that we can tell you about them; they are like trains in most other European countries.

There is a schedule available at news-stands, a thickish orange pamphlet called the *Pozzorario*. If you plan on doing a lot of train travel, this is a very useful booklet to have. Make sure you get the current one (they come out every June and October) and the one which covers this region ('Nord e Centro Italia').

Driving

If you've got a car, you're also going to have a map and should have no trouble getting to any of the starting-points for the walks.

If you're doing a walk which begins in one place and ends in another – the case with many of these walks – then you must either bus back to your car at the end or park your car at the end and bus to the beginning.

Places to Stay

While we have listed at least one place to stay in each of our destination towns, our suggestions are by no means exhaustive, and in most places there are several other choices. You can look in a general guidebook for other recommendations, or ask in the tourist office. If you like to live dangerously, you can wait until you arrive somewhere, and then ask around: '*Dov'è l'albergo più vicino?*' ('Where's the nearest hotel?') This method has all the advantages that attach to spontaneity. The down side is that you may find yourself having to hitchhike to a bigger town.

In addition to the usual hotel or *pensione*, there are two other interesting options that may appeal to you.

Affittacamere are rooms for rent in private homes. This is usually a less expensive alternative to a hotel or *pensione*. It is also sometimes the *only* option – if, for example, the single hotel in town is full. Tourist offices have lists of people letting rooms on this basis. Or, you can ask around: '*C'è qualcuno che affitta camere?*' ('Is there anyone who lets rooms?').

Agriturismo indicates private accommodation in the countryside, in anything from villas to extremely basic rooms in rustic farmhouses; the accommodation may come in the form of a room, a suite or an apartment. Sometimes the property is a working farm, complete with livestock, sometimes a wine estate set in the midst of acres of vineyards and olive groves. There may be a

pool, a tennis court or horseback excursions available. You may (especially in the case of apartments) get a kitchen, or you may – and this is the usual format – get to eat with the family and any other guests. When you take into account the Italian way with food (and we found that a lot of the best cooking is done at home), the fresh, home-grown produce, splendid rural setting, and the fact that even the smallest of farms seems to cultivate a bit of vineyard and that the product of this vineyard ends up in seemingly unlimited quantities on your dinner table, you begin to form a picture of what this experience can be like.

And yet, *agriturismo* seems to be some kind of secret. In 1993 about seven million people chose to stay in an *agriturismo* lodging, but only 3 per cent of these were non-Italians. It's true that in most of these places the proprietors speak little, if any, English. But the food, the very relaxed and friendly atmosphere, and usually the location, can easily make up for this. We had more fun staying in *agriturismo* accommodation than anywhere else.

Many of the more expensive establishments offer self-contained accommodation by the week (weeks often running eccentrically, for example Wednesday to Wednesday); but sometimes even these places will rent you a room for a single night. Tourist offices have lists of many of the *agriturismo* lodgings in the area, and there are also agencies which print a catalogue (in Italian, but there are pictures) every year. If you're planning ahead, request a catalogue from one of the agencies, or contact either the local tourist office or the regional tourist office (e.g., Florence, Siena, etc.), or from the regional *agriturismo* offices listed below. (We never booked more than a day ahead, because it was logistically impossible for us to do so. This only caused us a problem once, but we may have been lucky.)

Catalogues are available from:

TUSCANY

Terranostra Regionale
c/o Coldiretti
Via dei Magazzini, 2
50122 Firenze
Tel. 055-280539; fax
055-2360288

UMBRIA

Terranostra Umbria
Via Campo di Marte, 10
06124 Perugia
Tel. 075-5009559/
5007196; fax
075-5092032

or
Via Montanini, 63
53100 Siena
Tel. 0577-46006

Agriturist Regionale
Piazza San Firenze, 3
50122 Firenze
Tel. 055-287838; fax
055-2302285
or
Via della Sapienza, 39
53100 Siena
Tel. 0577-46194

Agriturist Umbria
c/o Federumbria
　Agricoltori
Via Savonarola, 38
06121 Perugia
Tel. 075-32028/36665;
fax 075-32028

Turismo Verde
　Regionale
c/o Confcoltivatori
Viale Lavagnini, 4
50129 Firenze
Tel. 055-489760
or
Via dei Termini, 6
53100 Siena
Tel. 0577-47157

Turismo Verde Umbria
Via Campo di Marte,
　14/I
06124 Perugia
Tel. 075-5002953; fax
075-5002956

The regional tourist office of Umbria publishes a free brochure *Agriturismo Umbria Ospitalità* that lists many establishments in the region. You can contact them at:

Regione dell'Umbria – Ufficio Promozione Turistica
Corso Vannucci, 30
06100 Perugia
Tel. 075-5041; fax 075-5042483

There are also at least two agencies in the US who have *agriturismo* listings, but these will be more expensive:

Barclay International
Tel. 800/845-6636 or
212/832-3777; fax 212/
753-1139

Villas International
Tel. 800/221-2260 or
415/281-0910; fax 415/
281-0919

Camping is another possibility. As we have never camped in Italy ourselves, we can't offer much advice on the subject. You will usually find campsites near the larger cities and in the major tourist areas. During the peak season, in popular places, these campsites are generally quite crowded, and without a reservation you may find it difficult to get a spot. If you're prepared for it, you can usually pitch a tent in some out-of-the-way spot, as long as it's not in a National or Regional Park, where camping is forbidden. The parks have *rifugi*, or mountain huts, where you can stay overnight.

Getting Information from Tourist Offices

Tourist offices are great sources of local information, including lists of places to stay. Many tourist offices print glossy brochures listing everything from *affittacamere* to luxury hotels, and also including *agriturismo* accommodation.

Note that the main tourist office of a region will have information covering the whole region, and most of the smaller towns in that region will have their own local tourist office as well.

It is essential to know, when perusing the lists of places to stay, that the abbreviation 'loc.' (*località*) before an address indicates that the establishment in question is situated somewhere outside the centre of whatever town it's listed under. The trick then is to find out *where* the location indicated actually is, as it may be at some distance. If you cannot find it on your map ask at the tourist office.

Towns that are too small to have their own tourist office often have a *pro loco*, a village association, at which you can ask about renting rooms.

For information before you leave on your trip, you may want to try the Italian State Tourist Board. They publish a useful pamphlet called 'Italia: Travellers Handbook'.

630 Fifth Avenue, 1565
Rockefeller Center
New York, NY 10111
Tel. (212)245-4822

500 N. Michigan Ave.
Chicago, IL 60611
Tel. (312)644-0990

360 Post Street
San Francisco,
CA 94108
Tel. (415)392-6206

1, pl. Ville Marie, 1914
Montreal, Quebec H3B 3M9
Tel. (514)866-7667

1 Princes Street
London W1R 8AY
Tel. 0171-408 1254

Miscellaneous

CAI

The Club Alpino Italiano, CAI, is a large, state-subsidized organization with branches (*sezioni*) in every city and in most towns of any size. Along with public services such as mountain and cave rescue, avalanche forecasts and the training of professional guides, they also administer over 500 mountain huts, and mark and maintain thousands of miles of paths all over the country. The CAI has been almost everywhere, and their prodigious efforts have made their red/white/red paint blaze a familiar sight to walkers.

Local tourist offices usually have current CAI information, at the very least the address and telephone number of the local chapter. Everyone we met who was connected with the CAI was extremely helpful and friendly. Most sections run hikes on the weekends, which is always an option if you're up for this kind of adventure. While most CAI members don't speak English, if you're doing a lot of walking in a region, a visit to the local headquarters may still prove useful – or at the very least, interesting.

One thing about the CAI, however, is that while they are largely responsible for the existence of marked trails in the region covered by this book, the marking can be a bit hit or miss, and their marks may sometimes have been obliterated. So don't feel the ship is going down if we refer in our directions to a CAI waymark which you can't find.

CAI National Headquarters
Via Ugo Foscolo 3
Milano
Tel. 02-864380

Electricity

Italy runs on 220 volts, so Americans will need to adapt any electrical gadgets (like contact-lens heaters, electrical shavers or battery rechargers. Radio Shack is a source, as are some department stores. (We bought adaptor plugs at the watch repair department of Macy's.) Mail ordering from The Civilized Traveller is another option. When buying a transformer, be sure to specify that you're going to Italy. Britain like Italy, runs on 220 volts, but has a different shaped plug, so an adaptor plug will be necessary. It's a lot easier and a lot cheaper to get this end of the operation together before you leave.

The Civilized Traveller
Mail Order
54 W 21st Street, Suite 505
New York, NY 10010
Tel. 800-604-5556; fax 212-229-0572

Mail

Your mail can be addressed to the town where you'll be picking it up, with the words *fermo posta*. You'll need to show your passport when you go to the post office to claim any mail sent to you in this way.

Stamps are for sale at post offices and from any Sale e Tabacchi shop (with the T sign outside).

Telephones

Public telephones take coins or phonecards, for sale at post offices, many train stations and airports, and at Sale e Tabacchi shops. Stock up with the largest denomination cards you can get, and ask for the glossy little card that Telecom Italia (the Italian phone company) puts out explaining the long-distance system.

As well as being the most convenient way of making calls within Italy, phonecards are also the cheapest way to call home. To use your credit card, dial 170 and you'll get an English-speaking operator. ATT has a much-advertised service called 'USA Direct', and while easy, it's also expensive: they charge about $4.00 for the first minute.

When dialling numbers within Italy, you don't dial the area code if it's the same as the one you're in.

Holidays and Closings

Everything closes down from around noon or 1 p.m. until 3 or 4. If you're planning to pick up lunch on your way, make sure you do it before then. Otherwise you'll have to be in a town large enough to have a restaurant: these stay open through lunchtime, but shops don't.

Every restaurant has by law to be closed on one day of the week, its *giorno di riposo*, which will usually be posted in the window of the restaurant.

Everything will be shut on:

1 January
Easter Sunday and Monday
25 April, Liberation Day
1 May, Labour Day
15 August, Assumption Day
1 November, All Saints' Day

8 December, Feast of the Immaculate Conception
25 and 26 December, Christmas

Emergencies

Dialling 113 on the telephone will summon police or ambulance.

For serious health problems US citizens should contact the US Embassy. British nationals should take their E.111, which enables them to use the Italian national health service.

In Florence we found the 'Tourist Medical Service' useful. They are a small practice, and speak English.

Tourist Medical Service
Via Lorenzo il Magnifico, 59
Tel. 055–475411

Laundry

If the idea of becoming a millionaire appeals to you, you may want to consider opening a chain of laundrettes while you're in Italy – if we haven't already done it. In all of the area covered by this book, there is one laundrette, in Florence.

Of course, you can always have your laundry done by a hotel or inn, but it's extremely expensive, and may take more than one day; so check their price and their time frame before parting with your dirty clothes.

Another option in the bigger towns is a *lavanderia*, where you drop off your clothes in the morning and pick them up at the end of the day. Again, this is expensive, but not as expensive as having the hotel do it.

By the way, remember not to have any Gore–Tex items dry-cleaned.

Private Property

Many of our walks pass through *proprietà privata*. Though you will see signs to this effect posted all over, they seem to be directed more towards cars than walkers. Many CAI routes go through private property, and we had no problems on any of our routes. Just remember that it *is* someone's property, and be respectful, as you would want other people to be when passing through *your* property.

Dogs

The Italian benevolence towards children does not apparently extend to dogs, and the neglected, lonely, forsaken lives most of them lead was a source of repeated despair to at least one of the authors. We heard much hysterical – often frightening – barking, but we never had any problems. The usual cause of their hysteria is that they are tied up, fenced in or even caged; your – perhaps distant – passing is probably the most exciting thing that's happened to them all year. You'd be hysterical too.

If you do meet an aggressive, untethered dog, the best thing to do is walk away. If in doubt, carry a large stick (or steak).

Wine

While real connoisseurship continues, unfortunately, to elude us, we still appreciate a good bottle when it comes our way, and many did in the course of writing this book. We seldom spent much on wine, but we drank well. Occasionally we have recommended a wine in the text, and more occasionally still have recommended avoiding one. The best tip we can give is that if you're buying wine, it's appoximately 50 per cent cheaper to buy it directly from the *fattoria* (estate), than from an *enoteca* (wine shop), though of course if you've got to carry it on your back, this may not be practical.

Updating

We have done our best to make this guide as accurate as possible. But things change: dirt tracks become paved roads, landmark oaks are axed, restaurants slide downhill or out of business. We would greatly appreciate any corrections or comments you may have. Please write to us care of Penguin Books, at 375 Hudson Street, New York, New York 10014 or 27 Wrights Lane, London W8 5TZ. Or e-mail us directly at 102642.16@compu-serve.com.

How to Use This Book

The region covered by the book is not terribly large, and none of the walks is inaccessible from any city within this region. With the exception of 'A Walk in the Garfagnana' (p. 181), all the walks in the Tuscany section of the book are easily accessible from Florence and Siena; the Umbria walks lie further afield. With a couple of exceptions (duly noted) any of the walks within a chapter can be done in a day, including any travel time, from the centre of that region.

The Chianti region which leads off the book lies between Florence and Siena, and is more or less equally convenient from either. The walks in the chapters 'Around Florence' and 'The Casentino' are centred on Florence, while those in 'West of Siena' and 'South Tuscany' are centred on Siena. But as Florence and Siena are themselves only about an hour's bus ride apart, a walk's being 'centred' on one of the cities hardly renders it unfeasible from the other.

The walks that assume a Florence or Siena base do not actually begin inside the city, but require a bus or train ride to reach the trail head. The reason for this is that the outskirts of those cities do not make for pleasant walking. The time the bus or train ride takes is listed in the 'Logistics' section of each walk, and is usually minimal, so that you can complete an outing in a single day or less.

★

The book is intended to be flexible enough to serve for day or half-day walks, and for longer walks of two or more days. To arrange a shorter walk, either take one of the single-day walks, or do one stage of the longer, 'sequential' walks.

All of the sequential walks can be adapted to fit your time frame. That is, you could do one, two, three or four days of a five-day walk. There are one or two exceptions (cases in which there is no public transport to the overnight locale), and these are duly noted in their place.

The 'Logistics' section of each walk lists various bits of practical information. Hotel and restaurant recommendations in the 'Logistics' will generally apply to the *destination* of the walk. Thus, in the sequential walks, the information pertaining to the town from which any day's walk *begins* will be found in the 'Logistics' section of the previous day's walk.

If you opt for a walk of more than one day, you won't want to carry the bulk of your luggage (see 'What to Take and What to Wear' above for suggestions on what to bring on these extended walks). What we usually did was leave our suitcases behind at the hotel where we'd stayed the night before leaving on the walk. The hotel-keepers were always very accommodating, storing our bags behind the desk or in a closet somewhere, free of charge. At the end of the walk – however many days it was – we'd bus back to the hotel, often staying that night there: in this case the hotel became the 'base' to which we returned.

Another option would be to take your suitcases to the hotel at which you plan to end your walk, booking yourself in for that future night, and asking them to hold your bags until you arrive.

Yet another alternative is to leave your suitcases in the left luggage (*Deposito bagagli*) of a railway station, where for a small fee your bags can be securely stored. The stations in larger towns have these, and in smaller stations the *capo di stazione*, or stationmaster, may agree to perform the same service.

Distances

1 kilometre = 0.621 miles
1 mile = 1.609 kilometres

That's official, and useful to know when you're reading a map. (As a rough and ready guide, 5 miles is more or less equal to 8 km.) The grid squares on the maps each represent a square kilometre.

Unofficially, a yard is much the same as a metre. At least to us it is, and in keeping with that model of inexactitude, you must take all our distances with more than a grain of salt. We were definitely not out there with a measuring rod.

To walk a kilometre generally took us between 10 and 20 minutes, depending on whether that kilometre was over particularly steep or otherwise difficult ground, and on how energetic we happened to be feeling at the time. On fairly flat, easy-going terrain, at a fairly easy pace, you might estimate about 15 minutes to walk a kilometre. The walk times given at the beginning of each walk were based on the non-stop walking time it took us to complete the walk, but you will need to adjust these times to reflect your own speed of walking, and add in time for stops.

While on the map a kilometre is a kilometre, bear in mind that a kilometre on a very steep incline is going to feel a lot different from a kilometre over flat ground.

One last note on our directions technique: when the directions say 'T-junction', this junction will not necessarily be an exact T, but it will be in the same family.

Maps and Guidebooks

All the best hiking maps of the region are based on the old 1:25,000 Italian military maps produced by the Istituto Geografico Militare (IGM). The Kompass series of maps is generally more up-to-date, but at 1:50,000 they are not nearly as detailed.

For some of the areas covered by our book there are no hiking maps, but the whole of Italy is covered by the

IGM. One problem with the IGM maps is that they are hopelessly out of date and many things have changed since they were drawn up. For us, the worst thing about this was that once-open land had been fenced off by the time we arrived, necessitating a rethink of the entire walk. But with rare exceptions, the IGM maps are very accurate topographically.

Another problem is in locating these maps. They are all available at IGM headquarters (at the address given below). There are also specialist travel bookshops in Florence that carry a selection of them, and there will be at least one bookshop in all the larger towns that will carry a selection, but usually just for the surrounding area – if that. The other source for these maps is the town *comune*, or town council office, which will always have the map covering the immediate vicinity, and will usually xerox it for you if you ask them to (maps are located in the 'Ufficio Tecnico' of the *comune* building).

One last word on the IGM maps: they don't come cheap: L. 10,000 each.

If there's a hiking map that covers the area you're going to be walking in, we recommend your buying it (or copying it as above). Maps are available in bookstores, sometimes at news-stands in train or bus stations, and in various other shops, restaurants or hotels you come across when you're walking. Sometimes the local tourist office will have maps or other information on walking, hiking or, as it is often called in Italy, trekking. There is almost always someone who speaks English in a tourist office, and they can usually tell you where to get local maps or guidebooks.

Istituto Geografico Militare (IGM)
Via di Novoli, 93
Firenze
Tel. 055-27751

Specialized bookshops in Florence:

Libreria il Viaggio   Libreria Stella Alpina
Via Ghibellina 117r   Via Corridoni 14b/r
Tel. 055-240489   Tel. 055-411688

Libreria Esercizio
   Promozione Turismo
Via Condotta 42r
Tel. 055-294551

Finally, a note about our own maps. General in nature, these maps are provided as a back-up to the much more detailed written instructions. As mentioned above, it is always best to have a detailed map of the area, if one is available.

We have often marked turnoffs and other seductive deviations from the correct route, as little 'tabs' off the main route, indicated by a series of dots that lead nowhere. But we haven't done this for every deviation or potential wrong turn that presents itself, nor is the inclusion of these 'tabs' strictly consistent between the maps and the written directions. Therefore, use them only as a general guideline.

Getting Lost

Almost certainly there will come a time (perhaps many times) when – though you are quite sure you've followed the directions to the letter – the map, the directions and the landmarks around you cease to corroborate each other. Outlook is everything in these situations.

With perhaps one exception (the Sibillini walk), being lost is unlikely to pose any real danger, so it's pretty much up to you how the experience affects you. Of course, it's easy to be philosophical now, from the comfort of a padded desk chair in a temperate, sunny room, but the fact is that there were many, many times when we cursed not just the writer of any particular guidebook we were using, but *all* guidebook writers. Naturally, we assume that our directions are going to be incalculably superior to any that we ourselves used. But whether we are terribly mistaken in that assumption, or whether directions written by someone else are by nature difficult to interpret, or whether you are waylaid by changing landmarks (dirt roads are paved, new roads may appear that weren't there before, signs or other markers may be taken down — CAI signs especially tend to come and go a bit), it is bound to happen to you. And when it does, you will probably be better off if you encounter the situation with a spirit of adventure, and the sense that it's really not such a terrible thing to be lost occasionally.

Many of our walks are through farmland or other 'civilized' areas, and the maps give the names of some of the farmhouses, names that have been in place for decades. If you find someone, you can ask them to identify the nearby farmhouses, or to show you where a farmhouse you've located on your map is actually situated. Or you can try showing them your map and asking them to locate your current position on it.

Nitty Gritty

- Tap water and the water at public drinking fountains is OK to drink.
- Prices: most of the hotels and restaurants we list are in the low-to-moderate range, which is to say that for a hotel room (in 1997) you might expect to pay on the average L. 70,000–90,000 per night, with exceptions on either end frequently encountered. *Affittacamere* rooms are usually around L. 50,000–60,000. The average cost of a dinner for two people with either a bottle or a carafe of good (but not expensive) wine

will probably be between L. 45,000 and L. 65,000, again with plenty of exceptions either side. Significant exceptions will be noted where they appear.

- We haven't rated the walks for difficulty, because other than the Sibillini walk, none of them are particularly difficult. The difference in difficulty is essentially one of length: a three-hour walk is 'easier' than a six-hour walk.

- When there are other tracks branching off the route you've been following, assume if they are smaller tracks than the one you're on that you don't take them. Usually we haven't mentioned them individually, though occasionally we have given the general advice 'ignore deviations'.

- It would sometimes be very difficult, if not impossible, to do the walks in reverse, and attempting to do so could well be an exercise in frustration.

And Finally . . .

Our opinions and recommendations are not coloured by bribery. Other than a piece of cake and a coffee, which it later transpired had been graciously offered rather than sold, we did not get anything for free while we were researching this book. Only occasionally did any of our hosts even know we were writing a book; thus we expect that any other decent, courteous travellers will receive the same treatment at the establishments listed as we ourselves did.

Abbreviations

ATW   at time of writing (i.e., be aware that things may
         have changed since)
CAI   Club Alpino Italiano (see p. 22 above for address)
IGM   Istituto Geografico Militare
km   kilometre(s)
m   metre(s)

The Walks

TUSCANY

CHIANTI

This is the heart of Tuscany, bounded north and south by Florence and Siena; east and west by the rivers Staggia and Elsa. With its dense concentration of vineyards, olive groves, old farmhouses, kitchen gardens, orchards, hilltop cypresses, terraced slopes and wooded valleys, it remains the definitive embodiment of the idea of the 'Tuscan landscape'.

Partly because of its popularity with wealthy ex-patriots (especially British ones), recent travel books have tended to take a somewhat catty tone in describing the region, dwelling on its gentrification, its adoption as the honorary British county of 'Chiantishire', rather than its spectacular beauty: a peculiarly harmonious blend of the natural and the man-made that Fernand Braudel justifiably described as 'the most moving countryside that exists'.

Recent developments have certainly had an impact, but this has never been a static landscape; indeed its charm lies precisely in its continuous adaptation to and absorption of human history. Every age has left its mark. Castles and fortified hamlets survive from the medieval period, when much of the area was essentially a theatre of war. With the discovery of the Americas a profusion of new crops (tomatoes, green beans, peppers, corn, numerous fruits and squashes) made their way across the Atlantic, radically altering European agricultural

practices. Chianti is a warm, fertile, but hilly region, and every nook and cranny of land is scrupulously cultivated with whatever crop its microclimate best suits, and this is reflected in a pleasantly rich irregularity in the textures of the landscape. In the eighteenth century, the *mezza-drile*, or sharecropping, system was consolidated, whereby the *contadini* (peasants) were given some rights over the land they cultivated in return for a fixed share of the fruits of their labour. One of the conditions for leasing a farm was that the *contadini* family would build a new terrace every year. Matthew Spender describes the process in his fascinating account of Tuscan life, *Within Tuscany*:

The terraces would be made parallel to the horizon, following the contours of the hills, starting at the bottom of a hillside, removing the forest and scrub oaks and pulling the earth down to the side of the new wall, which was made from the stones found right there in the ground. Vertical gullies at regular intervals ensured that the run-off would not cause erosion of the precious earth. It could take a decade to rebuild a hillside from the bottom to the top.

A great many of these dry-stone terraces still stand today, adding to the overall hand-hewn, sculptural quality of the landscape.

It was in the mid nineteenth century, with the pioneering viticultural work of Baron Bettino Ricasoli (who succeeded Cavour as leader of a newly united Italy), that Chianti acquired its modern identity as a wine region. At the family castle of Brolio, Ricasoli developed the process of double fermentation – the second time with dried grapes – known as *governo*, and still used today. The baron also established the proportions of Sangiovese, Canaiolo Nero and Malvasia grapes that came to be adopted (with minor variations), by the whole Chianti region. Naturally enough the immense popularity of these wines persuaded landowners to turn increasing amounts of their property into vineyards. This certainly hasn't helped preserve the region from the general drift towards monoculture afflicting all farming regions today, but it's worth remembering that of the 70,000 hectares of Chianti Classico territory only 6500 are dedicated to the exclusive cultivation of vines.

The sharecropping system survived until the 1960s,

when it was dismantled by a series of new statutes, socialist in intent, if not altogether in their effect. The *contadini*, whose labour had supplied the landlords' *fattorie* (farms) with produce to sell, as well as feeding their own families, became salaried agricultural workers. Wages could not compete with those of factories in the nearby towns and the result was a rapid, large-scale exodus from the countryside. On almost all of the walks in this book you'll see the results of this, in the form of abandoned farmhouses – picturesque, forlorn; some of them still more or less intact, with the ground floor where the animals were kept (a kind of live heating system for the rest of the house) still bedded with straw from their last occupants; others in ruins, overrun with the brambles that mark the first stage in the forest's repossession of its original domain.

'Gentrification' more often than not has simply meant converting these otherwise doomed buildings into private homes, obviously a less appealing option than having them continue as working farms, but better than complete annihilation. More to the point, an emerging generation of younger wine growers has already begun reviving traditional methods of organic cultivation and low-tech production, with encouraging results. Depending on their success it may be that the industrial-scale agriculture of big landowning consortiums will one day become a thing of the past.

'It is queer that a country so perfectly cultivated as Tuscany, where half the produce of five acres of land will have to support ten human mouths, still has so much room for the wild flowers . . .' D. H. Lawrence's observation in the 1920s still holds good for much of Chianti today. For all the indelicacy of mechanized farming, the quantity and variety of wild flowers blooming along the margins and ditches, among the crops themselves, in woods and orchards, down the verges of roads and old mule tracks, is fantastic, and forms one of the many great delights of walking in this area. The iris, once the symbol of Florentine freedom, no longer grows wild, but there are poppies, asphodels, cyclamens, orchids, campanulas, wild culinary herbs and dog-roses in abundance. Giant thistles – more artichoke than thistle – open up great purple brushes in summer, and the prolific yellow broom flowers brilliantly all over the landscape from May to August, filling the air with a pleasant soapy fragrance. The naturalist Gary Paul Nabhan lists filaree, gypsywort, comfrey, timothy, chicory, butter-and-eggs, cheese-weed, hawkbit, foxtail, sow thistle, lambs' quarters, hogweed, mustards, false basils, borages and sages, among the commoner roadside weeds and herbs. On almost any of these walks you're likely to find your socks covered with a mass of burrs, seeds and pollen.

Mixed oaks, hornbeam and dwarf maples (survivors of the old *vite marittita* system, in which they were used to support the vines) make up most of the woods and coppices. Higher up on the northern slopes grow chestnut groves and white firs (brought into the region by the Vallombrosan monks when they established their abbey at Badia a Coltibuono in the twelfth century). A more Mediterranean mixture – cypress, juniper, arbutus – prevails on the southern slopes.

As for the birds and beasts, watch for the splendid crested hoopoe, fairly common around here, as are the porcupine and the wild boar. The porcupine is mainly nocturnal, so you are unlikely to see the creature itself, but it has a habit of shedding its needle-sharp black and white spines along woodland paths, providing one of the more elegant souvenirs of these walks. Boars too, while numerous, are elusive, though you may well spot their hoof prints, or the mud-slides they revel in, or, if you're lucky, the occasional dropped tusk. The indigenous

Tuscan variety has been all but ousted by a larger, more fertile breed imported from Hungary after the war. Given that it enjoys nothing better than uprooting a vineyard, its ubiquitousness tends to be appreciated more by restaurateurs than local farmers.

The Walks

These are some of the most enjoyable and easily managed of the walks in this book. Almost all of them combine stunning landscape with historical, cultural, oenological and gastronomical points of interest. Most of them are rugged without being excessively strenuous, and all of them score high in terms of *ambiente* – the general feel and atmosphere.

The three-day 'Chianti Excursion' takes in some of the most interesting country in Chianti, including the wine towns of Greve and Radda, the park of San Michele (the highest point in Chianti), the ancient castle of Volpaia and the lovely little hamlet of San Sano. You can follow this itinerary as it's laid out, or tailor it: other possibilities for this route could include incorporating the Lamole ring walk, or beginning the itinerary in Gaiole. For example, you could walk to San Michele from Lamole rather than from Greve (Lamole is quite a bit closer to San Michele than Greve is). Or, you could walk from Greve to San Michele, and then do the San Michele to Lamole portion of the Lamole ring walk, thereby ending in Lamole and bussing back to Florence from there. Or, you could walk from Lamole to Greve via San Michele. You could start from the town of Gaiole, doing the Gaiole to Radda walk, and then pick up the Radda to San Sano portion of the 'Chianti Excursion'.

All but one of the eight itineraries in this chapter can be done as a single-day walk with bus connections back to Siena and, in most cases, Florence (the exception is the San Michele–Radda walk, since there is no bus to San Michele, though there is one to Lucolena, 3 km away). Several of them can be connected with each other to form excursions of two, three or four days: a wonderful way of seeing the region if you have the time, and the weather is good.

Food

There's no Chianti cuisine as such, or at least none as distinct as the wine. Simple, generally well-prepared Tuscan food with Florentine and (such as they are) Sienese accents is the basic fare. Its roots are in peasant cooking – *cucina povera* – where leftovers are assiduously recycled. Bread in particular is never allowed to go to waste: reheated, garlicked and flavoured with oil, it becomes the basis for *bruschetta* or *fettunte*, or *crostini* – toasted slices spread variously with chopped tomatoes, white beans, a paste of chicken livers and spleen, or anchovies and capers, and so on. Soaked in water, squeezed out and crumbled, it is mixed with tomato, onion, basil and cucumber, to form the delicious summer salad called *panzanella*. Simmered with tomatoes and olive oil it becomes the substantial soup known as *pappa al pomodoro*, and cooked up with leftover vegetables (generally cabbage, beans, potatoes and carrots) it provides the comforting, porridge-like texture for the famous *ribollita*.

In country restaurants, almost always congenial places to spend an evening, the 'kitchen' often consists of little more than a large wood-burning grill where veal chops and steaks, or pork studded with garlic and rosemary sizzle over the embers. Considering the superb produce available in the markets, side dishes can be disappointingly meagre in range and quality. The white cannellini beans are an exception: often available, generally cooked in an earthenware terrine with oil, salt and pepper, and almost always delicious.

There are a number of flossy restaurants catering to rich tourists. On the whole these are places to avoid; Tuscan food as a rule is best when it's at its most straightforward. It doesn't respond well to the complicating and fussy touches by which these establishments justify their inflated prices.

The region abounds in *fattorie*, the old estate houses, where you can taste and buy wine (usually for about 50 per cent less than in the *enoteca*) as well as olive oil, honey and other local products.

Agriturismo

If you've got a car, you may be interested in the list of accommodation put together by the Consorzio del Marchio Storico, Chianti Classico. They'll fax or mail it to you: Via Scopeti, 155, S. Andrea in Percussina, 50026 San Casciano VP (Fi); tel. 055-8228245/6/7; fax 055-8228173.

I | CHIANTI EXCURSION

GREVE TO PARCO SAN MICHELE

This is a steady climb connecting Chianti's unofficial capital, Greve (home of an annual wine festival), with the old chapel and converted villa of San Michele in the wooded ridge of the highest part of the Chianti hills. The itinerary follows a little-used dirt road all the way, so it's impossible to get lost. As you climb from the cultivated valley, past the villas and *fattorie*, the views

Volpaia
?
See p
8 1

over east Chianti's vineyards and olive groves widen impressively. High on the ridge you'll see the cross marking Mt Domini, from which you can see spectacular views over the Chianti and Valdarno regions.

Greve is a pleasant little market town, famous for its funnel-shaped, arcaded Piazza Mercatale, with a statue of the sixteenth-century explorer, Verrazzano, in its centre. The old stone buildings of San Michele are now a restaurant and hotel with rooms varying from very cheap to moderate. It's a friendly, clean, somewhat ramshackle place, popular with hikers as well as local wine growers, who occasionally organize sumptuous (and surprisingly inexpensive) wine-tasting banquets. A wonderfully peaceful place to spend a night or two.

Food

There is a handful of reasonable, moderately priced restaurants in Greve. The best is probably the Ristorante Bottega del Moro, off the main piazza, which offers a good choice of Tuscan dishes in friendly surroundings. Several readers of the first edition of this book have reported that the Ristorante Giovanni da Verrazzano has gone terribly downhill, and all have recommended instead the basement pizzeria Gallo e Nero (also located off the main piazza). Otherwise, the *rosticceria* on the other side of the square sells superb baked pastas and roasted meats to take away. On Saturdays the square becomes a busy market with stalls selling *porchetta* as well as some of the best cheeses and salami of the region. The restaurant in San Michele serves excellent, straightforward Tuscan home cooking. Especially good are the gnocchi with *pesto*, the vegetable side dishes, and the *tiramisu* – one of the best in Tuscany.

LOGISTICS

GREVE TO PARCO SAN MICHELE, 3–4 hours

🚌 Transport
Ⓜ Maps, guidebooks and trail info
🍴 Eating
⊞ Accommodation
ⓘ Miscellaneous info

🚌

FROM FLORENCE, AND RETURN

SITA bus (tel. 055-214721) route 353 (Firenze–Castellina). Buses between Florence and Greve are fairly frequent.

SITA bus 347 goes between Florence and Lucolena, Lucolena being 3 km from San Michele (which you have to walk); so you could use this to start the walk from San Michele, or if you walk to San Michele from Greve, stay the night and want to return to Florence the next day. On Saturdays there are also buses on this route that go between Greve and Lucolena.

Length of journey: Florence–Greve, about 1 hour; Florence–Lucolena, 1¼–2 hours.

Ⓜ

- Carta dei Sentieri e Rifugi, sheet 10, 'Monti del Chianti', 1:25,000
- Kompass Carta Turistica, 'Trekking del Chianti, Sentieri nel Chianti Fiorentino (parte 1)', 1:50,000

🍴

GREVE
Bottega del Moro
Piazza Trieste, 14/r
Tel. 055-853753

PARCO SAN MICHELE
Villa San Michele
Parco Naturale di San Michele
Tel. 055-851034
Closing day: Monday
Price: very inexpensive

PICNICS
The Saturday market at Greve has good *porchetta*, roast meats and game, among other things. There are also several *salumeria* (delis) in Greve.

⊞

GREVE

Del Chianti
Piazza Matteotti, 86
50022 Greve in Chianti (Fi)
Tel. 055-853763; fax
055-853764
Price: double rooms, L. 90,000–
135,000

Giovanni da Verrazzano
Piazza Matteotti, 28
50022 Greve in Chianti (Fi)
Tel. 055-853189; fax 055-853648
Price: double rooms, L. 75,000–
100,000

SAN MICHELE

Villa San Michele
Parco Naturale di San Michele
Tel. 055-851034
Price: very inexpensive
Essentially a hostel. Rooms very
plain; one exceptionally nice
room in the front (slightly more
expensive) has its own terrace
with table and chairs, others have
access to a communal terrace.
Restaurant closed Mondays – and
there is nowhere else to eat up
there!

OTHER

Fattoria di Rignana
Loc. Rignana
50022 Greve in Chianti (Fi)
Tel. (for accommodation, not
restaurant) 055-852065; fax
055-598729
Closed Monday, November.
Inexpensive to moderate. If you
have a car, this *agriturismo* is a
really nice place to stay. Located
down a country track (sign-
posted) about 6 km south-west of
Greve (and about 3 km SE of
Badia a Passignano), off the
Montefioralle road; 5 apartments;
also nice big rooms furnished with
country antiques in the old
farmhouse. 40 beds in total. Pool.
    Their restaurant is the
Cantinetta di Rignana (tel.
055-852601). Specialities include
*crostini in 16 modi, cannelloni con
sugo e ricotta di Rignana*, grilled
meats, and Chianti Classico from
the estate. Closed Tuesday.

ⓘ

Tourist office: Greve tourist office
is in Piazza Matteotti, in the town
hall.
Local CAI: Via dello Studio, 5,
Florence; tel. 055-2398580

Directions

Leave Greve from the narrow end of the funnel-shaped main square, Piazza Matteotti **A**. This leads into Piazzetta Santa Croce and its church, where you turn left. Cross the main road there, and continue to the end of the road you're on. At the end of the road, turn right, following signs for the cemetery and Villa San Michele.

Follow this road as it climbs up to the cemetery **B**, winding to the right of it, after which you will notice the CAI mark 24.

This itinerary is a fairly steady climb all the way, but the steepest part is at the beginning.

Pass Melezzano vineyard and its sign announcing that (happily for us and the consumer) they use no weed-killer. The asphalt ends just after the enticing (but unfortunately private) Melezzano villa. Carry on straight ahead.

About an hour out of Greve you'll reach the turning to Canonica on your left **C**, marked by a sign on a tree. This is a tiny old village of seven houses and an old church (the detour is a little less than ½ km).

Beyond the turning, the road passes through the Pian della Canonica area, a high, fairly level ridge.

When you reach Monte Domini, marked by a cross on a hill to the left of the road, take the short detour to reach it and climb to the top for one of the most vast and beautiful views over the Chianti and Valdarno regions.

Continue to follow the road as it winds its way to the top. A little more than 1 km from Monte Domini the road forks **D**. Take the right fork, very well signed, for Villa San Michele, which is about another 2 km from here. You will know you have reached the villa – and its charming chapel – by the small stone gateway set a bit off to the right of the road (where CAI 00 and 28 diverge **E**) as CAI 00 continues on to the left.

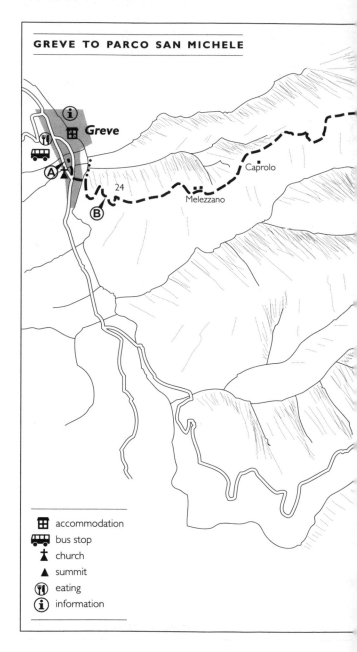

GREVE TO PARCO SAN MICHELE

Greve

A

B

24

Caprolo

Melezzano

	accommodation
	bus stop
	church
▲	summit
	eating
(i)	information

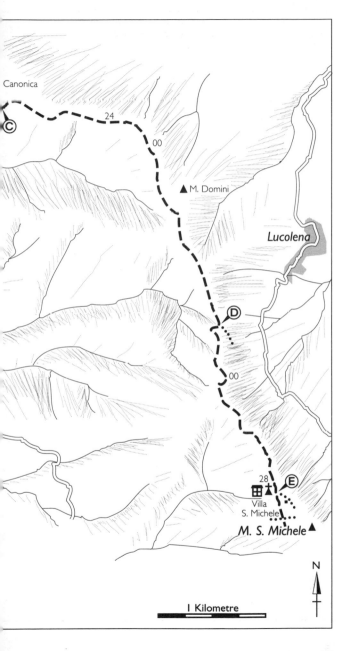

From the villa there is a huge view over Chianti; dramatic, not in an Alpine way, but over splendid, rolling hills.

PARCO SAN MICHELE TO RADDA
via Badia Montemuro and Volpaia

This is a long but exceptionally pretty and generally easy walk from the highest point in the Chianti hills down along meandering woodland paths and farm tracks, through the stunning fortified village of Volpaia and on through vineyards to a steep but brief ascent into the hill town of Radda, capital of the old 'League of Chianti'. The little village of Badia Montemuro has an old abbey built by the Camaldolesi monks (to visit, see Signora Finaghi in Badia a Montemuro). Volpaia, with its cool, stone-covered alleys, is one of the most interesting villages in Chianti, and the landscape between here and Radda, with views across the valley to the little Romanesque church of Santa Maria Novella, is stunning.

Food

You can get sandwiches at the bar in Volpaia, or lunch at the restaurant, La Bottega, there. The tiny *osteria* in Badia Montemuro (though it comes a little early in the walk) is a great place to eat: friendly, unspoiled by tourism, quietly dedicated to excellent cooking. The *panzanella* and fried polenta are especially good. The grilled meats are fairly unadorned, but come in large, succulent portions. The local, unmarked bottles of wine and *vin santo* (a sweet white wine) are cheap and remarkably good.

For descriptions of the restaurants in Radda, see pp. 82–3.

LOGISTICS

SAN MICHELE TO RADDA

San Michele to Montemuro, 30–45 minutes; Montemuro to Volpaia, about 2 hours; Volpaia to Radda, 2–2½ hours

Total c. 5 hs.

🚌 Transport
Ⓜ Maps, guidebooks and trail info
🍴 Eating
🏨 Accommodation
ⓘ Miscellaneous info

🚌

FROM FLORENCE

There are no direct buses from Florence to San Michele. If you're not walking up from Greve (as per the previous itinerary) you could try hitching from there, though cars are few.

SITA bus (tel. 055-214721) route 347 goes between Florence and Lucolena, Lucolena being 3 km from San Michele (which you have to walk). On Saturdays there are also buses on this route that go between Greve and Lucolena.
Length of journey: Florence–Lucolena, 1¼–2 hours, depending on which bus you get

RETURN FROM RADDA

To Florence: ATW there are two SITA buses from Radda to Florence: Mon.–Sat. at 7.15 a.m.; Mon.–Fri. at 8.45 a.m.
Length of journey: 1½ hours

To Siena: on weekdays there are five TRA-IN buses (tel. 0577-204111/204245) back to Siena, between 6.55 a.m. and 6.35 p.m. No Sunday buses.

Ⓜ

• Carta dei Sentieri e Rifugi, sheet 43, 'Monti del Chianti', 1:25,000
• Kompass Carta Turistica, 'Trekking del Chianti, Sentieri nel Chianti Fiorentino (parte 1)', 1:50,000

The Comune (top floor) in Radda will xerox the local IGM; the shop connected with the Giovannino Affittacamere sells the 'Monti del Chianti', 1:25,000, listed above (preferable).

🍴

BADIA MONTEMURO

L'Osteria
Loc. Badiaccia
Montemuro
Tel. 0577-738036

Hours: lunch, 12–1.30, dinner
5–7.30; shop open (for
sandwiches, etc.) 9–12 and
5–7.30
Closing day: Tuesday
Price: inexpensive

VOLPAIA
La Bottega
Tel. 0577-738001

RADDA
See pp. 82–3 for Radda
restaurant descriptions.
Il Vignale
Via XX Settembre, 23
Tel. 0577-738094
Closing day: Thursday
Price: expensive

Le Vigne
Loc. Le Vigne (1.5 km from the
centre of Radda)
Tel. 0577-738640
Closing day: Tuesday

Pizzeria Michele
Viale XI Febbraio
Tel. 0577-738491
Closing day: Monday

PICNICS
The Osteria in Badia Montemuro
(see above) sells *panzanella* and
other takeaway food. Their
house wine and *vin santo* are also
good.

Giovannino (Affittacamere)
Via Roma, 8
Radda
Tel. 0577-738056
Price: inexpensive

Fattoria Castelvecchi
(*agriturismo*)
Loc. Castelvecchi (between
Volpaia and Radda)
Tel. 0577-738050
Price: expensive
Thirteen apartments and 8
rooms, 80 beds total.

Fattoria Castello di Volpaia
(*agriturismo*)
Castello di Volpaia
Loc. Volpaia
53017 Radda in Chianti (Si)
Tel. 0577-738066; fax
0577-738619
Price: expensive
Three apartments, 18 beds total
(Casa Olinto, two single
bedrooms which can be
combined; the Tower, a
three-bedroom apartment;
Casetto, a five-bedroom
farmhouse. Minimum 3-night
stay.) Dinners can be arranged,
and are reputed to be good.
English spoken.

Tourist office: Pro Loco, Piazza

Ferrucci, 1, 53017 Radda in
Chianti (Si); tel./fax 0577-738494
Forest ranger station (Stazione
Forestale): tel. 0577-738249

Castello di Volpaia: lunch available
for groups of 15 or more.
Wine-tasting available for groups
of 15 or more; tel. 0577-738066.

Directions

Leaving the Villa San Michele by the pagoda–style gate
A, turn right on to CAI 00.

Very soon you reach a fork, with CAI signs on a
pole in the middle for 'Panzano 32' and 'Volpaia 52' as
well as '00'; take 52/32 to the right. Follow along here
for a short distance until you meet an intersection of
several paths **B**. The path immediately to your left and
uphill is also CAI 00. You *don't* want that, you want
the next one to the left (at about 90 degrees).

Keep following this path, ignoring deviations.

When you meet the asphalt road **C**, go right.

Soon you'll come to a turning on the right for Badia
Montemuro; take this, into the hamlet. To visit the
abbey, either arrive around the time of a Mass, or ask
around for Signora Finaghi. Other than that, there isn't
really anything here, except the *osteria*, well worth a stop
(See above.)

FROM BADIA MONTEMURO

Passing the *osteria* **D** on your right, in 10 m or so you
will see on the right a flight of cement stairs leading
down to a dirt road. Go down these stairs and take a
right on the dirt road at the bottom. Follow this road as
it winds leisurely downhill, soon passing a small sawmill.

After 10–15 minutes, the road forks, a seemingly
newer, wider track going downhill to the left, the right
fork remaining level. Take the right fork. As this path
nears a stone house, it looks a bit like a private driveway,

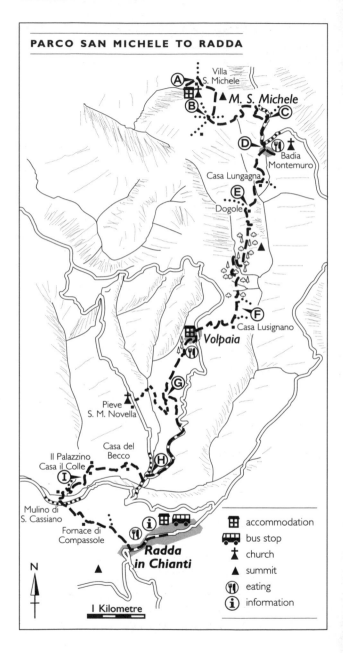

PARCO SAN MICHELE TO RADDA

Villa S. Michele
Ⓐ
Ⓑ
▲ *M. S. Michele*
Ⓒ
Ⓓ
Badia Montemuro
Casa Lungagna
Ⓔ
Dogole
▲
Ⓕ
Casa Lusignano
Volpaia
Ⓖ
Pieve S. M. Novella
Casa del Becco
Il Palazzino
Casa il Colle
Ⓗ
Ⓘ
Mulino di S. Cassiano
Fornace di Compassole
ⓘ
Radda in Chianti
▲

🏠 accommodation
🚌 bus stop
✝ church
▲ summit
🍴 eating
ⓘ information

N

I Kilometre

but it isn't. On reaching the house (Casa Lungagna), take the right fork, which curves downhill around the back of the house, rather than the left, which goes in front of the house.

Follow this path as it winds downhill to where it crosses a stream and then begins to climb uphill. During this climb (about an hour out of Badia Montemuro) you will encounter the large abandoned farmstead of Dogole. The path forks here **E**; take the left fork, which passes in front of these stone structures.

Follow this path as it goes downhill alongside the buildings. After 50 m or so, downhill, the path will bend around to the right and begin to go uphill, into the woods again. Stay on this pleasant, shaded, peaceful woodland path for about 2 km. It twists and turns, crosses streams, proceeds sometimes gently up hill and sometimes quite steeply down. It would be hard to get lost; just keep to the main path. Firs give way to chestnuts and oak.

After 30–40 minutes the path comes out at a dirt road **F**. Turn right. Follow the road past Casa Lusignana, where there's a nice panorama over the Val di Pesa. Then, when the road ends in a T-junction soon after, go right; this road leads to Volpaia.

FROM VOLPAIA

From the door of the Castello di Volpaia (now an *enoteca*) in the main piazza, go down the steps at the right-hand corner of the piazza (to the right of the bar). Cross the little stone gutter and go out through the lowest of the three arches facing you. A gravel road takes you down through a row of cypresses with magnificent views of Chianti ahead of you. The hilltop town with the tower in the distance is Radda. Keep to the main gravel road, ignoring deviations to the right and left.

After about 15 minutes, across the valley to your right

you'll see the Pieve di Santa Maria Novella, a twelfth-century Romanesque church. A few minutes later, just where the road makes a hairpin turn to the left, there's a branch off to the right **G**, marked with a 'CAI 52' sign (but note that this is in fact only a subsidiary of the main CAI 52 route marked on the 'Monti del Chianti' map). If you want to visit the church, take this right and continue across the valley keeping to the main path, ignoring a couple of steep turns up to the right. (Request the key from Signora Bini, who lives next door.) Otherwise, ignore this deviation and continue on past it.

In another 10 minutes (about ½ hour out of Volpaia) you'll come out on a little-used asphalt road. Turn right.

After about 20 minutes you'll come to a junction **H**. Turn left towards Radda; almost immediately, about 30 m farther on, take the dirt road off to the right. This is a delightful farm track that offers a more pleasing access to Radda than the main road.

Passing an abandoned building after 5–10 minutes (Casa del Becco), you come in another 5–10 minutes

to a house (Il Palazzino), where you fork down to the left, soon passing a farmhouse (Casa il Colle) with a covered sheep pen 50 m beyond it. Ignoring a couple of minor lefts at the sheep pen, proceed another 50 m to where the path forks again **I**. Take the left fork.

In a few minutes the path crosses a stream and a few minutes after that it comes to a T-junction with another path. Go left, coming to another house (an old mill, Mulino di San Cassiano) in 100 m. Pass around this to the left, crossing a bridge. In another 150 m the path comes out at the main asphalt road. Across this, and a little to the left, is a smaller road signed 'Fornace di Compassole'. Take this.

A steep 15-minute climb brings you to the *fornace* (pottery). This produces all kinds of terracotta tiles, planters, pots, etc. You may want to wind up through it.

From here a more gentle slope leads you to the main road, where you turn left into Radda, reaching the town in about 10 minutes.

RADDA TO VAGLIAGLI OR SAN SANO

A beautiful, meandering walk through woods and farmland, and down along a peaceful forgotten valley. The San Sano ending is probably the prettier: you don't have to walk along a busy road, and the village itself has more charm than Vagliagli. The Vagliagli route takes you past the Villa Dievole, to which legend attributes a former diabolical inhabitant, though it's now in the hands of a private mortal. Both routes take you past the Romanesque church of San Giusto and the delightful little castle of San Polo in Rosso, now used by the vineyard of the same name as its business office. (The wine itself is sold in the nearby village of Lecchi.)

You can get a bus into Siena from both places, though you should check timetables in advance. ATW, there are also two afternoon buses from San Sano to Gaiole, a 15-minute ride.

Food

Il Poggio, near San Polo, is a very good place to eat: imaginative but unpretentious cooking, a lively atmosphere, and gorgeous views from the outside tables. Vegetables are treated with unusual care here. The *zuppa di verdura* (vegetable soup) is fresh and tasty, and you should also sample the spicy marinaded aubergine with pancooked onions. The pasta speciality – *al Giannneto* – is a delicious spicy meat sauce with parsley, over tortellini or spaghetti.

Vagliagli isn't particularly well served with places to eat. In San Sano there's the popular little Trattoria della Rana, connected to the grocery store. The atmosphere is friendly, and it's an attractive, inexpensive place to spend an evening, but the cooking is erratic: a disappointing pasta with *porcini* mushrooms which turned out to be preserved even though they were in season at the time; a less than thrilling gnocchi with mascarpone and spinach (to sample this rich but delicate Tuscan dish as it should really taste, go to La Finestre in the Piazza del Mercato in Siena). As with many of these country restaurants, you can expect to wait a long time before eating, and a long time between courses.

LOGISTICS

RADDA TO SAN SANO/ VAGLIAGLI

Radda to San Sano, about 4 hours; Radda to Vagliagli, about 4¹/₂ hours

---

🚌 Transport

Ⓜ Maps, guidebooks and trail info

🍴 Eating

🏨 Accommodation

ⓘ Miscellaneous info

🚌
TO RADDA

From Siena: five TRA-IN buses (tel. 0577-204111/204245) leave Piazza S. Domenico for Radda daily on weekdays, the first at 7.30 a.m., the last at 7.15 p.m. As always, check current schedule. No buses on Sundays.

Length of journey: ³/₄ hour

From Florence: ATW there are SITA buses (tel. 055-214721) from Florence to Radda as follows: Mon.–Sat. 7.00 a.m.; Sat. only 1.35 p.m.; Sun. only 5.00 p.m.

Length of journey: 1¹/₂ hours

RETURN TO SIENA

From San Sano: TRA-IN bus

Length of journey: 40 minutes

Frequency: infrequent, so check schedule before embarking.

From Vagliagli: TRA-IN bus; if you don't want to do the last stretch up the asphalt road into Vagliagli, you can catch the bus at the point where the itinerary meets the asphalt road; check schedule beforehand

Length of journey: 25 minutes

Ⓜ

- Carta dei Sentieri e Rifugi, sheet 43, 'Monti del Chianti', 1:25,000

🍴

Trattoria Grotta della Rana
San Sano
Tel. 0577-746020
Closing day: Wednesday

Ristorante Il Poggio.
Loc. Poggio S. Polo
53010 Lecchi in Chianti (Si)
Tel. 0577-746135/7461176
Closing day: Monday
This restaurant is located on the wide dirt road that leads to Castel San Polo, and is indicated in the walk directions.

⊞

Hotel Residence San Sano
Loc. San Sano 21
53010 Lecchi in Chianti (Si)
Tel. 0577-746130
Price: L. 90,000–170,000 (dinner
L. 30,000)
A renovated thirteenth-century
fortress. 11 rooms. Restaurant.
Pool. German owner speaks

English and knows a lot about
walks in the area.

ⓘ

Tourist office: Pro Loco, Piazza
Ferrucci, 1, 53017 Radda in
Chianti (Si); tel./fax 0577-738494
Forest ranger station (Stazione
Forestale): tel. 0577-738249

Directions

Leaving Radda by the long flight of steps that go down behind the stone wall on the main street by the bus stop (ATW they lead down to the Da Michele Pizzeria/ Ristorante), turn right at the bottom of the steps and follow the gravel path sloping downhill. Where it ends on an asphalt road, turn left.

Reaching the Convento Santa Maria, turn right, downhill, by the stone wall near the stone well **A**. Bear left past the wall on to a stone road.

Follow this track as it leads downhill between a stone wall (behind the convent) and a very long building lined with cypresses. At the end of the wall and of the building, take the first right-hand path, downhill **B**.

Follow this path downhill to the bottom of the valley, where it crosses an old stream bed. There's a farm track to the left, immediately after the stream bed; take this.

Follow this path as it bends right uphill along the periphery of the field. Keep climbing as you pass on the left a field of grapevines and then, where vines give way to olive trees, follow the path left, immediately passing a stone water-hole or tank on your right.

Just before reaching the house (Casa Bereto), turn

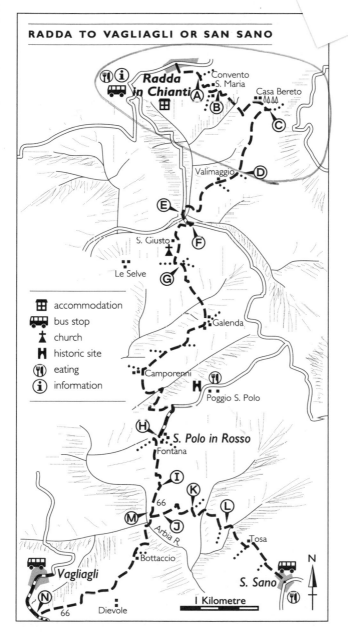

RADDA TO VAGLIAGLI OR SAN SANO

Radda in Chianti Ⓐ

Convento S. Maria

Ⓑ

Casa Bereto

Ⓒ

Valimaggio Ⓓ

Ⓔ

S. Giusto

Ⓕ

Le Selve

Ⓖ

accommodation
bus stop
church
historic site
eating
information

Galenda

Camporenni

Poggio S. Polo

Ⓗ

S. Polo in Rosso

Fontana

Ⓘ

Ⓚ

66

Ⓛ

Ⓜ

Ⓙ

Arbia R.

Tosa

Bottaccio

Vagliagli

Ⓝ

66

Dievole

S. Sano

N

1 Kilometre

right again, ascending along the edge of the olive grove. When you reach the top of the grove, bear left, where you will find a small path leading along the right-hand side of a thick hedge.

Follow this path uphill until it comes out at a wider path opposite a little wayside cross surrounded by four cypress trees. (This is about ½ hour from the start.) Turn right here **C**.

Stay on this path, ignoring deviations. It is a very pleasant ridge walk along here, with views of the Chianti hills on both sides. After about 20 minutes, the path merges with another similar-size path coming from the left **D**. Continue on here, bearing right.

About 150 m later, when the path forks, bear right past the farm of Valimaggio.

The path soon joins with another, slightly larger gravel road; continue downhill.

This road comes out on an empty asphalt road. Turn left **E**. Walk down to the fork and bear left, towards San Sano.

Take the next right-hand turn, towards San Giusto and Le Selve **F**. The asphalt leaves off here, giving way to gravel again.

Soon you come to a very pretty Romanesque church, San Giusto, with a handsome bell tower and the parish buildings still intact. (This is about 1½ hours from Radda.)

Continue along the road past the church, beginning to climb. After about 350 m of steady climbing, at a right-hand bend in the road, a more minor path branches off to the left, uphill (if you reach another sign for Le Selve, you've gone too far, by about 70 m). Take the path on your left, passing a vineyard on your right, and then almost immediately fork again (this fork is almost a three-way fork, if you count the very much smaller track all the way on the left); take the right fork **G**.

After another 150 m or so, you'll reach another fork (that comes immediately after a smaller path coming up from the right to join ours). Take the right (lower) fork.

Shortly after this, fork right again, taking the lower, downhill fork.

At the top of the hill, the path comes out on a T-junction at a big old stone house. This is Galenda (about ½ hour from San Giusto); as you reach it, turn right on the dirt road rather than carrying on through the arch.

Keep to the main path, which climbs up and then turns along the ridge of a hill with good views either side (including the little tower of Castel San Polo).

After a little less than 1 km (about 10 minutes) the path begins descending, until it reaches the abandoned farmhouse of Camporenni. Here, before passing the house, turn left; stay on the main track as it winds to the bottom of the valley and crosses a stream, after which it climbs for about 15 minutes, coming out at a wide dirt road, which is the car road from Poggio San Polo. Go right here (left for the Ristorante Il Poggio); after about 200 m you come to the charming Romanesque Castel San Polo (2½–3 hours from Radda).

After visiting the castle, turn left out of the main entrance (i.e., continuing along the road by which you arrived), and then when the road forks again almost immediately, bear right on a dirt track **H**.

Passing a group of houses on your left (Fontana), follow the path round to the left as it descends below the driveway (which ATW is blocked by a large stone). About 100 m past the houses, where the path curves around into a T with the driveway, continue on to the right.

From here a rugged stone track winds down through a nicely wooded valley. You'll pass one or two red and white CAI signs (route 66). After 10–15 minutes on this track you cross a little stream **I** amidst very lush vegetation.

If you are doing the San Sano ending, be alert here: in about 5 minutes (during which you'll be walking roughly parallel with a larger stream down to your right, not to be confused with the little stream you've crossed at **I**) you'll come to a little tabernacle half hidden by the vegetation on your left, with a delightful painted Madonna in it. Retrace your steps a few paces, and you'll see a grassy path going off to the right (to the right now that you've turned round; i.e., it would have been on your left originally) **J**. This is where the San Sano and Vagliagli endings go their separate ways. If you're going to Vagliagli, there's no need for you to find the little tabernacle; just continue on along the original path (CAI 66), and pick up the Vagliagli directions below.

SAN SANO ROUTE

Having found the grassy path mentioned above, take it. It looks overgrown at first, but is in fact a really great path – amazingly peaceful.

In 5–10 minutes, after some minor twists and turns, the path swings around sharply to the right and then bends left. In another 5 minutes, you come to a T-junction with another path; go right **K**.

The path winds down, crossing a little stream (hidden by vegetation). Soon afterwards, it starts climbing and in a few minutes forks. Go round to the left **L**.

After a couple of minutes the path crosses a tiny stream and climbs around the other side of the small valley, coming out at a gravel road. Turn left, passing the farm-house, Tosa.

After a couple of minutes the gravel gives way to asphalt, and the path winds into San Sano.

VAGLIAGLI ROUTE

About 10 minutes after crossing the little stream **I** (you are still continuing along CAI 66) you'll cross a somewhat dilapidated bridge over a nice stream **M**.

Perhaps 10 minutes beyond that, the path ends at a T-junction with a bigger track. Turn right here, past an old stone building on the left (Bottaccio). In another 10 minutes, the path widens as it meets the stone wall surrounding the estate of Villa Dievole. Follow this road until it comes out on the main asphalt road **N**. Go right there and on into Vagliagli, where you can get a bus to Siena. Alternatively, you can get the bus at this intersection with the main asphalt road if you've checked the schedule beforehand and know that one is imminent.

2 | LAMOLE RING WALK
via San Michele

This is one of the best walks in the region, taking you up into the high ridges of east Chianti, with fine panoramic views in both directions, and then down blackberry-bordered footpaths and ancient stone roads through a classically picturesque and unspoiled stretch of the Tuscan landscape. As an added incentive, the tiny hamlet of Lamole has one of the most pleasant restaurants in Chianti.

Food

There are in fact two good places to eat on this route, one in San Michele (see Greve to San Michele walk, above), the other in Lamole: the Ristoro di Lamole. It's worth timing your walk to eat at the latter as this really is an exceptionally appealing restaurant. Prices are moderate, the setting – overlooking a vast hillside – is gorgeous, and the beautifully cooked food manages to be far more original and adventurous than the usual rather circumscribed fare, without seeming in the least bit contrived or fussy. There are daily specials, and a regular menu featuring gnocchi with gorgonzola, a wonderful garlicky *penne* with rocket and ricotta, *saltimbocca* (slices of veal and *prosciutto* with sage, braised in butter and marsala wine), imaginatively prepared vegetables and salads, and superb desserts, among them an amazing, light, creamy cheesecake with a perfect crust and a sauce of fresh blueberries.

LOGISTICS

LAMOLE RING WALK

Lamole to Monte San Michele, 1 1/2 hours; Monte San Michele to Lamole, 1 1/2 hours

🚌 Transport
Ⓜ Maps, guidebooks and trail info
🍴 Eating
▦ Accommodation
ⓘ Miscellaneous info

🚌

FROM FLORENCE

SITA bus (tel. 055-214721), route 353 (Florence–Castellina). ATW there are direct buses on workdays (*feriale*) to Lamole at 7.00 a.m., 2.15 and 6.45 p.m. All of these buses stop at Greve, so you could go from Florence to Greve, stay in Greve for a few hours and then catch one of the later buses from Greve to Lamole. (On Saturdays there's also a bus from Greve to Lamole – 20 minutes – at 11.30.) On Sundays and holidays, ATW, direct buses at 10.50 a.m. and 7.00 p.m.
Length of journey: 1 1/2 hours

RETURN TO FLORENCE

SITA bus 353 (Castellina – Florence). ATW there are direct buses back to Florence at 6.35 and 8.35 (connects with 9.20 bus from Greve to Florence), and 3.45 p.m. (connects in Greve). On

Saturdays there's a bus from Lamole to Greve at 11.55 a.m. Check Sunday/holiday schedule.
Length of journey: 1 1/2 hours

You can take the bus back from Casole rather than walking back to Lamole at the end of the route. Check bus times before leaving, as there's nothing happening (not even a bar) at Casole.

Ⓜ

• Carta dei Sentieri e Rifugi, sheet 43, 'Monti del Chianti', 1:25,000
• Kompass Carta Turistica, 'Trekking del Chianti, Sentieri nel Chianti Fiorentino (parte 1)', 1:50,000

🍽

LAMOLE
Ristoro di Lamole
Lamole
Tel. 055-8547050
Closing day: Wednesday

PARCO SAN MICHELE
Villa San Michele, see p. 51

🏨

LAMOLE
Le Volpaie (*agriturismo*)
Fattoria di Lamole
50020 Lamole
Greve in Chianti (Fi)
Tel. and fax 055-8547065
Price: double room and breakfast for 2, L.150,000; suite (with kitchen) and breakfast for 2/4 persons, L.250,000.
This is an old farmhouse on the Fattoria di Lamole estate. Pool.

Filette di Socci Guido
Lamole
Tel. 055-8547017
A farmhouse in Lamole with apartments to rent.

SAN MICHELE
Villa San Michele, see p. 52

ⓘ

Local CAI: Florence: Via dello Studio, 5; tel. 055-2398580

Directions

From the bus–stop, with your back to the church **A** and just before coming into Lamole, turn left.

There is a four-way fork here. The furthest-left option goes by the church. The next one to the left is a stony path leading uphill; take that.

Soon this comes out on a small asphalt road; turn left along it.

When you reach the first left (about 100 m), a stone road going uphill, take it **B**.

This comes very soon to a T-junction with another dirt road in front of a stone wall and vineyard. Turn left **C**.

After 2−3 minutes you'll pass a shed housing a water pump (or some similar thing) on the right, and the path climbs into the woods (there's a C A I band on a tree to the left, just where the wood begins).

Soon after this the path skirts to the left of a vineyard, and then passes the tail-end of a stone wall. Ignore a small path to the right here (parallel to the wall) and continue straight on.

About 30 m after this, the path forks **D**. Take the left fork. This would appear to be C A I 30, marked on a tree.

Reaching the point where pine trees start (about 40 minutes out of Lamole), A T W there is a newly made clearing, which may mean there will be a house here in the future. The trail continues across the clearing (C A I band on a tree on the left of the path), heading upwards into the pines.

In a few minutes this path reaches a T-junction **E** with another dirt track; turn left.

Up to this point there's been a lot of climbing, but you can always take it slowly. All the serious climbing is finished at this point, and it's all downhill on the way back.

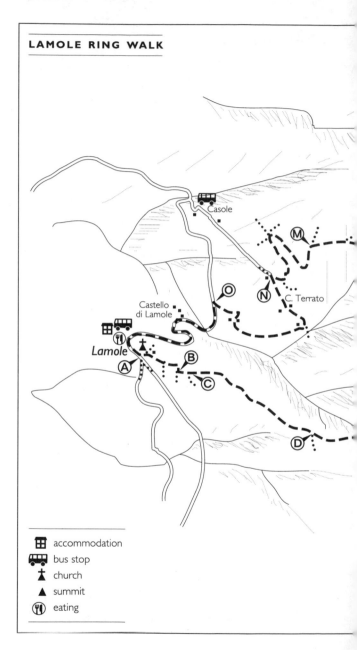

LAMOLE RING WALK

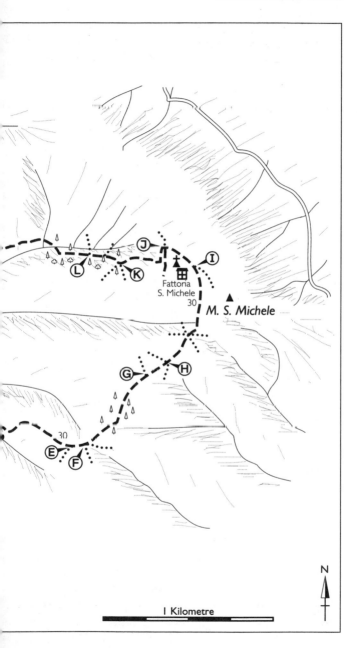

Fattoria
S. Michele

30

M. S. Michele

N

I Kilometre

Very soon the track comes out on a more open area, at more or less a T-junction; i.e., there's a path coming in from the right and we join it **F**. About 10 m from where these paths join, there's another turning to the right. Ignore this, and continue straight ahead, slightly uphill, towards the pine trees.

There are really nice views up here. In the morning the whole valley to the east can be filled with a level plain of white clouds below you. To the west, there is a wide view of Chianti countryside.

Follow the main path, which bends to the left as you reach the pine trees, and skirt to the left of them. You soon reach a vague T-junction **G**. Go right, downhill.

The path then descends (straight ahead on the hilltop beyond, and also off to the left, are two examples of Italy's ubiquitous mountain-top TV aerials) and at the bottom of the short descent meets a crossroads **H**. Keep straight on.

The next intersection, soon reached, has four major paths ahead of you. Take the one straight ahead, the biggest one, second from the left, and level (not uphill or downhill). This is CAI 00 (but so is another of these four).

Arriving at the next T-junction **I**, go left (there are signs on a painted pole to the right here, 'Panzano 32/ Volpaia 52', which is the path we have been on, and '00' and 'M. S. Michele').

Arrive at the Villa San Michele.

LEAVING SAN MICHELE

Passing through the pagoda-style gate **J**, immediately turn sharply left on the path which drops below the gate. Follow this path down the hill, ignoring lesser deviations. There is a tremendous view of Chianti below you. Soon the path begins to ascend slightly, and reaches an intersection **K**; the main path goes straight on, but we turn right. (There are CAI signs on trees here.)

This track soon comes to a T-junction. Go left, downhill.

The path descends rather steeply here; then, as it levels out, just *before* it bends right and crosses a stream bed, take a lesser fork to the left **L** (CAI mark on a tree to the left of this path). This lesser fork is just a small foot-path, and follows along to the left of the stream bed.

This section of path can get fairly overgrown, but it's a beaten dirt track, and follows – descending – the line of trees growing along the stream.

After a short distance (100–200 m) you'll reach trees coming in from the left side to meet those you've been following along on your right side. The path bends right here, still descending, crosses over a stream bed and levels out.

As you begin to climb again, notice the fine old stone-work along the path here.

Follow this path now, which goes very gently down-hill (ignoring a small deviation coming in sharply from uphill on the right). There are CAI marks along here.

The path comes out on a T-junction with a gravel path **M**. (This is about ½ hour after leaving San Michele.) Turn left.

Follow this path downhill, passing three houses, and with very wide views over the valley to Lamole, includ-ing the Castello di Lamole on the nearest of the hills. This is one of the most stunning panoramas on all our walks in Chianti.

Just follow the main path as it winds downhill, ignor-ing deviations (including one big one, downhill to the right with a big wooden cross).

After 15–20 minutes this gravel road starts bending sharply to the left around a house. Just *before* this bend, there's a hairpin left-hand turn **N** by the house. This smaller road has a little sign (ATW) 'Il Terrato'. Take this.

(Note: alternatively, you can just follow the main road down to Casole, about ½ km away, where you can get a bus or hitch back to Lamole or Greve.)

This path passes between two old stone houses (Casa Terrato) and carries straight on, passing a vineyard on the right and a hedgerow and stone wall on the left, and soon reaching another old house on the right. Turn right here, passing in front of this house and following the gravel road downhill.

When you reach the next house (or two houses – it's not clear which) the path turns right between the two buildings.

When this road comes out on the small asphalt road O (about 15 minutes after the hairpin turning to Il Terrato), turn left to Lamole, just under 1 km away. There is a SITA request stop (*fermata richiesta*) here, if you've timed your walk to coincide with a bus.

3 | RADDA RING WALK
via Volpaia

A 45-minute bus ride from Siena, Radda sits on a high hill at the heart of the comparatively rugged part of the region known as the Monti del Chianti. It was the capital of the old League of Chianti, and still has the old concentric streets circling the historic Piazza Ferrucci, where there's a stately old Palazzo Comunale encrusted with shields.

This is a very pretty walk, much of it along old farm tracks, with wonderful views over one of the loveliest parts of Chianti. Points of special interest are the

S.L.96

See p49?

twelfth-century Romanesque parish church of Santa Maria Novella, and the beautiful fortified hill village of Volpaia with its extraordinary little maze of covered stone passageways, and its church, the Commenda di Sant'Eufrosino, designed by Benedetto da Maiano. There's also a terracotta works – the Fornace di Compassole – fantastically tiled in its own products, and worth strolling through.

Food

There's a restaurant in Volpaia, La Bottega, where you can eat lunch (check closing day), or you can always bring a picnic, especially if you're coming from Siena, where you can assemble a portable banquet of such delicacies as *vitello tonnato*, stuffed *zucchini*, *panzanella*, *sfumato* (a kind of vegetable soufflé) or *tonno e fagiole* (tuna with beans), at the Rosticceria on Via Calzoleria, or at Morbidi on Banchi di Sotto.

In Radda there are a number of restaurants to choose from, among them Il Vignale, touted as one of the major gastronomic venues of the area. The food here is certainly good, and the place itself is fairly pleasant, in a somewhat studiedly rustic way (it's part of a large, up-market concern comprising also a *fattoria* and an *agriturismo* establishment), but there's a curious chilliness about the atmosphere – not helped by the sign in the window announcing a hefty minimum price per head – and a slight pretentiousness in some of the dishes. The *affettati* (sliced hams and salami) come with different-flavoured *crostini* for each meat: fig, lemon zest, *pesto* and so on. We had a beautiful dish of pasta triangles filled with ricotta and walnuts, and a tender but dull serving of grilled chicken. A plate of grilled vegetables was marred by the common fallacy of thinking the vegetables should be barely singed before being served, whereas they need to be cooked thoroughly to release their true flavours. A dessert of strawberry pudding was small, tasty and like everything else, overpriced.

A little below the main part of town, in a pretty setting, with good views from the terrace, is the similarly named Il Vigne. Though more modest (in every way) than Il Vignale, and altogether friendlier, this too seems to be aspiring somewhat beyond its capabilities. The duck stuffed with *porchetta* was distinctly lame, and the pasta with tomatoes and basil tasted as though it had come out of a can. In their defence it should be said that we ate there on the night of the World Cup semi-finals, and the kitchen staff (along with the rest of Italy) were understandably distracted. We had heard good reports of the place generally, and it may have been that we chose the wrong night.

For a completely straightforward, decently cooked meal, your best bet is the popular San Michele Pizzeria, serving standard pastas, grills and pizzas.

LOGISTICS

RADDA RING WALK
Radda to Volpaia, about 2½ hours; Volpaia to Radda, about 2 hours

---

🚌 Transport
Ⓜ Maps, guidebooks and trail info
🕅 Eating
🏥 Accommodation
ⓘ Miscellaneous info

🚌
TO RADDA
From Siena: five TRA-IN buses (tel. 0577-204111/204245) leave Piazza S. Domenico for Radda on workdays (*feriale*), the first at 7.30 a.m., the last at 7.15 p.m.; no buses on Sunday
Length of journey: ³/₄ hour
From Florence: ATW SITA

buses (tel. 055-214721) run from Florence to Radda as follows: Mon.–Sat., 7.00 a.m.; Sat. only 1.35 p.m.; Sun. only 5.00 p.m.
Length of journey: 1½ hours

RETURN FROM RADDA
To Florence: SITA bus: ATW, Mon.–Sat. 7.15 a.m.; Mon.–Fri. 8.45 a.m.
Length of journey: 1½ hours
To Siena: workdays there are five TRA-IN buses back to Siena, between 6.55 a.m. and 6.35 p.m.; no Sunday buses
Length of journey: ³/₄ hour
Taxi info: Sig. Gemini Giovanni: tel./fax 055-852025 (Panzano) Sig. Colella Michele: tel./fax 0577-749258 or 746119 (Gaile)

Ⓜ
- Carta dei Sentieri e Rifugi, sheet 43, 'Monti del Chianti', 1:25,000
- Kompass Carta Turistica, 'Trekking del Chianti, Sentieri nel Chianti Fiorentino (parte 1)', 1:50,000

The Comune (top floor) in Radda will xerox the local IGM; otherwise the shop connected with the Giovannino Affittacamere sells the 'Monti del Chianti', 1:25,000, listed above (preferable).

🍽

VOLPAIA

See p. 58

RADDA

See p. 58

PICNICS

From Rosticceria, Via Calzoleria, 12, Siena (NB, opens at noon) or Morbidi, Banchi di Sotto, 27, Siena.

🏨

See p. 58

ⓘ

Tourist office: Pro-Loco, Piazza Ferrucci, 1, 53017 Radda in Chianti (Si); tel./fax 0577-738494.
Forest ranger station (Stazione Forestale): tel. 0577-738249
Castello di Volpaia: see p. 59

Directions

Leaving Radda from the south-west corner by the Enoteca/Bar Dante, take the main asphalt road (Via Pianigiani) **A** leading west towards Castellina; pass the four-star Relais Fattoria Vignale on your left.

After walking for several minutes (about ½ km), you arrive at an intersection with a small stone and mortar chapel building on the left. On the right are signs for 'Fornaci Laterizi a mano' and 'Fornace di Compassole'. Take a right. The road immediately forks again; take the lower branch, downhill and to the right, on to a little-used asphalt road.

Coming to the *fornace* (kiln, pottery) on your left, you

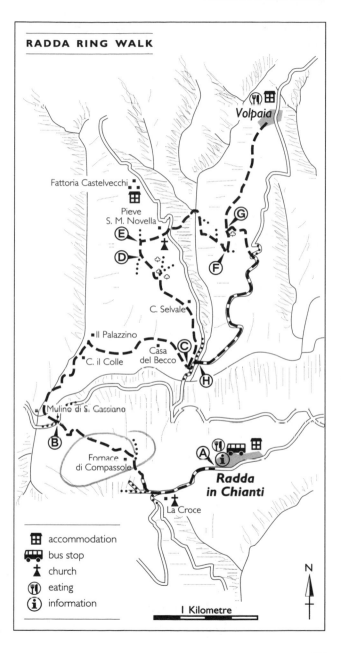

RADDA RING WALK

Volpaia

Fattoria Castelvecchi

Pieve
S. M. Novella

E

D

G

F

C. Selvale

Il Palazzino

C

Casa
del Becco

C. il Colle

H

Mulino di S. Cassiano

B

Fornace
di Compassole

A

Radda
in Chianti

La Croce

accommodation

bus stop

church

eating

information

N

1 Kilometre

may want to look round and pick up the road a little further downhill. The *fornace* produces all kinds of terracotta tiles, as well as planters and pots, etc.

Follow the road as it winds along downhill. About 10−15 minutes past the *fornace*, you'll reach a main road **B**; cross directly over this, on to the gravel road, which soon crosses a small bridge and winds through the stone buildings of an old mill (Mulino di S. Cassiano), where it bends round to the right and begins to climb uphill.

After 150 m, there is a slightly smaller fork to the right and downhill; take this.

Following this track, ignoring any deviations, you'll pass a sheep pen and the farmstead (Casa il Colle), and then pass a bit later to the right of another farmstead (Il Palazzino).

Always following the path, you will next pass the ruined farmstead of Casa del Becco (about an hour after leaving Radda).

The path leads out to an asphalt main road. As you approach this asphalt road, there is a dirt-track fork up to the left about 10 m before the asphalt. Take this **C**.

(Note: if you continue on to the asphalt and turn left, you come immediately to a fork. The right, asphalt, road is signed to Volpaia; the left, gravel, road Montemaggio and Santa Maria Novella. This is the path shown on the IGM map Monti del Chianti, but it is not our route.)

Turning on to the dirt track before the asphalt road, follow the dirt track uphill until it comes to a vineyard; turn right, skirting the edge of vines, up towards the house (Casa Selvalle). The path bends to the left in front of the house, staying between the vines and the stone wall that runs in front of the house. At the end of the wall bear left, keeping to the wide track that now leads between two large vineyard plots, with panoramas on both sides.

When you get to the end of the vineyard, the path reaches the beginning of a wood, where it winds left into another section of vineyard, through an opening in a wire fence. (There's a 'No hunting' sign at the entrance to this vineyard, but you can walk along the path. There is also, just where the path begins to turn towards this vineyard, a very narrow track into the woods, and also a wider track round the right side of the woods. Ignore both of these.)

Take the path which bends left into the vineyard and then immediately turns right along the edge of the vineyard, with the woods to your right. Carry on straight along here, until in a few minutes you see an old stone and terracotta tabernacle **D**, where the path turns right. Follow along, with vineyards to your left and a hedge and olive groves to your right.

To the right below is visible the Pieve di Santa Maria Novella, a twelfth-century Romanesque church. When you reach a break in the fence and hedge, and a stone road turning off to the right **E**, take it, down to Santa Maria Novella. (To visit the church, ask for the key from Signora Bini, who lives next door.)

(Note: if your destination is the Fattoria Castelvecchi *agriturismo*, continue on past the turning for Santa Maria Novella, following the path as it continues along the vineyard, and then bends left and climbs towards a stone building now used as a garage for tractors. Bear right past this and follow the path as it leads up to a group of old stone buildings – Castelvecchi, with rooms and apartments available.)

Take the stone path down to the church. Pass round the right-hand side of the church to the front, where a short driveway takes you down to a white gravel road. (Turning left here would bring you to the little agriturism hamlet of Castelvecchi.) Straight across the road from the main entrance to the church is a path heading down into the valley. Take this. It looks rough at first, but is actually a well-maintained, shady footpath.

After about 3 minutes you cross two branches of a small stream, winding along for another 2 minutes to where a path forks steeply up to the left; ignore this, and continue straight on. After 5 minutes ignore a second left fork that heads uphill. Follow the main path as it bends sharply to the left **F**, ignoring a fork to the right, until you come out at a T-junction with a 'CAI 52' mark on a tree **G**. Go left (signed, ATW, towards Volpaia). This is a pleasant old farm track with views across the valley to Santa Maria Novella.

The thirteenth-century tower of Volpaia itself soon comes into view. Climb steadily towards it on the main path, ignoring all digressions to the right or left. A lovely row of cypresses marks your entrance to Volpaia.

FROM VOLPAIA

Retrace your steps back to **G**. From the door of the Castello di Volpaia (now a wine shop) in the main piazza, go down the steps at the right-hand corner of the piazza (to the right of the bar). Cross the little stone gutter and go out through the lowest of the three arches facing you. A gravel road takes you down through a row of cypresses with magnificent views of Chianti ahead of you. The hilltop town with the tower in the distance is Radda. Keep to the main gravel road, ignoring deviations to the right and left.

Across the valley to your right after about 15 minutes you'll see Santa Maria Novella. A few minutes later, just where the road makes a hairpin left **G**, there's a branch off to the right, marked with a 'CAI 52' sign (but note that this is in fact only a subsidiary of the main CAI 52 route marked on the Monti del Chianti map). Ignore this branch. (This is the way you came from Radda.)

In another 10 minutes you'll come out on a little-used asphalt road. Turn right.

After about 20 minutes you'll come to a junction **H**.

Turn left towards Radda; *almost immediately* (about 30 m) you'll see a dirt road off to the right; take this. This is the path you came on, and from here you are retracing your steps.

Passing an abandoned building (Casa del Becco), you come to a house after 10–15 minutes (Il Palazzino), where you fork down to the left, soon passing a farmhouse (Casa il Colle) with a covered sheep pen 50 m

beyond it. Ignore a couple of minor lefts at the sheep pen and proceed for another 50 m. Where the path forks again take the left fork.

In a few minutes the path crosses a stream and a few minutes after that it comes to a T-junction with another path. Go left, coming to the old mill (Mulino di S. Cassiano) in 100 m. Pass round this to the left, crossing a bridge. In another 150 m the path comes out at the main asphalt road **B**. Across this and a little to the left, is a smaller road signed 'Fornace di Compassole'. Take this.

A steep 15-minute climb brings you to the *fornace*. From here a more gentle slope leads you to the main road where you turn left back into Radda, reaching the town in about 10 minutes.

4 | GAIOLE TO RADDA

Gaiole is a busy commercial centre and not particularly attractive in itself, but this is a pleasant walk that takes you through a landscape that on the whole shows a harmonious interplay between the human and the natural. Pretty farms, old villas, a working *fattoria* and cypress groves line the way. Early on in the walk you pass by the quaint, perfectly preserved little village of Vertine, worth a look round.

A nice option for extending this walk would be to pick up the Radda to San Sano portion of the Chianti Excursion, pp. 63–4.

Food

See Radda Ring Walk, pp. 82–3.

LOGISTICS

GAIOLE TO RADDA
about 3 hours

🚌 Transport
Ⓜ Maps, guidebooks and
     trail info
🍽 Eating
🏨 Accommodation
ⓘ Miscellaneous info

🚌
TO GAIOLE
From Siena: a TRA-IN bus (tel.
0577-204111/204245) leaves
Siena for Gaiole early in the
morning, and the next one is at
12.50; check schedules ahead of
time, as the service is infrequent
Length of journey: 40 minutes
From Florence: SITA bus (tel.
055-214721)

RETURN FROM RADDA
To Florence: SITA bus; see p. 83
To Siena: on workdays there are
five TRA-IN buses (tel.
0577-204111/204245) back to
Siena between 6.55 a.m. and
6.35 p.m.; no Sunday buses
Length of journey: 1 hour

Ⓜ
• Carta dei Sentieri e Rifugi,
  sheet 43, 'Monti del Chianti',
  1:25,000
• Kompass Carta Turistica,
  'Trekking del Chianti, Sentieri
  nel Chianti Fiorentino (parte
  I)', 1:50,000

🍽
RADDA
See p. 58 and p. 82.

🏨
RADDA
Giovannino (Affittacamere)
Via Roma, 8
Tel. 0577-738056
Price: inexpensive

ⓘ
Tourist office: Gaiole tourist
office: Palazzo Comunale, Via B.
Ricasoli, 3 (upstairs); tel.
0577-749405
  Radda tourist office: Pro Loco,
Piazza Ferrucci, 1, 53017 Radda in
Chianti (Si); tel./fax 0577-738494
**Forest ranger station (Stazione
Forestale):** Via Ricasoli, 51,
Gaiole; tel. 0577-749569
Radda: tel. 0577-738249

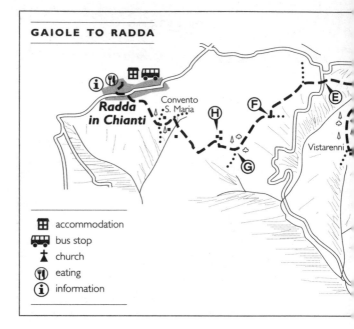

GAIOLE TO RADDA

Radda
in Chianti

Convento
S. Maria

Vistarenni

⊞ accommodation
🚌 bus stop
✝ church
🍴 eating
ⓘ information

Directions

From the bus-stop in Gaiole (the bus-stop at which you get off if you're coming *from* Siena – buses going in the other direction will stop across the street somewhere) on Via Casabianca **A** (near Via B. Ricasoli), walk a short distance along Via Casabianca until you reach a church on your left. Take the road that turns left here **B** between the church and the post office. Near the top of the hill, take a right **C** (still asphalt) towards Cavarchione.

About 20–30 minutes from the bus-stop, you'll reach Vertine, a tiny, charming village; it's interesting to take a short stroll through here.

After visiting the town, return to the T-junction where you turned left in order to visit Vertine. Take what would have been the right turn as you approached from Gaiole, i.e., uphill, the road leading away from

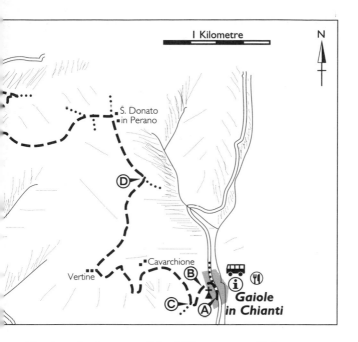

Vertine. At the top of the hill you pass a little cemetery on your right, and the asphalt gives place to gravel.

Follow this road, which after 10 minutes or so meets with another and turns left **D**.

When you reach the top of the hill (where the very large villa of San Donato in Perano will be on your right and a stone house on your left) take the smaller dirt road that turns off here to the left, alongside the stone house and downhill. Keep on along this gravel road, ignoring the first left fork, which passes the entrance to a villa.

About ½ hour past San Donato in Perano, the road reaches Fattoria Vistarenni. (You may see them bottling the wine, which they sell in their small shop.) Continue on the road, and just below the *fattoria* and its villa (sixteenth century; private), bear right, entering an avenue of cypresses. This is a lovely stretch, lined with pine, cypress and oak, gentle up-and-down walking, and the sound of a brook which runs alongside for a while.

The road ends at an intersection with an asphalt road **E** (this is about 2 hours out of Gaiole). Cross over the asphalt road and take the path leading uphill directly on the other side.

After a five-minute climb uphill, the path converges with another path, which it joins, heading left and towards Radda, which is visible from this intersection.

About 10 minutes later, the path comes out on to a slightly bigger dirt road **F**. Turn right on to this and follow it as it immediately bends to the left.

After a few minutes, watch on your left for a wooden cross (about 4 feet tall) on a stone base and surrounded by four cypress trees **G**. Here, take the small path that branches down to the right.

The path soon passes alongside a grove of olives and vines, on the left side of a villa with a pool **H**. Continue to wind round between the grove and the villa (with Radda visible on the hill straight ahead). Near the front of the villa (if the back is considered to be where the pool is), where the last row of vines is (but the olive trees go on), take the track that turns left: there are actually two tracks turning left here, parallel to each other, one on each side of this last vine row. Take the first one (the upper of the two), so that you have this last vine row on your right, and pass under the electric line.

At the end of the grove, the path turns right. Follow it, first downhill, then left at the bottom of another field, and then right across a little stream and uphill along a dense hedge. (This may sound a bit complicated, but in fact is all very easily followed, and takes only 5–10 minutes.)

When you intersect with a bigger stone road, turn left

(between a very long shed lined with cypresses, and the back of the Santa Maria convent). This road comes out on an asphalt road on which you turn right, and then immediately left and on into town.

5 | GAIOLE RING WALK
via Badia a Coltibuono

The variety of the Chianti landscape is well displayed on this walk, which takes you through woods and vineyards with views of hilltop castles, up through the hamlet of Montegrossi, past a strange, rather desolate quarry, and on to the stunning monastery of Badia a Coltibuono. The Vallombrosan monks who took over this monastery in the twelfth century established a tradition of expert viticulture which is continued by the present owner, Giannetto Catinari, who has combined it with a more modern expertise in public relations, turning the place into one of the most fashionable vineyards in Chianti, with its own restaurant and estate shop, as well as a cooking school run by Lorenza de' Medici.

If you're thinking of buying wine, save some money (and some space) for the less-well-advertised but probably better wines of the Riecine estate which you pass on the way back down to Gaiole.

Much of this walk is without shade, so spring or autumn would be the best times to do it.

Food

The restaurant at Badia a Coltibuono is the obvious place to have lunch. It's somewhat fancier and more expensive than the usual, but the cooking is good and the setting

is delightful. The menu sticks to Tuscan standards; *salumi*, *crostini*, home-made ravioli with sage and butter, braised rabbit, good mushroom dishes in season. Chocolates made by the owner's brother Roberto are a speciality.

LOGISTICS

GAIOLE RING WALK

Gaiole to Badia, 2½–3 hours;
Badia to Gaiole, under an hour

🚌 Transport
Ⓜ Maps, guidebooks and
   trail info
🍴 Eating
🏨 Accommodation
ⓘ Miscellaneous info

🚌
TO GAIOLE

From Siena: a TRA-IN bus
(tel. 0577-204111/204245)
leaves Siena early in the morning
(ATW 7.05), and the next one
is not until 12.50; check schedules
ahead of time, as the service is
infrequent.
Length of journey: 40 minutes
From Florence: SITA bus (tel.
055-214721)

Ⓜ

• Carta dei Sentieri e Rifugi,
  sheet 43, 'Monti del Chianti',
  1:25,000

• Kompass Carta Turistica,
  'Trekking del Chianti, Sentieri
  nel Chianti Fiorentino (parte
  1)', 1:50,000

🍴

Badia a Coltibuono
Coltibuono
Tel. 0577-749031
Lunch is served from 12.30 to
2.30: Plan your walk to arrive
closer to 12.30, so that if you get
lost you don't also miss lunch.
Closed: Monday, and for a period
in winter.
   Sometimes it's necessary to
reserve a day or two in advance.

🏨

For places to stay in Gaiole,
consult any general travel guide.

ⓘ

Tourist office: Gaiole tourist office
in Palazzo Comunale, Via B.
Ricasoli, 3 (upstairs); tel.
0577-749405
*Forest ranger station (Stazione
Forestale):* Via Ricasoli, 51,
Gaiole; tel. 0577-749569
Badia a Coltibuono: Vallombrosan
abbey founded in the twelfth
century on the site of an
eighth-century hermitage; one of
Tuscany's finest Romanesque
buildings. There are regular
Masses on Sundays (autumn/
winter 3.30; spring/summer

4.00/4.30). Masses for groups can be arranged by calling 0577-749087. Visits and wine tastings can be arranged by appointment (0577-749498); and tastings are always available at the estate's shop.

Azienda Agricola Riecine: 53013 Gaiole in Chianti (Si); tel. 0577-749527/731110. They've got a red and a white *super-vino da tavola.* Visits: Mon.-Fri. 10–12; 3–5.30. This vineyard has established a fine reputation for

their Chianti. A maximum of only 25,000 bottles a year is produced, entirely from grapes grown on their own land. The Gioia di Riecine red *vino da tavola* (one of the 'super-Tuscans') is aged in *barriques,* while the white is fermented in small wooden barrels. English spoken. If you're walking down from Badia a Coltibuono, stop in here; we thought their wine better than the Badia's.

Directions

The street just behind the bus-stop at Gaiole is Via G. Marconi **A**. As you face it, from the bus-stop, take it to the right, away from town.

After about 1½ km, the road bends round to the right across a little stone bridge over a stream. Take the dirt road off to the left **B** immediately before the bridge. Bear left, uphill, past the first fork (a smaller path) that goes downhill to the right.

When the path forks again, where you have the right branch crossing over a stream (you can see a big pipe under the path conducting the water) and the left branch continuing alongside the stream, take the right fork over the stream **C**.

After about 1 km (perhaps 25–30 minutes, because it's an ascent), there is a good-sized fork (nearly comparable in size to what we've been on) making a hairpin turn to the left and behind, and uphill. Take this **D**. If you miss it, you'll come in a minute or two to a stone

house (Frabecchi on the map; note that the IGM map shows the path – CAI 56 – continuing on past the house, but in fact it doesn't) on the right of the path, with the path pretty much ending in their yard. Then you'll know you've gone too far and can simply turn back and pick up this fork. If you are in any doubt, you may want to check (to see if the house is up ahead), because there are one or two forks off the road before this one, though they are smaller than the main path.

Note: owing to changes in the pathways, this next section may not conform topographically with the shape of the path on the map, so be particularly alert to the written instructions here.

After a climb of 15–20 minutes (during which you should ignore turnings to the left), there is a similar-sized path turning off to the left **E**, north and steeply uphill, at what appears to be the top of the hill we've been climbing. It is a wide, steep, stony path, and well marked by CAI. Take this. (If you miss this turning, the path will bend to the left and level out, so go back.)

In another 5 minutes or so you'll see another path leading off at 90° uphill, the same size but rougher. Ignore this. Just after that, you'll enter a stretch of the walk with a dense evergreen forest on the right and beautiful chestnuts on the left.

GAIOLE RING WALK

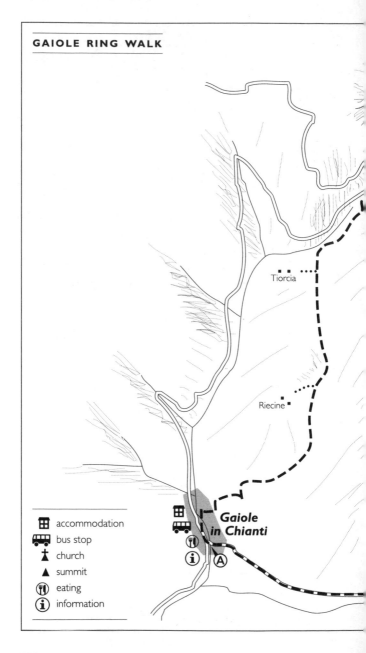

Tiorcia

Riecine

Gaiole in Chianti

🏢 accommodation
🚌 bus stop
⛪ church
▲ summit
🍴 eating
ℹ️ information

Ⓐ

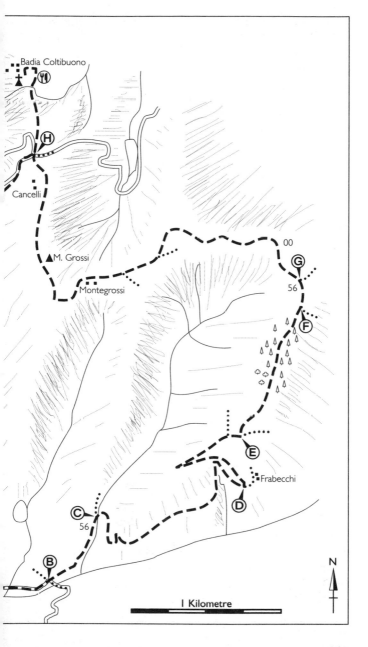

Badia Coltibuono

H

Cancelli

▲ M. Grossi

Montegrossi

00

G

56

F

E

Frabecchi

D

C

56

B

N

1 Kilometre

The path becomes dense pine forest on either side, making a very dark passage. Passing a 'CAI 56' marker and another path at 90° to the right **F** (which you ignore), continue straight ahead.

A couple of minutes later, the path slopes down to a T-junction **G**, where there's a fence straight ahead of you. Turn left here. This is CAI 00.

This is a beautiful hilltop path, with occasional views of Badia a Coltibuono ahead of you on the distant hillside.

Keep following the main path, ignoring deviations off it. Soon you will see the ruined castle of Montegrossi on a hill off to the right. Fine view as you come into the hamlet of Montegrossi.

Follow the road through the middle of the hamlet, ignoring two forks to the right just as you enter. The road turns to asphalt here, but there's nobody on it.

Following along the road, a short way after Montegrossi you will pass a huge, interesting stone quarry on your left and on the right a road up to the ruins of the castle.

Passing the little tower, Cancelli, the road drops down to a junction **H**. Cross straight over the main road, and turn in immediately on the right for the Badia a Coltibuono Osteria (shop). Following the road on which the shop is located you will come to the abbey itself, and its restaurant.

LEAVING BADIA A COLTIBUONO

From the road by the shop, turn left on to the road that drops down to the main junction **H** and turn right there. Very soon you will see a dirt road branching off to the left and downhill. Follow this road all the way down, passing the Tiorcia and Riecine estates on the right. Eventually the road turns to asphalt, Via B. Bandinelli, and leads on into Gaiole.

6 | BROLIO RING WALK

This is a good walk through some of the most delicately attractive parts of Chianti, and a pleasant way of turning a visit to the famous winery and castle of Brolio into a full day's outing, easily accessible from Siena. Little hamlets, abandoned farmhouses (including the splendid old buildings of Torricella, once part of the Brolio estate), a trellised 'vitiarium' (vine-covered walkway), a stream where the intrepid can take a dip (and which even the un-intrepid may have to wade across if the weather has been wet), punctuate this fairly gentle meander through serious wine-growing country.

The handsome, turreted Castello di Brolio was bought from the monks of Vallombrosa by the Ricasoli family in 1067, and provided the backdrop for innumerable battles between the Florentine and Sienese factions during the medieval period. It sits in its landscape with a glorious (and highly photogenic) air of permanence. It was here, with the invention of the formula for the wine we now associate with the region, that modern Chianti was born.

Note: when we initially did this walk for the book, the house of 'Podernovi', near the end of the walk, was abandoned. Since then it has been privatized, and the owner is not friendly to walkers. Therefore, a small portion of the route has been modified, and what was originally a path through the woods must now be done on a gravel road (until such time as we can return to map out an alternative). While unfortunate, this 2 km on the gravel road is still a pleasant enough walk, and is no longer in distance than the original. Therefore, we still highly recommend the walk.

Food

The Brolio estate runs a small restaurant – Da Gino – for its workers, as well as visitors. It's nothing special, but it's friendly, serviceable and moderately priced. The menu has more seafood on it than you normally find in central Tuscany, including a tasty *riso nero con seppie* (risotto with squid and squid ink). The *penne del Barone* is also good, with a creamy, spicy tomato sauce sprinkled with parsley. The *insalata mista* is large, fresh and good; but avoid the *ribollita*, which was the worst we tasted in Tuscany.

LOGISTICS

BROLIO RING WALK
about 3 hours

🚌 Transport
Ⓜ Maps, guidebooks and
   trail info
🍴 Eating
🆗 Accommodation
ⓘ Miscellaneous info

🚌

TO/FROM BROLIO
From Siena: ATW there is only one TRA-IN bus (tel. 0577-204111/204245) per day (Mon.–Sat.) from Siena, route 127; be sure to check return times too. The journey is 20–30 minutes. There are also buses between Brolio and Gaiole, a

15–20-minute ride. If the schedule doesn't suit you, there are buses (route 134) between Siena and San Felice (see itinerary map for location of San Felice), a 50-minute ride, but it may fit your schedule better.

The bus drops you at the entrance to Brolio estate; you have to walk up the hill to the castle.

Ⓜ
● Kompass, sheet 661, 'Siena – Chianti Colline Senesi', 1:50,000

🍽
Da Gino
Tel. 0577-747194
Closing day: Tuesday

Carlino
San Regolo
Closing day: Tuesday

⊞
There is an expensive hotel at San Felice, tel. 0577-359260; fax 0577-359089.

ⓘ
Brolio Castle: visits, Mon.–Fri. 8–17.00. Appointment necessary only for groups; tel. 0577-749710. The immense modern winery is located below the castle and is well organized for visits and tours. English spoken. There are also apartments for rent at Brolio (tel. 0577-749066).

Vinicultural pioneer Baron Bettino Ricasoli's apartments can be visited 9–12 and 3–6.

Directions

From the bus-stop, go up through the Brolio estate entrance (across from the Madonna di Brolio church) and arriving at the top **A**, turn left for the trail, or right to visit the castle.

From **A**, follow the road, passing vines on the right and trees on the left.

After about ¾ km, there's an intersection with a house, La Grotta, on your right. Ignoring the road most

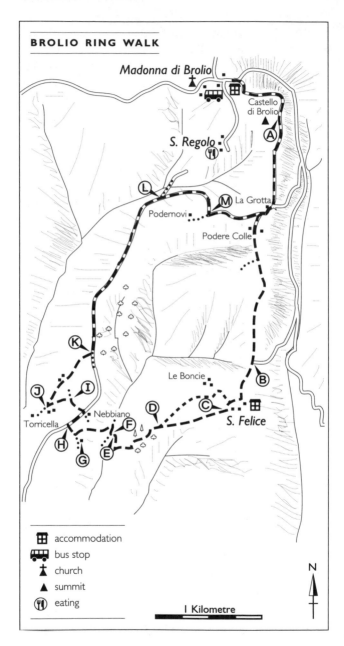

to the left, ahead of you the road forks: take the left fork, passing a small tabernacle on your right.

Very soon you pass a small chapel on the right, and then reach the dwellings of Podere Colle. Stay on the road as it passes between these two houses; just beyond them (about 75 m) there is a fork; take the left, downhill, slightly smaller one, CAI signed.

This path skirts a vineyard, and then, nearing the far corner of it, forks away from it to the left. (There are CAI marks along this stretch too.)

This path comes out to a T-junction with a small asphalt road, across from a tabernacle **B**. Go right here. In a few minutes (and about 45 minutes after leaving Brolio), you'll reach the Borgo San Felice (a hotel complex and an expensive restaurant).

Follow the little asphalt road you've been on, which now passes to the right of the buildings and soon reaches a parking lot on the right. (There's a gravel road here to the right signed for Le Boncie and Poggio Rosso, but don't take it.) Continue along the asphalt road a bit further, until you come to a couple of brick pillars on the right, marking the entrance to the 'vitiarium' **C**. This is a vine-covered trellis that cuts across the vineyard from San Felice in a straight line. Take this covered way.

NOTE: *if this walkway is for any reason closed, go back to the parking lot and take the gravel road signed to Le Boncie and Poggio Rosso. Take the first left turn, after about 75 m, soon passing La Ca' del Guagliumi on the right, and getting a long panorama towards Siena. Follow this road as it bends left and passes between vineyard and olives and more vineyard, until you reach a T-junction with the vine-covered trellis walkway that comes across the vineyard from San Felice* **D**. *Turn right here.*

At the end of the walkway, continue straight on, passing a path to the right, which is where the alternate path mentioned in the note above meets the walkway route **D**.

You soon enter some woods, where, bearing to the left, the path dwindles to a footpath that descends gently. Attention is needed along here. Watch for a tiny deviation to the left. Keep on the main path past this tiny deviation. Then, when you near the bottom of the valley (about 5 minutes past **D**), there's another of these small deviations, a hairpin to the left, just where the footpath begins to flatten out rather than descending as it has been. (If you follow this little hairpin left for about 55 paces, you'll come to a very tiny footpath bearing sharply down to the right, where the stream pools, good for taking a dip on a hot day.) Otherwise, ignoring this hairpin left, the path very soon comes to a shallow pool in the stream on your left **E**. Cross this pool, and then turn right on the path you will find on the other side of it **F**.

This stony path ascends for about 70 m from the pool, and then turns sharply to the left. (Ignore the tiny path that goes to the right here.)

The path continues to climb. Soon on your left the view begins to open out and there's a little fork dropping down to a vineyard; follow this to the end of the vineyard (20 m or so). Bear right (away from the house **G**) and

follow the track that climbs up on the right and then drops back down towards the house **G** where there's a dirt road, more or less their driveway. Take this dirt road to the right.

This soon comes out on a T-junction with a bigger dirt road **H** that leads back to Brolio; turn right.

Soon you pass on the right the old church of Nebbiano, now a private residence.

Just past this there's an entrance on the left into a vineyard. Take this. Stay on this path as it drops down through the vineyard to the bottom of the shallow valley and there meets a T-junction **I**. Turn left here, following along as the path first winds and then goes straight along the valley bottom between vineyards, and then turns right and climbs.

At the top of the vineyard, turn left at a break in the hedge. In about 20 m reach a T-junction **J**. Go left to visit Torricella or right to carry on.

This track soon passes Podere Casanuova on your left.

In about 10 minutes the path comes out on a T-junction **K** with the main gravel road. (ATW there are two yellow signs here pointing the way to La Torricella.) Turn left on this gravel road.

In about 1½km, the road forks; bear right **L**. Just under 1km from here, the road bends sharply left (at the junction with the driveway of Podernovi) **M**. Stay on the gravel road until, after about ⅔ km, you come to the crossroads you passed earlier, with La Grotta on your left. Turn left here, following the road up the hill past La Grotta, and go back to Brolio the way you came.

AROUND FLORENCE

For obvious reasons, the immediate environs of Florence don't make for particularly pleasant walking. We had hoped to find interesting routes linking some of the great Renaissance villas such as Poggio a Caiano or Petraia with nearby Etruscan sites, or with one or two of the more celebrated outlying restaurants such as Da Delfina in Artimino, but despite pleasant stretches here and there, these areas are pretty dreary, and the proximity of the industrial plain just beyond doesn't help. Curzio Casoli, from whom we've adapted some of our other walks, does have routes connecting these places in his excellent booklet *Trekking and Mountain Bike around Florence and Siena*, but you'd have to have quite a tolerance for boring suburbs to enjoy these particular itineraries.

Still, you don't have to go far to find unspoiled countryside. From the hill town of Fiesole, a short bus ride from the centre of Florence, there are pleasant walks that can give you at least the illusion of being deep in the heart of the countryside. Better still, take a day off to picnic in the Mugello – the pretty area of farmland and wooded slopes stretching between Florence and the Apennines. A little further afield are the forest and abbey of Vallombrosa, something of a resort area, but none the less attractive, as well as cool and shady; desirable qualities in the Tuscan summer.

LOGISTICS

FLORENCE

(**¶**) Eating

(**🚌**) Transport

(**ⓘ**) Miscellaneous info

(**¶**)

There is no shortage of restaurants in Florence (a city which, after all, caters to millions of tourists every year), and all the travel guides have substantial lists of these. What we can offer are four restaurants that were still unknown to tourists when we wrote this book (although one of them, Trattoria I Raddi, was apparently covered in French travel guides), all four well above average and each with its own unique atmosphere. Two of them are on the 'other' side of the river (the Pitti Palace side), but only a five-minute walk from it, which makes a lovely stroll of an evening.

Cavolo Nero Trattoria
Via dell'Ardiglione, 22
Tel. 055-294744
Closed: Sundays.
We almost hate to give this one away. Tucked away in a quiet

side street (in the same neighbourhood as I Raddi), this tiny place with its young, creative chef was a real find. They also have a garden at the back with a few tables. The chef made something special of *pici* with *zucchini* and ricotta. A terrine of baked cheese and pepper was rich, but great if you're in the mood for cheese. Good pasta with clams. The menu always had departures from the old standards that you find day after day in Italian restaurants, and the food was always imaginatively handled.

Moderately priced and, when we were there, serving dinner only.

Trattoria I Raddi
Via Ardiglione, 47/r
Tel. 055-211072
Closed: Sundays
The romanticized version of the old-style trattoria come true. The menu is fairly basic, the food done reliably, honestly, well.

Low to moderate price.

La Giostra Club
Borgo Pinti, 10/r
Tel. 055-241341
This dining club, fairly invisible if you're not looking for it, is

something of an adventure. A complimentary glass of good sparkling wine and *bruschetta* kick things off. The kitchen is more or less open, and you watch beautiful plates of food go by. A huge mozzarella, basil, radicchio and lettuce salad. *Penne* with *zucchini* flowers in an interesting reduced onion sauce. Paper-thin slices of beef roasted on a dish full of fresh herbs. Superb, smoky *tiramisu*.

Rather more expensive than our usual recommendations, but not extravagantly so.

Gauguin
Via degli Alsani, 24
Tel. 055-2340616

This vegetarian restaurant was uneven but well worth going to, despite its high cover charge. Excellent home-made *tortellini* stuffed with asparagus, a good baked gnocchi in a basil sauce, a wonderful mozzarella with truffles (*tartufato*). Beware of the mediocre *caponata*, and by all means avoid the salad advertised as huge but in fact quite modest and a rip-off at L.14,000 (ATW).

PICNICS

Check out the huge Mercato Centrale, not only for buying of picnics, but as an experience in itself.

🚌

SITA bus station: Via Santa Caterina da Siena, opposite the railway station. Tel. 055-214721. English spoken.

Railway station: Santa Maria Novella. Train information: tel. 055-288785. English spoken.

ⓘ

Tourist Office: there are two main tourist offices in Florence:
- Via Cavour, 1r; tel. 055-290832; fax 055-2760383. This is the basic tourist information office.
- Via Manzoni, 16; tel. 055-23320; fax 055-2346286. This is the principal office for administration and correspondence, as well as being a tourist information office.

Bookshops: there are several bookshops in Florence that deal in maps and guidebooks. See p. 32

CAI: Via dello Studio, 5; tel. 055-2398580

7 | TWO WALKS FROM FIESOLE

Just 8 km north-east of Florence, the little hill town of Fiesole has been a summer retreat for rich Florentines ever since Boccaccio sent his aristocratic storytellers up to its leafy villas to escape the plague which was devastating the city below. With its aerial views over Florence, fine buildings, well-preserved Roman and Etruscan ruins, and cool breezes, it has become an obligatory day's outing for tourists in Florence. A short walk through the town leads to the park-like slopes of Monte Ceceri, where Leonardo experimented with his flying machines and the dark *pietra serena* used in old Florentine buildings was once quarried.

FIESOLE TO PONTE A MENSOLA

Considering how close you are to Florence, this tranquil walk has a remarkably bucolic feel to it, offering a taste of classic Tuscan countryside with olive groves, poplars and old farm buildings. After crossing Monte Ceceri (a 40-minute climb, mostly quite gentle), the well-marked track descends through farmland with immense views, passing the crenellated tower of the eleventh-century Castel di Vincigliata, and finishing at the suburb of Ponte a Mensola, where you can get the bus back to Florence. Ponte a Mensola itself isn't particularly interesting, though Boccaccio spent his childhood there; some good Trecento works are to be found in the church of San Martino.

Food

Rather than eating in one of the flossy, overpriced Fiesole restaurants, we suggest buying a picnic at the *rosticceria* just off the Piazza Mino, at 21 Piazza Garibaldi, which makes gourmet sandwiches, excellent grilled vegetables and good salads.

LOGISTICS

FIESOLE TO PONTE A MENSOLA, 2–2½ hours

🚌

FROM FLORENCE
ATAF bus 7 to Fiesole from the station, the Duomo or Piazza San

Marco (tel. 055-580528)
Length of journey: 20 minutes

RETURN FROM PONTE A MENSOLA
Pick up ATAF bus 10 to Florence in Ponte a Mensola

Directions

Take Via Giuseppe Verdi **A** at the lower left corner of Piazza Mino as you're facing down from the cathedral. Passing some pretty houses and a panoramic view of Florence, you pick up red and white CAI 1 signs; follow these. At Via Adriano Mari, the route branches down to the right towards Monte Ceceri, through cypress woods. Take this.

Keep an eye on the signs, as the route to the top of Monte Ceceri takes a sharp left at one point, off the main path; take this. (It is 40 minutes from Fiesole to the summit at a slow stroll.)

After admiring the view, cross the summit and take the *left* trail 1. In 15 minutes you come out on Piazza

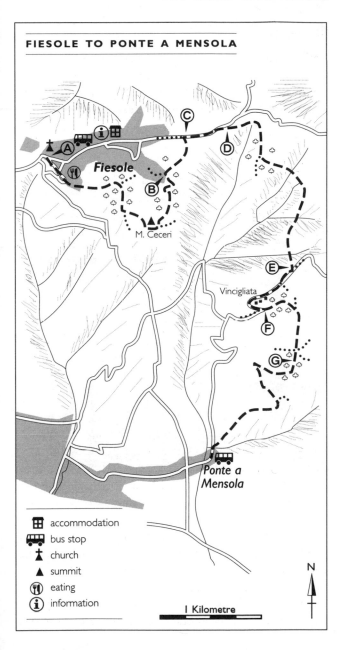

FIESOLE TO PONTE A MENSOLA

Fiesole

M. Ceceri

Vincigliata

Ponte a Mensola

	accommodation
	bus stop
	church
	summit
	eating
	information

N

1 Kilometre

Prato al Pini **B**. Turn right, again following route 1 (Via Peramonda). Here you glimpse real rural Tuscany: olive groves, old farmhouses. Florence, though just the other side of Monte Ceceri, seems a million miles away. At the end of the road, go right **C**. Follow this somewhat busy road (marked C A I 1, red and white) for 100 m to the S T A M bus-stop on the right **D**. C A I 1 trail goes off down a little track (by the bus-stop) by the green recycling containers; follow it. Well marked, it is a lovely path with immense views. The crenellated tower of Vincigliata is visible over distant poplars.

Pass through a farm with horses and olive groves, gently downhill all this time. After 45 minutes, the path comes out on a little road **E**. Turn right towards the tower of Vincigliata. Though not open to the public, you can see enough of this eleventh-century ruin to get a sense of its brooding, monumental qualities.

Coming round it, take the dirt road **F** that branches off to the left through olive groves. Pick up red and white markings again at a farmhouse, and go on. There is a fine, almost eye-level view of the Duomo to your right. Pass to the right of the gates of a villa, and then, where the path splits into '1' and '2', take '2' **G** to the right, a rugged little path down through oaks and laurels. This comes out on a small road. Turn right to Ponte a Mensola, where you can take the ATAF bus 10 back to Florence from the STAM bus-stop.

FIESOLE TO MAIANO

A short, pretty walk through the cypress woods of Monte Ceceri and down a rugged mountain path (wear strong shoes) with gorgeous views over rural Tuscany. Maiano has two outstanding restaurants; it is well worth timing your walk to arrive there for lunch or dinner.

Food

Le Cave di Maiano in the quiet little village of Maiano has been attracting gourmets for years. A peaceful, unpretentious place, with a terrace, this is the perfect setting for a long relaxing meal of northern Italian cooking at its best: beautifully prepared pastas and risottos, mouth-watering roasts of pheasant, pigeon and guinea-fowl, excellent desserts. There's a L.40,000 four-course set lunch, or you can eat à la carte.

Further up the hill – just as you come into the village from the walk – is a newer, more modest, but extremely pleasant Sardinian restaurant, La Graziella (also called Trattoria Casalinga). *Pane carasau*, a paper-thin fried bread, and *spaghetti alla bottarga*, a delicately flavoured pasta sprinkled with dried, grated fish roe, are among the delicacies served here. For the full island effect, get a bottle of the robust Abbaia, but don't expect to do much walking afterwards.

LOGISTICS

FIESOLE TO MAIANO,
1–2 hours

🚌 Transport
🍽 Eating

🚌
FROM FLORENCE
ATAF bus 7 from the station, the Duomo or Piazza San Marco to Fiesole
Length of journey: 20 minutes

RETURN TO FLORENCE
You can walk all the way back, or you can take an ATAF bus 17 back into town from Il Salviatino (tel. 055-580528).

🍽
Le Cave di Maiano
Maiano
Tel. 055-59133
Closing day: Thursdays and August
Price: Moderate to high
Reservations advisable

La Graziella (also called Trattoria Casalinga)
Maiano
Tel. 055-599963
Closing day: Monday
Price: Moderate
Reservations advisable

Directions

Take Via Giuseppe Verdi **A** at lower left corner of Piazza Mino (as you're facing down from the cathedral). After passing some pretty houses and a panoramic view of Florence, you pick up red and white CAI 1 signs; follow these. At Via Adriano Mari, the route branches down to the right towards Monte Ceceri, through cypress woods. Take this.

Keep an eye on the signs, as the route to the top of Monte Ceceri takes a sharp left at one point, off the main path; take this to the summit, which is about 40 minutes from Fiesole, at a slow stroll.

Cross the flat area at the summit, to the path at the far left corner; almost immediately the Maiano path branches off to the right **B**. (It's signed.) Follow this; it's marked with CAI red and white signs (it's route 7, though no numbers are visible at this point). The path winds steeply down. BE ALERT: watch for a sharp left turn where the path levels after 70 m. Take this and you'll soon see CAI 7 marked. Ignore the many side tracks; the path is well marked in red and white.

After 10 minutes, as you reach a concrete telephone pole, there's a path down to your right **C**: take this (there's a sign on a rock indicating that this is the way to Maiano), immediately branching right again at the fork. After another 10 minutes, there's another well-marked turn to the left **D**. Take this.

After 10 minutes, you come out on a dirt road; go right **E** (still marked 7). In a few minutes you'll come to an iron bar across the road marking the entrance to Maiano.

There is no bus to Florence from Maiano itself, but you can walk on straight down the road for about 15 minutes, to Il Salviatino, where you'll find a 17 bus-stop.

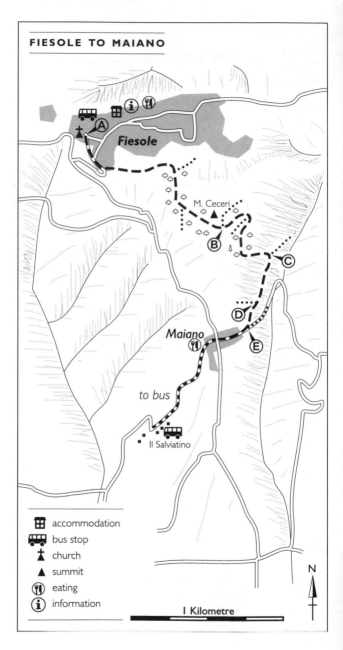

FIESOLE TO MAIANO

Fiesole

M. Ceceri

Ⓐ

Ⓑ

Ⓒ

Ⓓ

Ⓔ

Maiano

to bus

Il Salviatino

⊞ accommodation
🚌 bus stop
✝ church
▲ summit
🍴 eating
ⓘ information

N

1 Kilometre

8 | MADONNA DEL SASSO RING WALK
with Optional Spur to Santa Brigida

A perfect day walk from Florence, in the area of farmland and wooded slopes between the city and the Apennines known as the Mugello. The route takes you through a forest of massive evergreens, and out past the Sanctuary of the Madonna del Sasso (see below). There's an optional spur to the pleasant old village of Santa Brigida with its small but exquisite Romanesque church, well worth seeing. A somewhat rugged 40-minute climb on the way back rewards you with an excellent shaded walk through chestnut woods and sweeping views over the Mugello.

The Madonna del Sasso

In the year 800 a pilgrim (St Andrea) built a small oratory at Madonna del Sasso. Several centuries later, in 1484, some local shepherdesses had a vision of the Virgin Mary while praying for the recovery of their sick father. The father was cured, and in 1490 a church was built to commemorate the miracle. Wealthy Florentines adopted the church, hence its elegance. The altar contains a stone from the original oratory. Stairs to the right lead down to the chapel of the apparition and the cell of St Andrea.

Food

Not a gastronomic outing. There's a cheerful pizzeria opposite the bus-stop at Vetta le Croci (where you get off the bus from Florence), and a bar with food in Santa Brigida. For something more substantial you could try

Dino, a popular restaurant (also a hotel) in nearby l'Olmo, serving Tuscan basics at reasonable prices. Otherwise this might be the occasion to visit the great produce market in Florence (the Mercato Centrale) and put together a picnic.

LOGISTICS

MADONNA DEL SASSO RING WALK (with optional spur to Santa Brigida), 3¹/₂–4¹/₂ hours

🚌 Transport
🍴 Eating

🚌

FROM FLORENCE, AND RETURN

SITA bus (tel. 055-214721) route 313 (Firenze–Grezzano) or 316 (Firenze–Borgo San Lorenzo), though the 316 route would be of use primarily for the return trip, as this bus runs only quite late in the day. Make sure the bus you're taking stops at

l'Olmo; not all the buses on route 313 do.

Length of journey: 30 minutes
The place you actually want to get dropped off is about a kilometre further on from l'Olmo. Ask the driver to drop you at Vetta le Croci.

🍴
Dino
Via Faentina, 329
l'Olmo
Tel. 055-548932

PICNICS
The Mercato Centrale, a few blocks east of the railway station, in Florence.

Directions

After getting off the bus at Vetta le Croci **A** (see 'Logistics' above), turn back, taking the Fiesole road **B** (left), and then go first left again, following the sign to

Madonna del Sasso. After a few minutes, coming to the brow of the hill, turn off the road on to a stony track on the left. You can leave your car here if you're driving. You'll see the red and white CAI marker here.

Follow the track round to the right to CAI route 8 **C** (iron bar across the path); take this.

The route is shady (nice in summer), fairly gentle and fairly well marked in red and white. Ignore turnings unless otherwise stated.

After a while you enter a wood of massive evergreens. Very sombre and pleasantly cool. Passing a ruined house, you come in a few minutes to a T-junction; follow red and white markers to the left. The path narrows and then soon after meets a small road **D**. Turn left on this road – the path merges with it. Look out for some bizarrely distorted chestnut trees on your right, survivors of the 1939 chestnut blight.

MADONNA DEL SASSO RING WALK

This road leads to the sanctuary of Madonna del Sasso, about an hour's walk from the start.

At the sanctuary the road ends, and path 8 resumes. Follow this, looking out for a branch that leads off to the right down steps. This is route 8; take it **E**.

The steep, downhill, stony path goes out through an old stone gateway and passes a very pretty farmhouse. Continue straight on, joining a dirt track that leads through an olive grove. At the end, it comes out at a metalled road **F**.

If you don't want to do the Santa Brigida spur, turn left here, and pick up the directions after spur.

*SANTA BRIGIDA SPUR (and buses to Florence). From **F**, go straight on down the road for 50 m. At the bottom, turn sharp left, continuing straight on into the village (45 minutes to here from the Madonna del Sasso).*

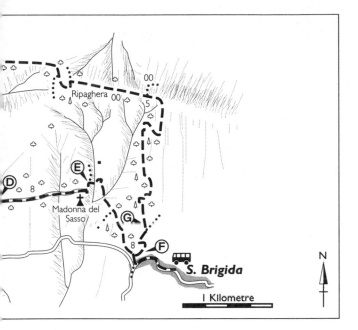

There are SITA buses from Santa Brigida to Florence.

*Leaving Santa Brigida, go back to where the CAI 8 dirt track came out on the tarmac road **F** and turn right uphill on route 5. You would have turned left on to this if you hadn't gone into Santa Brigida.*

TO CONTINUE WALK. After a steep 100-m climb, turn left off the road on to a path **G** (well-marked CAI 5 to Ripaghera); fine view back to Madonna del Sasso. A 40-minute fairly rugged climb follows, and then a fairly level passage through a chestnut glade. After another 20 minutes, follow the path left along the ridge.

In 5 minutes your path meets path 00. Take this left towards l'Olmo (signed). Your climbing is now more or less over. Sweeping views. Good places to picnic, though mostly wooded and shady with cool breezes.

Once your descent begins, continue along CAI 00,

ignoring a turn to the right and other deviations. Once you get back to where route 8 started, you'll see an easy short cut across fields to the bus-stop and pizzeria.

9 | VALLOMBROSA/SALTINO RING WALK
with Optional Spur

Fifty km south-east of Florence, at the edge of the Pratomagno (a range of mountains stretching between the Florentine Valdarno and the Casentino), lies the forest of Vallombrosa, site of an eleventh-century (but much restored) abbey, and favourite summer resort of the Florentines. Less wild than the Casentino forest, it nevertheless makes a pleasant outing from Florence, especially in summer, when the thick woods of beech and fir provide shade, and the higher altitude offers the chance of a cool breeze. Lush green meadows, spectacular views and an abundance of wild raspberries have made it a popular area for one of the great Italian institutions, the Sunday Picnic, which can mean traffic jams and hordes of people. However, since most picnickers seem to like to stick together, and to prefer a roadside site, it isn't too difficult to get away from them. Less easy to avoid are the military radar installations clustered on some of the mountain tops. These eyesores come as a terrible disappointment after you've slogged your way up to the ridges, and frankly they've more or less wrecked some of the classic walks in this region. Our own walk manages to skirt round them.

Vallombrosa itself is the site of an abbey, a restaurant, and not much else. The main resort centre is Saltino, a reasonably attractive village 2 km from the abbey. The tourist office here can give you a trail map, but even though the trails are generally well-marked, it's worth getting the real *sentieri* map. There's a ridge walk that runs from Monte Secchieta (1450 m) to Croce Prato-magno that many people recommend. However, you'd need a tent as there's no place to stay at the end, other than a rudimentary shelter, Rifugio Buiti.

The Abbey

The abbey was founded in 1038 by a Florentine, Gio-vanni Gualberto. The story goes that after his brother was murdered, Gualberto caught the murderer but decided to show him mercy, whereupon a crucifix (now in the church of Santa Trinità in Florence) miraculously bowed down to him. In 1193 Gualberto was canonized, and the Vallombrosan Order then became a powerful presence in Tuscany for several centuries. The abbey has been extensively rebuilt, and is no longer of great architectural interest, though the setting remains impressive. It still houses the Vallombrosan monks, and also functions as the arboretum for the Arezzo forestry institute, cultivat-ing more than 1500 species of forest plants. To arrange a visit, call either the Vallombrosa Forestry Office or the Sede di Vallombrosa (see 'Logistics').

The Walk

This is a half-day ring walk from Saltino, returning via the abbey at Vallombrosa, with an optional spur to Croce di Cardeto, well worth taking if you have the time (it adds about another 1½–2 hours to the itinerary). Much of it is through deep, sombre woods of beech and fir, though once you reach higher ground the woods give way to lush clearings with stunning views over the tree-carpeted hills of the Vallombrosa. Wild raspberries and blackberries grow along many stretches of the route. If you set off early in the morning you should have no trouble reaching Vallombrosa in time for lunch. Otherwise there are plenty of excellent spots for a picnic.

Food

Catering for Florentine weekenders and a resort clientele, the restaurants here tend to be a little fancier (though not at all pretentious) than in the nearby Casentino. Ristorante Giacomo in Saltino is a bustling, lively place, where the sight of the waiters lofting platters of appetizers such as *tonno e fagioli* or great dishes of wild blackberries and ice cream through the crowded dining-rooms, can hardly fail to raise the spirits. Prices are reasonable and the menu changes regularly. The *porchetta* (spit-roast suckling pig) spiced with juniper and lemon peel is well worth trying if they have it. Pizzas are served at night.

In Vallombrosa itself, the inexpensive little restaurant attached to the Pensione Medici serves the usual Tuscan standards, such as the thick vegetable and bread soup (*ribollita*), or ravioli with butter and sage, but done with care. The meats are well prepared, and on request, the chef made a particularly good, rather spicy *spaghetti carbonara* (cream, eggs and bacon). Our walk passes through here, and if you get off to a reasonably early start you should arrive in time for lunch.

LOGISTICS

VALLOMBROSA/ SALTINO RING WALK,

2½ hours without spur, 4–4½ with spur

🚌 Transport

Ⓜ Maps, guidebooks and trail info

🍽 Eating

🏨 Accommodation

ⓘ Miscellaneous info

🚌
FROM FLORENCE, AND RETURN

SITA bus (tel 055-214721), route 332 (Firenze–Saltino)
Length of journey: 1½ hours; easy trip, with fairly frequent service.

Ⓜ

- Carta dei Sentieri e Rifugi, sheet 31, 'Massiccio del Pratomagno', 1:25,000
- Carta Turistica e dei Sentieri, 'Parco Nazionale, Foreste Casentinesi, M. Falterona e Campigna', 1:50,000

🍽
SALTINO

Ristorante Giacomo
Via Carducci 12
Tel. 055-862185

VALLOMBROSA

Pensione Medici
Via Tosi Vallombrosa, 123
Tel. 055-862017

PICNICS

The Mercato Centrale in Florence, a few blocks east of the railway station

🏨

There is a good selection of hotels in Saltino, though in the summer you may have to ring round a bit before you find an empty room. We liked Hotel Le Terrazze very much, perhaps just for the novelty of it: very practical, straightforward and modern. Also very clean and bright.
Hotel Le Terrazze
Saltino
Tel. 055-862030

ⓘ

Tourist office: APT office (tel. 055-862003) in Saltino is open from 15 April to 15 September; they have a pamphlet with trail maps.
Forest ranger station (Stazione Forestale): Florence, tel. 055-862020;
Sede di Vallombrosa: tel. 055-862008

Directions

Heading downhill, south out of Saltino, pass the Ristorante Giacomo on your right; across from the Giacomo
on the left is a big parking lot. Here the main road bends
off to the right, and a smaller road continues straight
ahead uphill – signed 'CAI 13, Secchieta'; take
this **A**.

The road climbs, and then bends to the left where, as
the asphalt gives way to a stony road, there's a deviation
to the right, uphill, on a slightly smaller stony track **B**.
Take this (signed CAI 13 on a stone wall on the left of
this road).

The road climbs fairly steeply, passing (about 20 minutes out of Saltino) a big old stone house on the left, Bocca
del Lupo. (The IGM map is a little off here, as regards
the placement of Bocca del Lupo in relation to CAI 13.)

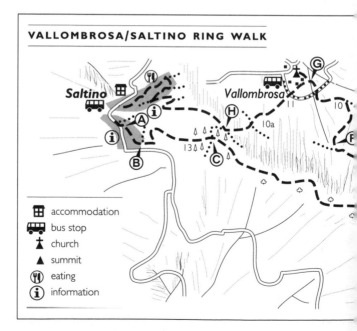

VALLOMBROSA/SALTINO RING WALK

☗ accommodation
🚌 bus stop
✝ church
▲ summit
🍴 eating
ⓘ information

Passing through a very dark stretch of pine forest, there's an intersection of several paths **C**. On the right is a little shrine to the Virgin. The path to the left is signed CAI 11; straight ahead and uphill is signed CAI 13, the path we take.

Another 5 minutes of climbing leads to a clearing giving a wide view over Regello, and a very nice pathway along the ridge (with many raspberries and blackberries), with views. It is very green and lush up here, even in summer: dwarfed beeches, yellow broom, ferns, flowers, and the tree-carpeted hills of the Vallombrosa stretching down into the valley. It is a very gentle, relaxing walk along here, with no climbing.

About an hour after leaving Saltino, you'll see our path being joined by path 12, coming in on the left **D**.

For a ring walk without the spur, turn left (on to

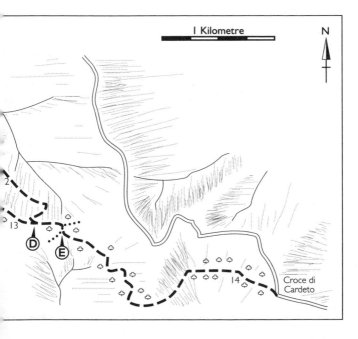

path 12) here and skip over the following spur directions.

*SPUR: Rather than turning left where the path is joined by
path 12, continue straight ahead here, quickly reaching a fork
by an old 'casetta forestale', forester's hut. Take the right
fork, signed 'Al CAI 14,'; there is also a yellow sign for
S. Antonio.*

*Watch on the left, in 50–100 m or so, for a smaller path
off to the left where the bigger path we've been on makes a
hairpin turn to the right. The bigger path (with the hairpin
turn) is signed 'CAI-FI-14 CR. CARDETO'. Don't
take this. Instead, take the smaller path off to the left **E** (which
is CAI path 14 on trail maps).*

*About 30–40 minutes after beginning the spur you'll pass
a promontory/lookout and then an old stone hut on the left,
with some stone seats outside, as you re-enter the woods. Just
past here, there's a little turning leading to CAI 15. Ignore
it, and stay on the main path.*

*In another 20 minutes or so, you will pass a gate across
the path (to stop cars). You now come out on a hilltop with
a big wooden cross, the Croce di Cardeto, and a splendid
view.*

*Return the same way you came, passing the forester's hut,
and reaching the fork where the spur began **D**. CAI 13 is
now on your left, CAI 12 on your right. Take the right-hand
path (CAI 12), signed for Vallombrosa.*

Continue along this way until you reach, after more
than 1 km, a fork downhill to the right (CAI 10); take
this **F**.

Stay on this very old path, descending towards
Vallombrosa (ignoring a deviation to the right signed
'al 9').

Eventually the path crosses an asphalt road and continues on the other side; soon after this there's a

T-junction **G**. Turn right here, reaching the monastery on the left about 20–30 minutes after spur reconnects with the ring portion of the route (about 3½ hours after leaving Saltino if you do the spur, or 1½ hours if you didn't).

Leaving Vallombrosa

(Note that you have the option of taking the SITA bus back to Saltino from here.)

Pass through the monastery. From the front of the Pensione Medici Ristorante (the side facing the monastery), turn left on to the main asphalt Via S. G. Gualberto. You can go back along the road – there's foot traffic paths off the asphalt, and it's flat, but trafficky.

Otherwise, return to the path you came into Vallombrosa on, by following CAI signs for '10 & 11'.

Reaching (in about 5 minutes) the fork where 10 and 11 split **G**, take the right fork, path 11 (you came down on 10). In a short while you cross the asphalt and continue up the other side.

There's a 10 minute steep climb here, after which you pass a turning on the right for 10/a; ignore it and carry straight on.

Shortly you will come to a T-junction **H**; go right (CAI 12), staying on this stony dirt road, bypassing the immediate turn on the left which is the continuation of path 11 (and will lead to path 13 if you want to go back the way you came).

About 45 minutes after leaving Vallombrosa, you'll reach a bar across the road as the path comes out on another dirt road; turn left (12/a).

In another 5 minutes, take a right downhill turning (at a lamp-post on your left with a yellow sign for

Vallombrosa); then take the first left (hairpin) turn you come to. This gravel road winds down in about 10 minutes to the main asphalt road where you turn left and go into Saltino.

THE CASENTINO

The vast forest reserves of the Casentino in the northern Apennines, where the Arno has its source, offer some of the most peaceful and fascinating walking in Italy. In easy striking distance of Florence, and yet utterly remote in atmosphere, the 26,200 acres of heavily wooded peaks running along the border of Tuscany and Emilia Romagna have been largely unchanged since the last Wurmian glaciation, ten thousand years ago.

Franciscan and Benedictine monks were attracted to the area in the late Middle Ages, and the three monasteries of Camaldoli, La Verna and Badia Prataglia are still the only major human settlements. The long association of these monastic orders with the idea of preserving wildlife (even today the monks at Camaldoli, still involved in the stewardship of the forest, observe a rule ordering them to plant five thousand trees a year) seems to have fostered an attitude of quiet respect for the area; not always the case with Italy's wilderness.

The forest is criss-crossed with well–marked trails that follow old mule tracks or paths between the monasteries. There are still traces of the *vie dei legni*, or wood roads, dating from centuries ago when the Grand Duchy of Tuscany used the tallest and straightest trees as masts for its navy at Pisa, dragging the vast trunks (they had to be at least 90 feet high to qualify) through the forest with teams of oxen. Streams, waterfalls (including the famous cascade of Acquacheta, immortalized by Dante in the *Inferno*), green alpine meadows, high breezy ridges with spectacular views, and the deep shade of the forest itself, make the area pleasant for walking even in summer; a perfect antidote to the stifling bustle of Florence in July and August.

From a naturalist's point of view, the Casentino is extraordinarily rich. Italy's first 'Natural Integral Park', the Sasso Fratino, was established inside the forest in 1959 as an enclave for ecological research. Entry is restricted, but you don't need to go inside it to experience the wealth of local wildlife. Populations of red deer, fallow deer, mountain sheep and the ubiquitous wild boar thrive. The Apennine wolf has made a comeback here, the most northerly extension of its territory to date. Woodpeckers – green, spotted, and the rarer black – flit through the trees (the hysterical chatter belongs to the green). From the high clearings you can see eagle-owls, kites, goshawks and allegedly even golden eagles circling over the valleys. Up to about 800 m the woods have a wide variety of deciduous trees: hornbeam, turkey oak, maple, lime, elm and chestnut (at one time a principal food source for the region). White fir, mountain ash and beech trees dominate the higher altitudes. The twisting, wind-stunted, silvery limbs of the ridge-top beeches in particular give the walks there a mysterious, enchanted quality. The flowers, too, are stunning: anemone, primula and violets in the woods; gentian and narcissi in the meadows. Rare species of saxifrage grow in the rocks at the top of Monte Falco, where you can also find black myrtle and the extremely rare red myrtle. Flower charts have been set up at one or two of the mountain refuges you pass on your way, to help you identify the mass of different species.

The Walks

The itineraries we have selected for this area include three to four days' worth of connected but separable walks, beginning at the monastery of Camaldoli and finishing in San Benedetto in Alpe. Public transport is available between Florence and all of the main staging-posts (though Campigna is a bit of a haul; see 'Logistics' for more details), making it easy to do only a particular section of the itinerary, if you prefer.

Also contained in this section are day or half-day ring walks in Camaldoli and Badia Prataglia.

These are mountain hikes of moderate difficulty, steep in places but with a high ratio of reward to effort. Remember to bring food and water, something to keep you dry and, if possible, a compass.

Food

Restaurants in the area go in for simple but robust dishes. The local fauna turn up in stews, salami and *scottiglie* (a form of grilling). *Porcini* mushrooms, raspberries and wild strawberries grow abundantly in parts of the woods; these are always worth ordering when the restaurant has them in fresh. Waverley Root, an authority on Italian cuisine, recommends the region's small juicy hams and delicately flavoured trout. He notes that the best chickens in Italy are raised in the Arno valley, below the forest, and awards the local *vin santo* (equivalent of the French Sauternes) second prize in all of Italy, after those of the Val di Pesa. Local dishes include *acquacotta* (an onion or vegetable soup thickened with egg), as well as cakes and polentas made of chestnut flour.

10 | CASENTINO EXCURSION

This three- or four-day route offers some of the best walking in the northern environs of Florence. If you have the time, it's a wonderful way to get a rest from the push and shove of sightseeing, and to experience a superb bit of countryside. The area is of great interest for its enormous variety of natural vegetation and, because of the prohibition of hunting, it's rich animal and bird life.

The ambience differs from that of other walks in this book (with the exception of those in the Sibillini) in that there is less interaction with human settlements. In this sense, it bears a closer resemblance to the system of hiking trails found across state and national forest reserves in the US than most of our other walks, which revolve more closely around the larger towns. For this reason, you should definitely have one of the trail maps listed in 'Logistics'. The 'Parco Nazionale, Foreste Casentinesi, M. Falterona e Campigna' 1:50,000-scale map covers the entire excursion. The 1:25,000 maps don't, so you will need three of them (see individual 'Logistics' sections).

The route begins at the monastery of Camaldoli, and then climbs through mixed woods and high mountain meadows, eventually crossing the Monte Falterona massif, the highest peaks of the Tosco-Romagnola Apennines, and the source of the Arno river. The last day of the itinerary brings you to the Acquacheta Falls, and the mountain village of San Benedetto.

If you haven't the time or the inclination to do the whole walk, any part of it can be done on its own (the only difficulty being with the Camaldoli–Campigna and Campigna–Castagno d'Andrea segments, as there is no easy public transport link between Campigna and Florence, though it's not too difficult to hitch between Campigna and Stia, from which there are both trains and buses to Florence.) If you opt for only a segment of the itinerary, we particularly recommend the Camaldoli–Castagno d'Andrea segment, which takes you through the best parts of the forests, and over the impressive Monte Falterona massif. If you leave early in the morning from Florence (though you might want to consider leaving Florence late in the day and spending the night in Camaldoli instead) this segment can be accomplished spending only one night (in Campigna) away from Florence, bussing back from Castagno d'Andrea at the end of the second day.

Because of the very limited overnight options in this neck of the woods (i.e., if one place is full, you don't have a lot of alternatives near by), we strongly recommend booking all your hotel accommodation before leaving Florence, unless you're camping. However, don't be overly concerned if you don't reach anyone at the Posto Tappa; it is unlikely to be full, and it is the policy of all the mountain refuges to accommodate anyone who shows up.

There is a shop or bar in each of the stopover points, that can furnish you with picnic provisions.

Finally, a note on Il Muraglione. While none of the stopovers on this excursion are big towns, Il Muraglione is not a town at all, but literally just the hotel/restaurant. Therefore, unless you're planning to bus back to Florence from Il Muraglione, you may want to consider either taking at a very leisurely pace the walk from Castagno d'Andrea to Il Muraglione in order to arrive there rather late in the day, or on the other hand, to get an early start from Castagno and plough on through to San Benedetto. Be forewarned, however, that this latter option is a real haul.

CAMALDOLI TO CAMPIGNA

One of the three great monastic centres of the forest, Camaldoli still draws a fair number of pilgrims and tourists, especially in summer. It's a tiny place, pleasantly set in its densely wooded mountains.

The village consists of the monastery, and little else; 300 m uphill is the hermitage (Sacro Eremo di Camaldoli), founded in 1012 by S. Romualdo, a Benedictine monk who wanted to revive the ascetic spirit of the earliest Christian communities, and was given the use of the forest by Count Maldolo (thus the name). Despite its remoteness and the austerity of its rule, the place quickly attracted large numbers of visitors – not only pilgrims, but also minstrels, jesters, drunken soldiers and even prostitutes, who drifted there from the nearby court of Count Guido of Poppi. Not surprisingly, these visitors interfered with the solitary meditations of the hermits. Romualdo's solution was to establish a monastery lower down the mountain, specifically to accommodate visitors and look after the forest domains. This has been remodelled considerably over the centuries, but remains interesting for portions of the original cloisters, and for its sixteenth-century pharmacy where the monks sell their herbal preparations. Also worth a visit is the church, the Chiesa Maggiore, the interior of which was decorated by Vasari.

The hermitage is as austere as ever. The twenty little cottages where the hermits still live in silence, each with their own kitchen garden and chapel, remain strictly off limits. There is a prototype of the cottages, however, which is interesting to visit. There is also a gift shop there, and a small snack bar.

One of the most enjoyable in the area, this walk begins with a fairly steep climb through fir and beech woods from Camaldoli to the Eremo (you can take a bus), and then climbs again just beyond the Eremo, though this second climb is alleviated in summer by more raspberry bushes growing along the side of the trail than most people will have seen in their lives. After this climb, the path is simply one delight after another, an easy amble through high mountain meadows and mixed woods (predominantly turkey oak but also black and white hornbeams, maples and other oaks), culminating at Poggio Scala, one of the best panoramic points of the park. In the meadows surrounding the knoll, violet crocuses grow in spring, followed later by the big yellow flowers of a rare ranunculus.

From there the trail carries on to Passo della Calla and then a short descent leads you into Campigna and the civilized delights of the eighteenth-century grand-ducal palace, now transformed into an *albergo*.

NOTE. All the guidebooks to this area that we've consulted give some variation of the walk from Camaldoli to Castagno d'Andrea, and all use the Rifugio La Burraia as their overnight point. However, La Burraia is closed indefinitely at the moment, ostensibly for repairs, but there is no projected date at which these repairs are to begin, much less the *rifugio* to reopen.

Food

Attached to the Albergo Camaldoli is the Ristorante Camaldoli, a friendly, unpretentious place, with attractive outdoor seating, and a menu that makes a good attempt to incorporate the local specialities. For dedicated carnivores, the huge *antipasto* of cured stag, fallow deer, roe deer and wild boar is a must, though there is no way of telling which meat belongs to which animal. The hare sauce on the *tagliatelle alla lepre* is less a sauce than a stew poured over the pasta – it's tasty and extremely substantial.

The Albergo Camaldoli has a deli that sells the above-mentioned cured hams and salami, and is a good place to shop for a picnic.

The Granduca in Campigna is something of a culinary oasis. The food, though not of huge variety, is extremely well prepared. The salads are excellent. There's a delicious *tagliatelle* with fresh *porcini* prepared, unusually, with a little tomato. The *tortello* stuffed with potato and onion in butter and sage is also good, and the *panna cotta* with myrtles is wonderful.

LOGISTICS

CAMALDOLI TO
CAMPIGNA, 3¹/₂–¹/₂ hours

🚌 Transport
Ⓜ Maps, guidebooks and trail info
🅨 Eating
🎟 Accommodation
ⓘ Miscellaneous info

🚌

FROM FLORENCE

Take the train (tel. 055-288785) to Arezzo (³/₄–1¹/₂ hours, depending which train you get), and then change for the 'Casentino' (the smaller line that goes from Arezzo to Pratovecchio/Stia), which you take to Bibbiena (45 minutes). From Bibbiena, change to the LFI bus (tel. 0575-370687) to Camaldoli (about 20–30 minutes; the bus will not stop automatically at Camaldoli, so make sure to tell the driver that's where you want to get off, or

you might miss your stop). There are about six buses a day, so check the schedule.

Or take the 330 SITA bus (tel. 055-214721) from Florence to Bibbiena, and then connect with the LFI bus as above. About 2–2¹/₂ hours.

RETURN TO FLORENCE

Getting back to Florence from Campigna is not very convenient. You have to take the ATR bus (tel. 0543-27821) to Forlì, a two-hour ride, and then go from Forlì to Il Muraglione, where you get a SITA or STAM bus (tel. 055-841210) back to Florence; and as ATW there are only two buses a day from Il Muraglione to Florence, you might have to stay overnight in Il Muraglione.

The only other option is to hitch from Campigna to Stia (about 10 miles, all on the same road), from which there are numerous train and bus connections back to Florence.

Ⓜ

The bar at Camaldoli has maps with paths and signed trails.

- Carta dei Sentieri e Rifugi, sheet 33, 'Appennino Toscoromagnolo', 1:25,000
- Carta Turistica e dei Sentieri, 'Parco Nazionale, Foreste Casentinesi, M. Falterona e Campigna', 1:50,000

🍴

CAMALDOLI

Ristorante Camaldoli (attached to Albergo Camaldoli)
Tel. 0575-556019

Foresteria S. Eremo (monastery)
Tel. 0575-556013; fax
0575-556001

PICNICS

The Albergo Camaldoli has a deli that sells cured hams and salami; it is a good place to shop for a picnic.

CAMPIGNA

Granduca
Tel. 0543-980051

Lo Scoiattolo
Tel. 0543-980052

🏠

CAMALDOLI

(There are several other hotels in Camaldoli; look in a general guidebook.)

Albergo La Foresta
Tel. 0575-556015

Albergo Camaldoli
Tel. 0575-556019

Foresteria S. Eremo (monastery)
52010 Camaldoli (Ar)
Tel. 0575-556013; fax
0575-556001
Office hours: 8.30–12 and 3.30–6.30

Camping: Campeggio Pucini (tel. 0575-556006) or Fonte al Menchino (tel. 0575-556157).

The local forestry authorities have set aside wooded camping sites at Camaldoli and Campigna. See the Stazione Forestale below. Camp-sites are usually only open from June to the end of September, so check ahead at other times.

CAMPIGNA

Granduca
Tel. 0543-980051; fax
0543-980016

Albergo Lo Scoiattolo
Tel. 0543-980052

Camping: There's a *rifugio* (Rifugio La Calla) at Passo della Calla. If you're interested, you can get the key from Albergo Lo Scoiattolo in Campigna.

The local forest authorities have set aside wooded camping sites at Camaldoli and Campigna; see above.

(i)

Local CAI: tel. 0575-355849
Forest ranger station (Stazione Forestale): Camaldoli, tel. 0575-556014; Campigna, tel. 0543-980174

• La Burraia is closed indefinitely.
• Make all hotel reservations before starting this walk.
• There are a couple of LFI buses (tel. 0575-370687) daily between Camaldoli and the Eremo (which cuts out some significant climbing).
• There is a small ornithology museum at Camaldoli, open in the summer.

Directions

Leaving Camaldoli, pass the monastery on your right and continue straight ahead (ignoring the right turn across bridge), passing PT (post office) on your left. Take the asphalt road here, not the footpath to its left.

Pass a chapel on the right and then cross a stone bridge; 75 m or so after this, take the footpath to the right (by a CAI 72 mark) **A**.

Following CAI marks, the path goes through firs, follows along a stream and crosses an asphalt road. The second time it crosses the asphalt, don't cross over, but turn left on to the asphalt (CAI signed); the path goes off again in about 10 m, to the left. The way is well signed here by the CAI; just follow their marks.

Shortly after this, the path crosses a stream and continues on the left side of the stream, but this isn't altogether obvious as there's a path going straight along the right side too. There's a CAI mark here, intimating that you cross the stream, but no CAI sign on the other side to confirm. You *do* cross however, and the path begins to climb steeply (and soon comes to a CAI mark).

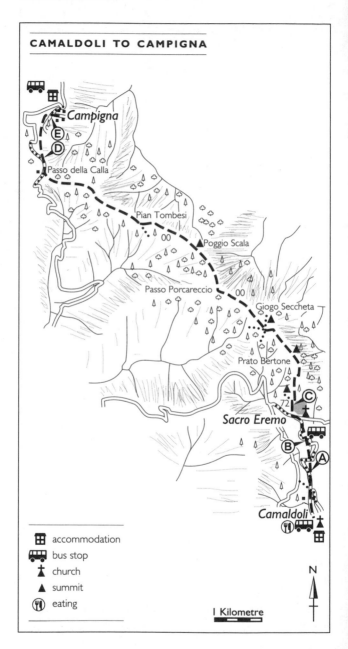

CAMALDOLI TO CAMPIGNA

Campigna

E

D

Passo della Calla

Pian Tombesi

00

▲ Poggio Scala

Passo Porcareccio

00

Giogo Seccheta

▲

▲

Prato Bertone

▲

72

C

Sacro Eremo

B

A

Camaldoli

⊞ accommodation

🚌 bus stop

✝ church

▲ summit

🍴 eating

N

1 Kilometre

About 40 minutes after leaving Camaldoli, the path comes out on the asphalt again at Tre Croci (three wooden crosses) **B**. Cross over; the CAI mark is just beyond crosses, though it's not visible from the road. Ten minutes later, you reach the Sacro Eremo di Camaldoli.

Leaving the Eremo, pass in front of it, keeping it on your right. At its edge, take the dirt and stone path leading uphill to the right of the asphalt road and skirting the wall of the Eremo. Follow the wall to the back of the Eremo, where you'll see the path straight ahead signed by CAI (72). (This is also a section of the long-distance GEA trail.)

After a short steep climb, the path turns right **C** for Passo Bertone – well signed – and continues to climb.

About 40 minutes after leaving the Eremo, you'll come out on a dirt road; turn left. There is a level walk along here, shady, which soon passes the beautiful little meadow, Prato Bertone, on the right.

Pass the sign and path for 'Batti Locchio, 1.580 km'.

About fifteen minutes later, after walking through mixed meadows and patches of woodland, come to an open space with several paths serving all directions. This is Giogo Seccheta. Follow the CAI-marked trail ahead to the right and uphill.

About 2 km later (at Passo Porcareccio), CAI 78 leads down to the left. *Don't* take it. In another 10 minutes or so (about 1 km), you'll come to the wayside shrine of the Madonna del Fuoco on your right. As you face it there's a hill to your right with a path up it: this is Poggio Scala, one of the great panoramic points of the park. Don't miss it.

Continuing on through beech wood, you'll reach in another half hour or so the pass at Pian Tombesi, 1403 m (sign on right of path), and another ½ hour or so beyond here the asphalt road at Passo della Calla.

At Passo della Calla there are several CAI routes marked. Our route is not, at this time, marked by CAI. Turn right on to the main asphalt road and follow it downhill towards Campigna.

About ½ km from Passo della Calla (past a metal guard-rail on the right) there's a small path off to the right downhill – you'll see a small wooden sign, 'Croce del Piccino 37; Campigna', with red CAI marks too. Take this **D**.

Follow the CAI marks.

The path comes out on a bend in the asphalt road again (about 10 minutes from Passo della Calla), but don't actually walk on to the road; instead, turn right and walk *behind* the guard-rail, following the path as it drops down to the right of the road here.

This is a really pretty path – either cut out of rock, or in the steep parts beautifully built with small slabs of stone driven vertically into the ground. Shady and all downhill.

The path crosses over a stone and wood bridge, and then climbs a bit to the left of a stone basin where the stream forms a pool. Just beyond there, the path comes out on an asphalt intersection – go downhill to the right **E**, reaching the hamlet of Campigna about half an hour after leaving Passo della Calla.

CAMPIGNA TO CASTAGNO D'ANDREA

This walk leads over the principal peaks of the Parco Nazionale di Monte Falterona, Campigna e Foreste Casentinesi, down through chestnut glades and meadows full of wild flowers (poppies, broom, gentians, irises, etc.) to the small town of Castagno d'Andrea.

The Monte Falterona massif divides the plains of the Mugello and Casentino. In reality Monte Falco, at 1658 m, is the highest peak, but because of its fame as the source of the river Arno, it is Monte Falterona's name which has been given to this group of peaks.

The slopes are covered with dense fir groves and beech woods. Anemone, narcissus, black myrtle and the extremely rare red myrtle grow in the clearings near the summit.

In spring it can be foggy up here, but on clear days the summit offers spectacular views over a large part of Tuscany. The cliff of La Verna and the Chianti valley beyond are visible to the south, to the north the mountains of San Benedetto, and to the west the peaks of Abetone and the Garfagnana.

Food

At present the only restaurant in Castagno d'Andrea is the Osteria, where you need to let the proprietor know a little in advance that you'll be eating there. The food is plentiful, though a bit rough and ready, and more or less limited to what the proprietor happens to have in his cupboard. We had ravioli in a robust tomato sauce, and a good *pasta in brodo* (pasta in broth). An otherwise straightforward (and fresh) salad had the perplexing addition of some large raw artichokes. Avoid the steak Fiorentina unless you enjoy chewing on shoe leather.

There's a kitchen at the refuge (Posto Tappa), but if you don't feel like cooking for yourself, this place is congenial and extremely cheap.

LOGISTICS

CAMPIGNA TO CASTAGNO D'ANDREA,

5 – 6¹/₂ hours

🚌 Transport
Ⓜ Maps, guidebooks and trail info
🅨🅘 Eating
🄷 Accommodation
Ⓘ Miscellaneous info

🚌

If you can get your hands on a STAM bus schedule, it's very useful for travelling between Florence and either Castagno d'Andrea or Passo del Muraglione, should you be picking up or leaving the itinerary at either of these points. It lists not only STAM buses but also SITA buses and train (FS) schedules. This is particularly useful because SITA and STAM sometimes connect with each other or with the FS in Dicomano or Pontassieve, rather than doing the whole route themselves.
Bus info: SITA, tel. 055-214721; STAM, tel. 055-841210
Train info: tel. 055-288785

FROM FLORENCE

Getting to Campigna from Florence is not very convenient. (See 'Logistics' p. 143) If you don't mind hitching, however, you can take the train from Florence to Arezzo, and then change for the 'Casentino' (the smaller line that goes from Arezzo to Pratovecchio/Stia), which you take to Stia. Then you have to hitch either to Campigna (about 10 miles, all on the same road) or to Passo della Calla (about 8 miles on the road to Campigna, where you can pick up our walk directions from the previous itinerary and walk the hour or so from Passo della Calla to Campigna).
Length of journey: about 2¹/₂ hours to Stia

RETURN TO FLORENCE

If you're eager to get back to Florence when you get to Castagno, ATW there are a couple of STAM buses (route 102) on workdays back to Florence from Castagno between 5 and 6 p.m. (connecting with the train in Dicomano), and a SITA bus (route 324) at 7.40 p.m. (also connecting with the train in

Dicomano). Alternatively, you could stay overnight in Castagno and take a very early bus back. (ATW there are SITA buses at 5.50, 6.20 and 11.40 a.m.)
Length of journey: 1½–2 hours

Ⓜ

- Carta dei Sentieri e Rifugi, sheet 33, 'Appennino Toscoromagnolo', 1:25,000
- Carta Turistica e dei Sentieri, 'Parco Nazionale, Foreste Casentinesi, M. Falterona e Campigna'. 1:50,000

🍴

There is only the Osteria, in Campigna. Drop by when you arrive in town and let the proprietor know if you're planning to eat there. It is very cheap.

For breakfast, down the road from the *rifugio* (in the direction of our walk) is a bar where you can have coffee under a grape arbour and trellises hung with flowers.

🏠

At Castagno d'Andrea, there is the Posto Tappa (*rifugio*, very primitive.) Ask either in the Osteria or the bar down to the left of it (as you have your back to it) for the keys to the *rifugio*. This is a clean, plain, pleasant place, with a clean kitchen and bathroom, 3 bedrooms with a total of 16 beds, blankets, pillowcases and pillows supplied (not sheets or towels). We had the whole place to ourselves on a weekend in May. In July it's best to book: tel. 055-8375133. It is very cheap; about L.10,000 per person
Camping: there are a couple of rudimentary refuges (no beds, but fireplaces, water on tap and grills) around the parking lot mentioned in the route directions (about an hour out of Campigna).

There's also free camping in pretty wooded sites set aside by the forest authorities at Castagno.

ⓘ

Tourist office: San Godenzo, tel. 055-8374023

Directions

The first part of this trail is well marked by CAI.

With the front of Albergo Lo Scoiattolo on your right (the Granduca Hotel down the road behind you) you are facing a fork. The right uphill prong of this fork has a little wooden sign pointing to La Calla. Take this **A**.

Very soon there's an intersection with a bigger asphalt road; cross over and take the smaller asphalt road leading off the main road on the right, uphill. This smaller road is signed by CAI, and there's also a small wooden sign 'Fangacci 371'. The asphalt ends almost immediately, and is replaced by a dirt and stone road which leads uphill through tall firs.

When the road forks (after about 100 m), take the right-hand uphill option **B**.

Soon you pass on your left a feature of these woods – beehives. The whole forest hums with the sound of the bees, too high overhead to be seen.

Continue on this path (also marked in green and white here), ignoring deviations (including one to the left about 20 minutes out of Campigna and another one 10–15 minutes later, a turning to the left over a stone and wood bridge crossing a stream, a CAI path marked by a small wooden sign on other side of bridge '371 Strada Provinciale' **C**).

About ½ hour later, the path comes out on a big parking lot. Cross to the far end. Across the main road from here you'll see a smaller tarmac uphill road (a military road), whose entrance is marked by the CAI on a tree to the left of it. Take this **D**.

Following this military road to the end, you'll see a military radar installation. A red and white marked path drops down from the left; take it to the right **E**. This is the long-distance GEA trail.

You may encounter fog along this stretch. Mixed

CAMPIGNA TO CASTAGNO D'ANDREA

beech wood and pasture. A huge structure looms: the top of the ski lift. The path is very clearly marked red and white '00', and sometimes GEA.

At the top of Monte Falco a signpost points right to Fontanella, but we keep going *straight on*.

In about 15−20 minutes, after a rough descent, the 00 path branches up to the right, marked red/white/red on a tree; take this **F**. There is then a steep, but mercifully short, ascent (about 10 minutes) across a small grassy knoll, back into woodland until you come to a turning on the right marked '16'; *don't* take this. The top of Monte Falterona is 50 m past this turning, marked by a rock with a brass plaque noting it as part of the Franciscan way, and a big cross. Be alert here, as it's very easy to take the wrong turn at the cross. Unless you want to go to the mouth of the Arno, DO NOT follow the leftward 00 path marked on a rock just beyond the path. Instead head to your right **G**.

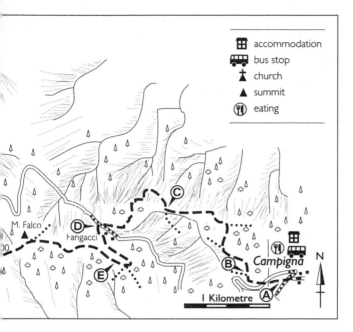

accommodation
bus stop
church
summit
eating

M. Falco
Fangacci
Campigna
N
1 Kilometre

The 00 path you do want is in the far right corner of the little pasture. (ATW the marks are painted on saplings.) After 50 m of grass descent, look for the red/white/red sign ahead of you leading into some woods across a wooden fence. Very steep at first, the path then levels off down along a wooded ridge with immense views.

About ½ hour from the summit you come to a grassy clearing. Path 17 is off to the right. It goes down to the top of the road to Castagno, but you can continue along the ridge by going straight ahead across the clearing, on the same red/white/red 00 trail. It branches to the left almost immediately – you want, not the broad uphill trail, but the narrow, less steep one.

After 15 minutes, you come to a long (100 m) grassy area with broom and purple columbines. The path re-enters the wood at the end of this on the right. Bear round to the right, as the path goes on in and out of woodland and meadow. It's usually easy to find the red and white marked trees at the end of meadows leading back into woods. The second big meadow is less easy, as the path is tucked away at the far left corner. A steep descent crosses a tiny stream, probably dry in summer.

There is a good picnic spot here, amidst a profusion of flowers, on a clearing overlooking Castagno.

Continue on 00 until you see a marked tree indicating '18' to the right (very easy to see as it's just in front of you). Take this right turning (18) downhill. The path winds a lot. Keep your eyes open for red and white markers; you should seldom be more than 30 m from one unless you're out of the woods. The path crosses a number of small streams, goes out of the woods across a scrub of broom and dog roses (fewer markings, narrow path) then goes back into the woods. Sound of streams everywhere in spring; violets, forget–me–nots.

Continuing on down, the path moves from beech to chestnut *castagno* trees; look for the saw-toothed leaves. The flora changes completely as you travel from a lovely chestnut glade full of flowers to an exquisitely fragrant pine grove.

In just over 1 km from the point where you left path 00 for path 18, path 18/a appears on the right. Both path 18 and 18/a will take you to the road into Castagno (on which you turn left), but 18 is the more direct of the two. However, you may find yourself on 18/a without realizing you ever left 18.

Path 18/a goes down into a valley full of ferns and delicate grasses, and then winds down through a series of small fields; always look for signs on trees, etc., before going too far in any direction. After crossing a little footbridge over a stream, the path comes out at a narrow tarmac road. This is the road into Castagno, to the left. CAI signs direct you to the centre of the village, about another 20 minutes from here.

CASTAGNO D'ANDREA TO PASSO DEL MURAGLIONE

A rugged, 3-hour walk, much of it through a heavenly valley with streams, ruined cottages overgrown with wild mint and oregano, and beautiful old farm buildings. A steep ascent at the end brings you to the high pass of Il Muraglione, with a memorial wall erected to mark the building of a road across the Apennines connecting the Adriatic and Tyrrhenian seas. It also marks the border between Tuscany and Romagna.

If you're feeling extremely energetic, you can go on from here to San Benedetto in the same day, but it's a very long day's march, and it would certainly be more relaxing to stay here in Il Muraglione, though be warned, there's nothing here except the wall, the *albergo* and the landscape.

LOGISTICS

CASTAGNO D'ANDREA TO PASSO DEL MURAGLIONE, about 3 hours

🚌 Transport
Ⓜ Maps, guidebooks and trail info
🍽 Eating
🎴 Accommodation

If you can get your hands on a STAM bus schedule, it's very useful for travelling between Florence and either Castagno d'Andrea or Passo del Muraglione, should you be picking up or leaving the itinerary at either of these points. It lists not only STAM buses but also SITA and train schedules. This is particularly useful because SITA and STAM sometimes connect with each other or with the train in Dicomano or Pontassieve, rather than doing the whole route themselves.

Another possibility in going to Castagno from Florence is to take the evening bus (ATW, SITA, 17.45, a 1³/₄ hour trip) as far as San Godenzo (on same bus route, earlier stop) and get the early (ATW, SITA, 6.05 – 6.20) bus to Castagno.
Bus info: SITA, tel. 055-214721; STAM, tel. 055-841210
Train info: tel. 055-288785

FROM FLORENCE

Both SITA (route 324) and STAM (route 102) have buses to Castagno d'Andrea
Length of journey: about 2 hours

RETURN FROM IL
MURAGLIONE

ATW there are two buses daily from Il Muraglione to Florence. There's the STAM bus 102

feriale, 8.20 a.m. *festivo* 8.15 a.m.) connecting in Dicomano with the train. There's also the SITA bus 324 every day at 4.25 p.m. which goes straight through to Florence. But check the current schedule.
Length of journey: 2 hours

Ⓜ
- Carta dei Sentieri e Rifugi, sheet 30, 'Appennino Toscoromagnolo', 1:25,000
- Carta Turistica e dei Sentieri, 'Parco Nazionale, Foreste Casentinesi, M. Falterona e Campigna,' 1:50,000

🍴 ⊞
Ristorante – Hotel Il Muraglione Passo del Muraglione, 87; 50060 San Godenzo (Fi) Tel. 055-8374019/8374393; Fax 055-8374393

Directions

Go down the hill from the *rifugio* at Castagno and turn right past the church out of the village.

Turn right at the stop sign, then left on Via San Martino, which is CAI route 14 **A**. There's a sign here with nature walks from Castagno marked.

The road crosses a stream and winds uphill. At the little cemetery, go left on CAI 14/b. After 25 m, the road forks; take the lower, right fork **B**.

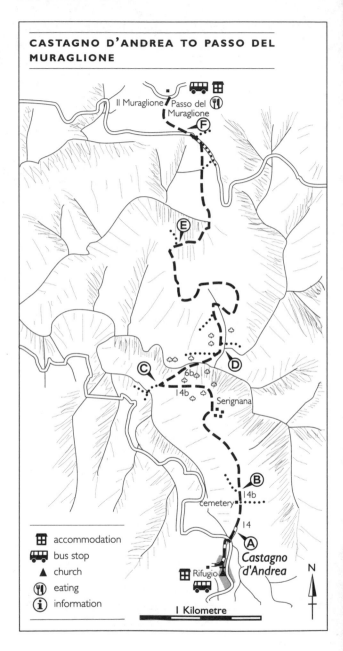

CASTAGNO D'ANDREA TO PASSO DEL MURAGLIONE

Il Muraglione Passo del Muraglione

F

E

C 6b D

14b

Serignana

B

cemetery 14b

14

A

Castagno d'Andrea

Rifugio

⊞ accommodation
🚌 bus stop
▲ church
🍽 eating
ⓘ information

1 Kilometre

N

The path climbs down this beautiful valley of woods and wild roses. As you approach the entrance to a stunning cluster of old farm buildings, the path cuts sharply down to the left (look for sign on tree) at Serignana.

The trail is well marked with red and white paint blazes. Go on down until you come to a little stone house. Just past it there's an intersection; take a sharp right **C**, on to trail 6/b (signed on a little tree) towards Il Muraglione.

For the next 3½ km you follow marked trail 6/b. In case you find it hard to pick up the marks (as always, they tend not to be there when you most need them), the following directions should make it easier.

Cross a narrow footbridge over a stream. Here is another gorgeous valley. Climb up, passing a waterfall down to your right. After about three minutes you come to a junction **D**; continue straight over it uphill, keeping to 6/b.

The steep ascent takes you through a little wooden gate. In another couple of minutes, where the path bends sharply to the left, there's a right turn across a stream: take this (you'll soon see a red and white marker).

The path zigzags past a ruined cottage, passing to the back of it, and then turns left again. Continue on up past some lovely old ruined farm buildings, where the path bends around to the right. You can look back across the valley and see where you came from.

Past the ruins you go through a wide gate, and then up to the *right* (not straight on). At the top, follow markings straight ahead (not right). You come to a clearly marked junction **E**. Go up to the right towards Il Muraglione (marked).

After 1 km you approach the road, with a concrete telephone pole ahead. Before you get to the road, the path forks. Take the left, downhill fork. In 75 m you reach the road. Turn left. Ignoring the first path up to the right, proceed about 100 m to a narrow path marked red and white leading up off the road to the right. Take this **F**. It is CAI 6.

A 15 minute steep ascent brings you to Il Muraglione – bar, restaurant, hotel. Magnificent view.

PASSO DEL MURAGLIONE TO SAN BENEDETTO IN ALPE

A long but exceptionally pretty walk through woods and meadows, ending at the attractive little mountain village of San Benedetto in Alpe. The high point of the walk is the Acquacheta waterfall – a wide veil of water shimmering over high rocks deep in a wooded valley. Dante, who spent part of his exile near here, paid memorable tribute to it in the *Inferno*:

> Straight my guide
> Pursued his track. I followed: and small space
> Had we past onward, when the water's sound
> Was now so near at hand, that we had scarce
> Heard one another's speech for the loud din.
>
> Even as the river, that first holds its course
> Unmingled, from the mount of Vesulo,
> On the left side of the Apennines, toward
> The east, which Acquacheta higher up
> They call, ere it descend into the vale,
> At Forlì, by that name no longer known,
> Rebellows o'er San Benedetto dell'Alpe, roll'd on
> From the Alpine summit down a precipice,
> Where space enough to lodge a thousand spreads;
> Thus downward from a craggy steep we found
> That this dark wave resounded, roaring loud,
> So that the ear its clamour soon had stunn'd.

> *Inferno*, xvi, translated by the Revd Henry Francis Cary

There are some primitive stone refuges you can camp in, as well as some beautiful fields in the last stretch from the falls. The whole falls area is popular on weekends and in summer.

Make sure you have one of the trail maps listed in the 'Logistics' section below.

LOGISTICS

PASSO DEL MURAGLIONE TO SAN BENEDETTO IN ALPE,
about 5 hours

🚌 Transport
Ⓜ Maps, guidebooks and trail info
🍴 Eating
🏨 Accommodation

🚌

FROM FLORENCE
ATW there's a STAM bus (tel. 055-841210), route 102, direct from Florence at 6.10 a.m., and a SITA bus (tel. 055-214721), 324, direct at 2.05 p.m.
Length of Journey: 2 hours

RETURN TO FLORENCE
The ATR bus comes through San Benedetto very early in the morning and connects to the early morning STAM bus at Il Muraglione to take you back to Florence. Either call ATR (tel.

0543-27821) or ask at your hotel for the exact time of the bus to Passo del Muraglione.

Ⓜ

The bar Il Muraglione has a good selection.

* Carta dei Sentieri e Rifugi, sheet 28, 'Appennino Toscoromagnolo', 1:25,000
* Carta Turistica e dei Sentieri, 'Parco Nazionale, Foreste Casentinesi, M. Falterona e Campigna', 1:50,000

🍴 🏨

Albergo Ristorante Pizzeria Acquacheta
Via Molino, 46
San Benedetto in Alpe
Tel. 0543-965314
Camping: Camping Vignale, San Benedetto in Alpe; tel. 0543-965245

Directions

Go around the back of the Hotel Il Muraglione. Red and white markings on a rock show the steep narrow uphill 00 path. Take this.

Continue following path 00, looking out for a sharp left (marked) uphill, which you take. There are various forks beyond here, but the route – a delightful, level trail through woods of evergreen – is generally well marked; just keep an eye out for the red and white trail blazes.

Half an hour from Il Muraglione you come to a T-junction. There are pink and yellow paint blazes on a tree at the right corner. Follow 00 up to the left **A**. Walk about 20 m on the track, and you'll come to a grassy opening. Path 00 leaves the track, bending to the right, up the incline.

About 5 minutes after this, the trail converges with an unpaved gravel road, follows it a very short distance and then takes off again on the left side (this is clearly marked), where it runs above the road.

Follow this ridge path for about 2 km through beech woods, until it comes out on a road. Turn right here (CAI 19). This is Colle della Maesta (about an hour or an hour and a half from Il Muraglione). From this point the path is well marked and easy to follow to the falls (Acquacheta) and on to San Benedetto.

After about 20–30 minutes, the road deteriorates a bit, into more of a rutted track. A few cars may be parked here (Il Crocione). There's a sign about Dante's having been there and described the falls in the *Inferno*. To the right of our trail, behind a bar, is a CAI trail to the eleventh-century hermitage visible in the distance away to the right, continuing on to Osteria Nuova and the state road connecting Il Muraglione and San Benedetto. (However, we do not go that way.)

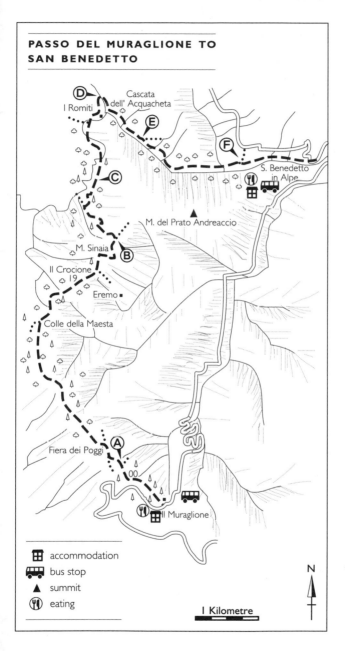

PASSO DEL MURAGLIONE TO SAN BENEDETTO

D
I Romiti
Cascata dell' Acquacheta
E
F
S. Benedetto in Alpe
C
M. del Prato Andreaccio
M. Sinaia
B
Il Crocione
19
Eremo ■
Colle della Maesta
A
Fiera dei Poggi
00
Il Muraglione

accommodation
bus stop
▲ summit
eating

N

1 Kilometre

Continuing along the track (crossing the summit of Monte Sinaia) in about 15 minutes you'll see a marked path that goes off to the right **B**. This path (409/a), leads fairly directly (by way of Prato Andreaccio) to San Benedetto in about 4 km. It is shorter, but it misses the falls.

Following the principal track, you now descend steeply, with a series of hairpin turns, into the Acquacheta valley, reaching the river after about ½ hour. At the river, turn right **C**.

Crossing the river several times (getting boots wet in the shallow water, unless you opt to remove them each time you cross) the path goes through several small meadows before reaching a bigger pasture, I Romiti, with old monastic ruins on the right just after a ford. Head towards the stone building on a little hillock at the far side of the field and go left. This is the start of the falls areas. The path from here to San Benedetto is extremely well constructed, with steps and some post fences (these latter primarily after the falls).

Keeping to the left of the hillock with the stone building on it, the path descends to a small waterfall and pool with stepping stones. Cross the river here **D**, and a little further on arrive opposite the falls, Cascata dell'Acquacheta.

From here to San Benedetto the path follows the left bank of the river (i.e., the river is on your right), sometimes rising well above it. Note that the path, after the falls, is signed with a yellow and red mark, rather than the usual red and white. Along the way the path forks **E**; take the lower route.

Ignore a CAI turning (179) about 2½ km past the falls **F**. It is about an hour and a half to San Benedetto from the falls.

11 | CAMALDOLI RING WALK

A half-day ring walk, climbing fairly steeply through the forest from the monastery to the Eremo (hermitage) and continuing along old wood trails through a pretty part of the Casentino, with occasional panoramic views, and plenty of wild raspberries along the route in late summer. If your time is limited, or you need to finish where you started, this would be a good way of sampling the Casentino's unique blend of the monastic and the primeval. Otherwise, the individual sections of the four-day itinerary (see above) are generally superior.

For a shorter version, you can walk up to the Eremo and take the bus back down to the monastery (check the bus schedule first, as they are not terribly frequent), or vice versa.

LOGISTICS

CAMALDOLI RING WALK, 4–5 hours
For information on transport, etc., see pp. 143–5.

Directions

Leaving Camaldoli, pass the monastery on your right and turn right on the asphalt road **A** leading to Bibbiena, crossing over the stone bridge. Just as you cross the bridge, there's a gravel path on the left, leading to a little log hut with public toilets. Before reaching the hut, however (just about 5 m from the asphalt), there is a small wooden sign for Cotozzo, marked with a CAI sign (trail 68). Take this.

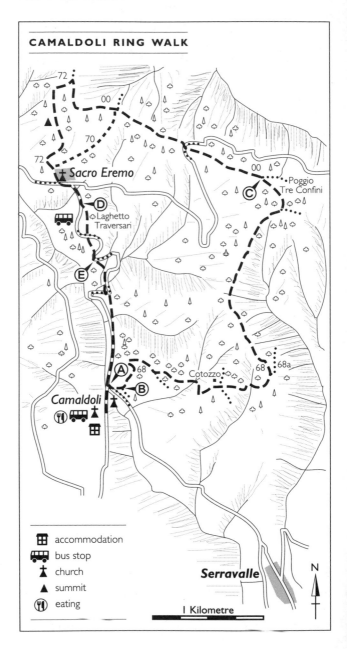

CAMALDOLI RING WALK

72

00

70

72

✚ Sacro Eremo

D

Laghetto
Traversari

E

Poggio
Tre Confini

C

00

Camaldoli

A 68

B

Cotozzo

68 68a

Serravalle

accommodation

bus stop

church

summit

eating

1 Kilometre

N

Soon you come to a big wooden cross (behind the monastery) at a fork **B**. Go left here.

The path climbs fairly steeply in this section, through mixed woods of beech, white fir and chestnut; but at least it's shaded, cool and windy even in the middle of summer. Just take it slow if you find it rough going; it's not too bad.

Follow this trail, ignoring smaller deviations and following the CAI markings. About 1 km out of Camaldoli, you'll cross a stream (Fosso del Ghiaccione). Soon after this you have a rather steep climb again, along an avenue of stately maples, leading you to the Rifugio Cotozzo.

When you reach the Rifugio Cotozzo on your left, turn right uphill. There is a little wooden sign about 10 m up the hill, 'Poggio Tre Confini', with CAI red and white markings. Stay on the main trail, following the CAI marks.

After passing an unmarked fork on the left, you come to another small fork to the left – this time, signed both ways. The larger path straight ahead is 68/a; the small one uphill to the left is 68: take this.

At Poggio Tre Confini (1½–2 hours after leaving Camaldoli), the path turns left (CAI signed) and descends.

Along here you can see the *cippus* (inscribed stones with goblets on them) marking the old boundaries between the holdings of the Grand-duke Leopoldo II and the property of the Camaldolesi monks.

After descending for a short time, you come to a T-junction **C** with a sign on the right to Poggio Tre Confini, and CAI on the left. Turn left, joining with the CAI 00/GEA ridge trail. You may be able to spot raptors along here, as they have a tendency to fly along the line of the peaks.

In 15 minutes or so, the path comes out on to asphalt.

Make sure to follow the path to the end, where it connects with the asphalt – by the little wooden sign 'Poggio Tre Confini/Fangacci'.

Across the asphalt from here (NOT path 70/a signed for Sacro Eremo; though it does lead to the Eremo, the last section of that route is on the road), find a path towards the right, going uphill: this is path 00, with signs for Porcareccio and Poggio Scali, as well as green and white and red and white paint marks on the trees.

Following this stone road you may notice traces of the old Franciscan stonework in it. After 10–15 minutes you'll reach a three-way fork. To the right downhill is signed 'Acuti: Lama'; to the left downhill is signed 'S. Eremo and CAI 70'. Our path continues straight on, but if you're tired, you can drop down to the Eremo from here on CAI 70, which is a more direct route. If you want to go on, there are lots of raspberry bushes as well as some panoramic views. But you do have to do another 10-minute climb.

If you continue, follow CAI 00/GEA for another 20 minutes or so until you reach a left-hand fork signed '72 Eremo' and GEA. Take this.

In this stretch you get your panorama, sun and raspberries. A 20-minute descent brings you to the wall of the Eremo; follow the path along the wall until you arrive at the front of the Eremo.

After visiting the Eremo, take the asphalt road towards Camaldoli. When you come to a fork with a dirt road on the left, take it **D**. You should see the CAI/GEA mark near by.

In 50 m or so, pass a fork down to the lake, Laghetto Traversari, on your left. Keep straight on, following the red and white markers.

The path crosses the asphalt road at Tre Croci (three wooden crosses). Where the path next comes out on the road, it will follow the road for a short distance; watch carefully for the path to resume on the right side of the road **E** where the road itself bends left.

The path will cross the road several times again before you reach Camaldoli, sometimes following it a short distance. Just follow the CAI marks.

Where the path comes out on the road, about 40 m above a stone bridge, stay on the road until the path goes down on the right about 10 m before the bridge, and continue on into Camaldoli.

12 | BADIA PRATAGLIA RING WALK

Badia Prataglia is a cheerful little mountain town (855 m) functioning as the main tourist centre of the Casentino region. Apart from its Benedictine abbey, founded in the tenth century, most of the town is fairly new, but it's pleasant enough, and so far seems to have escaped the kind of tackiness you find at other mountain resorts, such as Monte Amiata in southern Tuscany.

The Walk

This is a half-day (minimum) ring walk passing through deep woods of chestnut, fir and beech. Even in summer it can be fairly cool (and is much cooler than town, so bring something warmer to wear), especially along the ridge section, where surprisingly powerful winds blow more or less constantly. After the initial steep climb above the high pass at Mandrioli, the going is fairly easy. The relatively high altitude (about 1200 m mostly) adds a remote, other-worldly quality to the cloister-like atmosphere created by the tall trees arching over the old woodland paths.

Food

Food, unfortunately, is not a strong point here. There's a good bakery across the street from the Pensione Bella Vista in Badia Prataglia, where you can buy an excellent blackberry cake. But the restaurants – many of them in hotels that appear to double as retirement homes – are pretty unenticing. It's well worth going a few miles out of town to the little village of Serravalle (you can stay here too if you prefer), where the restaurant Italia Nuova/al Parco serves traditional Casentinesi dishes; a good way to sample the local cuisine. There's a L.10,000 sampler plate of *antipasto Casentino*, featuring, among other things, crispy fried ravioli with ricotta, *panzanella* (bread salad), and a dark, very intense grilled chestnut flour polenta. They make a delicious *acquacotta* (onion soup thickened with egg) and a respectable *funghi trifolati*, with fresh mushrooms (many places use preserved mushrooms for this dish). Main courses are a little hit and miss, but the *capriolo in umido* (venison stew) is succulent, full of flavour and generous.

LOGISTICS

**BADIA PRATAGLIA
RING WALK** 4–4¹/2 hours
from starting-point, or 4¹/2–5
hours from Badia Prataglia

🚌 Transport
Ⓜ Maps, guidebooks and
    trail info
🅨 Eating
🏥 Accommodation
ⓘ Miscellaneous info

🚌
FROM FLORENCE
From Florence take the train to
Arezzo (45 minutes–1¹/2 hours,
depending on which train you

get) and then change for the 'Casentino' (the smaller train line that goes from Arezzo to Pratovecchio/Stia) which you take to Bibbiena (45 minutes). From Bibbiena, change to the LFI bus to Badia Prataglia (about 20–30 minutes; make sure to tell the driver where you want to get off, or you might miss your stop). There are about six buses a day, so check the schedule.

Or take the SITA bus from Florence (route 330) to Bibbiena, and then connect with the LFI bus as above. About 2–2¹/2 hours.

Train info: tel. 055-288785
Bus info: SITA, tel. 055-214721;
LFI, tel. 0575-370687; ATR, tel.
0543-27821

Ⓜ
• Carta dei Sentieri e Rifugi,
  sheet 33, 'Appennino
  Toscoromagnolo', 1:25,000
• Carta Turistica e dei Sentieri,
  'Parco Nazionale, Foreste
  Casentinesi, M. Falterona e
  Campigna', 1:50,000

Ⓧ
Italia Nuova/al Parco
Serravalle
Tel. 0575-519180

PICNICS
Blackberry (*moro*) cake and flat
oily pizza bread from the bakery

across the street from the
Pensione Bella Vista in Badia
Prataglia.

⊞
Italia Nuova/al Parco
Serravalle
Tel. 0575-519180
There are other places to sleep
in Serravalle (*affittacamere*).
Serravalle is nearly two thirds of
the way to Camaldoli from Badia
Prataglia (a little more than 2 km
from Camaldoli), good striking
distance.
Camping: Il Capanno, tel.
0575-509246

Ⓘ
Tourist office: (summer only) tel.
0575-509054

Directions

The starting-point for this walk is about 2 km out of
Badia Prataglia. You can walk or hitch along the road
to the starting-point, or you can take the bus. You want
the bus to Corezzo, which ATW leaves at 6.20, 7.52,
13.30 and 18.40 (but ask in the tourist office for exact
times). You can ask the driver to let you off: '*Vorrei
scendere dove inizia il sentiero per Passo dei Mandrioli*' or, if
that's too ambitious, '*Il sentiero per Passo dei Mandrioli, per
favore*' should do it. If you want to take a bus all the way

to Passo dei Mandrioli, and start the walk there, you have the choice of two buses: the ATR bus to Raggio which ATW leaves at 8.05 a.m., and an LFI bus which leaves at 8.45 a.m. Again, check in the tourist office for current information, or ring the bus company (see 'Logistics').

Leaving Badia Prataglia towards the east, passing the Pensione Bella Vista on your right, come to a fork just outside town (towards the La Quercia hotel). Take the right fork.

The road soon forks again **A**; take the right, lower one, towards La Verna and Corezzo.

At the next fork take the right, lower one.

Pass La Quercia on the left (and a bus-stop). Soon there's a sign that you're entering Chiusi della Verna. Just beyond that on the left is a stone road **B** and a little cement hut (with CAI and GEA signs on it). Across from the hut, on the other side of the stone road, there's a little sign, barely legible, to Passo dei Mandrioli. Take this stone road, the actual starting-point of the walk.

Passing a sawmill on the left, you'll see a path leading up behind it, and immediately forking. Take the left, lower, fork.

Follow CAI and GEA markers up to Passo dei Mandrioli. The route passes initially through chestnut and beech woods, and then fir. It's steep, so you won't be going too fast, which gives you plenty of opportunity to keep an eye on the markers.

When the path comes out on a quiet asphalt road, you've reached Passo dei Mandrioli. Turn left on the asphalt, heading towards and passing on your right the sign marking the end of Emilia Romagna and the beginning of Toscana, and the Poppi sign. Passing those signs on the right, the curvy road turns right round some small stone cliffs (and passes on the left an iron cross mounted

BADIA PRATAGLIA RING WALK

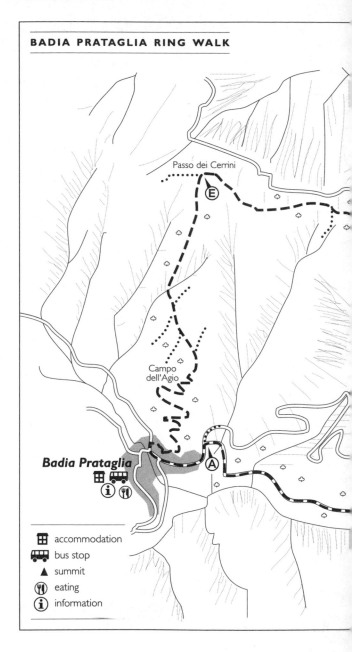

Passo dei Cerrini

Ⓔ

Campo
dell'Agio

Badia Prataglia

Ⓐ

	accommodation
	bus stop
▲	summit
	eating
ⓘ	information

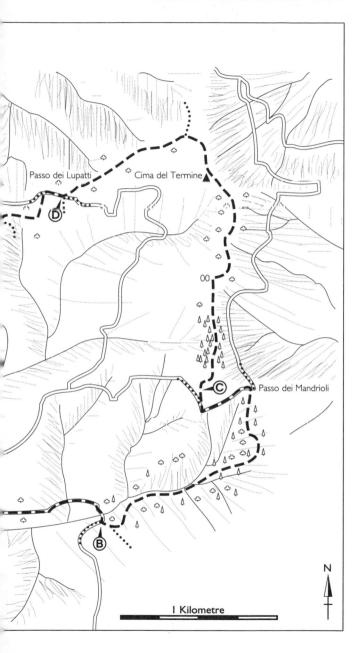

Passo dei Lupatti

Cima del Termine

Ⓓ

00

Ⓒ

Passo dei Mandrioli

Ⓑ

N

I Kilometre

in stone, marking the car death of a family) and then winds along past a little ANAS hut on the left. Just past the hut, the road makes the very sharp right turn (there are black and white road sign arrows marking the sharpness of this bend), and then straightens out for 50 m or so before bending left. Just where it's starting to bend left, see the CAI red and white 00 and some other green and white marks on a tree on the right side of the road. There's also a small wooden sign (like the one for Passo dei Mandrioli that you saw at the beginning of the walk) for Passo dei Lupatti. Take this **C**.

The path turns left immediately as you start on it at the bottom; watch closely for markings. Proceed slowly, following carefully the CAI or green and white signs. The CAI marks here, as on the first segment of this walk, are fairly frequent; you should not be in doubt as to being on the right path, but you have to watch the waymarks carefully. If in doubt, go back to the last mark you saw and try again.

As you begin to climb, you may notice the bed of a stream on the left, maybe 20 m away. Basically you're climbing straight uphill, parallel with that. It's steep, but just go as slowly as you need to; it's not far.

Soon (5, 10, 15 minutes, depending on how fast you take it) on your left you'll notice a clearing, and the path comes out on to this. It's very rocky – a slate sort of rock – with a clump of trees in the middle. There are some green and white markers (not in great shape ATW) along the right side of this clearing, on a tree and on the ground. But CAI seems to have abandoned us temporarily. Passing to the right of those trees, keep climbing up. You can see the ridge up ahead of you, and you just keep going towards it.

A few minutes later, after passing an area of barren rock just before the top, you reach the ridge and its tremendous views. Turn left, into the extraordinary-looking beech woods.

Follow along the path, keeping to the ridge (which divides Tuscany and Emilia Romagna). CAI is pretty spotty here, and there are several little deviations; but you just stay on the path which stays closest to the ridge edge on the right. It is very windy and cool. You can see the valley through the trees.

The path is fairly obvious – and CAI signs *do* appear intermittently. Keep to the ridge line as much as possible, joining at various points a slightly larger trail, a logging road. The route through these beautiful, tall beeches is fairly flat, with a bit of gentle up and down. When you notice the path has suddenly become extremely steep, you will be climbing Cima del Termine.

About 10 minutes after this, you come to the 'corner' of the ridge, where the path turns left (signed).

Always following the CAI route, you intersect a more major stone road about 15 minutes later **D**. Turn right here; *don't* follow the CAI trail straight ahead. The trail map and reality are two different things here.

Walk down this road a little way, until you come to a path forking up to the left (signed 'Crocina Fangacci 00. Km. 5020'). Take it. (There are several little signs along the right side of the road just past here, so if you reach these you know you've gone too far.)

In another 15–20 minutes, there's a turning to the left marked with green and white paint and a '44'. On the right side of the path is a stone with pink lettering; ignore this turn and keep straight on.

After another 15–20 minutes you'll pass another turning to the left, marked green and white with '43'. Turn left here **E**.

Follow this path down, waymarked in green and white. When the path forks, about 20–25 minutes later, bear left: there's a green and white sign. (Before this there was another path going left and uphill, but you wouldn't take it because it was going uphill.)

Another couple of minutes down there's an unmarked fork – take the left, bigger prong. Don't mind instructions too much – use common sense and just keep on downhill.

About ½ hour from the beginning of this descent, the path comes out by a grassy clearing with a wooden post fence around it and some picnic tables; this is Campo dell'Agio. Turn right and walk past the field (on your right), and follow the path that leads alongside it and then bends left at the corner of the field; and so into Badia Prataglia again, winding back and forth so that the descent is gentle.

NORTH OF LUCCA

13 | A WALK IN THE GARFAGNANA

The Alpi Apuane, Garfagnana and Orecchiella areas of north-west Tuscany offer extensive hiking opportunities, including two long-distance trails, 'Apuane Trekking' and 'Garfagnana Trekking'. This is a region catering for hikers, and as such is well mapped, well marked and somewhat beyond the scope of our book.

On the other hand, you may find yourself up in the north-west corner of Tuscany (on a visit to Lucca perhaps), and if this introduction to the Garfagnana encourages you to go the extra distance, it will have served a good purpose.

We've chosen the Garfagnana rather than the Alpi Apuane because the terrain is milder, better suited to a casual walk; and while less daunting than the Alpi Apuane themselves, the higher Garfagnana trails overlook the splendid, jagged peaks of their better-known neighbours. Moreover, whereas in summertime the high altitudes of the green Garfagnana valley offer a welcome respite from the furnace of lowland Tuscany, the heat can be blistering in the bare rocky summits of the Alpi.

The quiet little resort town of Corfino seems to be frequented solely by Italian families. It's an easy-going place, with little in the way of excitement, but at the La Baita hotel you'll get very good food, and if you're in the mood for a low-key environment well positioned

for an extensive network of walks, you'll see a side of Italy here that is completely tourist-free.

The Walk

This pretty walk begins amid farmsteads and streams, proceeds to the Botanical Garden of the Parco dell'Orec-chiella and then ascends to rocky outcrops, grassy hillsides and the towering cliffs behind them. After climbing to the top of the Pania di Corfino with its splendid views of the Alpi Apuane, the walk leads down to the Visitors' Centre of the park (and the Ristorante Orecchiella). The way back to Corfino passes through the tiny farming hamlet of Sulcina; when we passed through they were binding wheat into sheaves.

LOGISTICS

GARFAGNANA WALK

It is about 4 hours to the Visitors' Centre of the Parco dell'Orecchiella then another 1 1/2 hours back to Corfino.

A shorter option is possible, which skips the Botanical Garden and the ascent of Pania di Corfino, and goes directly to the Visitors' Centre, about 3 hours.

🚌 Transport
Ⓜ Maps, guidebooks and trail info
🅨🅘 Eating
🏠 Accommodation
ⓘ Miscellaneous info

🚌

FROM LUCCA TO CASTELNUOVO

By train: to Castelnuovo di Garfagnana from Lucca, on the Lucca–Aulla line

Train info: tel. 0583-47013 (Lucca) or 0583-62364 (Castelnuovo di Garfagnana)
Length of journey: 1 hour
Frequency: about ten per day
By bus: CLAP bus to Castelnuovo di Garfagnana; about ten per day
Bus info: tel. 0583-62039

FROM CASTELNUOVO TO CORFINO

CLAP bus, ATW three per day; the journey takes 25 minutes
Bus info: tel. 0583-62039 (8 a.m.–12 noon)

Ⓜ

Excellent information is available at the Comunità Montana in Castelnuovo di Garfagnana; see below.

- Carta dei Sentieri e Rifugi, sheet 15/18, 'Appennino Reggiano Modenese – Garfagnana', 1:25,000

🍴

CORFINO

La Baita

Via Prato all'Aia

Tel. 0583-660084/68680

Very friendly, family run. Reserve dinner; served at 8. Ravioli with ricotta and nuts. Pasta and chick-pea soup – very comforting. Pasta with very fresh, tasty artichoke sauce. Best gnocchi in Italy: home-made with a tomato–*pesto* sauce. Good garlicky turkey. The pleasant surprise of a tomato and borlotti bean salad. Everything beautifully cooked and inexpensive. Decent house red; avoid the white.

PARCO DELL'ORECCHIELLA

Bar Ristorante 'Orecchiella'

Parco dell'Orecchiella (near the Visitors' Centre)

Tel. 0583-619010

Closing day: Friday

Excellent salad, very good vegetable soups. Unusual *crostini* with a *salsa verde* and a red *salsa piccante*. Reserve.

CAMPAIANA

Bar Ristorante il Fungo Campaiana

Tel. 0583-68680 (or 660158 when the restaurant is closed)

Very friendly place up in the mountains; you can drive there if you've got a car, or take a day's hike there. (You can also stay overnight, but there is nothing there except this rustic restaurant. A nice ring walk would be to take CAI 56 to Campaiana, and the Airone 1 trail back to Corfino (make sure you have a map). Excellent ravioli with mushrooms. Open every day from 15 June to 30 September; otherwise only on Saturdays and Sundays (as long as the road isn't closed by snow).

CASTELNUOVO DI GARFAGNANA

Ristorante Triti

Via Garibaldi, 11

Tel. 0583-62156

A nice restaurant with very friendly service. Good, if minimal (you may want to get double orders of these) oven-roasted vegetables. Pizza. Excellent *pesto*. Substantial, robust, bacony *pasta all'amatriciana*: Nothing subtle, but fine.

⊞

CORFINO

Albergo La Baita
Via Prato all'Aia
Tel. 0583-68680/660084

Panoramico
Via Fondo la Terra, 9
Tel. 0583-660161

ⓘ

Tourist office. Castelnuovo di
Garfagnana: Comunità Montana
Garfagnana, Piazza delle Erbe, 1;
tel. and fax 0583-65169. Open
all year, and has excellent
information.
Listings for Corfino (in the phone
book, or in hotel guides, etc.)
will be found under 'Villa
Collemandina'.

Orecchiella Park Centre: tel.
0583-619098/65169.
Open daily July and August;
weekends only in June and
September, and by appointment
for groups October–May.

Next to the Visitors' Centre of
the park is a little shop that sells
some local specialities, such as
chestnut flour, honey, etc.

The alpine garden across the
road from the Ristorante
Orecchiella is preferred by some
to the Botanical Garden itself,
though the Botanical Garden
boasts the fascinating 'animal
faeces' exhibit.

Directions

Immediately before entering the grounds of the La Baita
hotel in Corfino, take the right-hand turn. In about 10 m
there's a left turn (signed CAI 58) up a path of large
stones; take this, passing La Baita on your left.

Continue to climb up this path, passing a tabernacle
and a fountain, both on the right, and ignoring deviations, stay on the CAI 58 trail.

Passing an old stone farm building on the right (currently a chicken coop), the path forks near a wooden
cross. Take the right fork, signed to CAI 56 and Campaiana.

When you come to a T-junction, turn right.

About ½ hour from La Baita, you'll reach the intersection with the Airone trail **A**. (*Airone* is an Italian magazine similar to the *National Geographic*, but perhaps more conservation-minded; they have created walking trails – several of them here in the Parco dell'Orecchiella – which are marked in blue and yellow.) Take a left and follow the Airone trail (which also, like the CAI route, goes straight on here).

In another 20 minutes or so, you'll reach a hut with a corrugated roof, currently painted red, just after an Airone sign (an actual sign, not paint marks), and the path turns left. You'll see Airone marks further along the fence here. The Airone trail is very well signed; if in doubt, just look for the marks.

Very soon after this, the path reaches a T-junction; turn right **B**, soon passing a working fountain on the left. The path follows on the right side of the stream now as it climbs. In summer, this area tends to be quite lush, with the result that the path is a bit overgrown in places.

About ½ hour past the thatched hut you'll come out on a T-junction **C** with a dirt road and signs of civilization (a fenced-in area with a lot of lamp-posts, actually a mountain hut, the Rifugio Isera).

SHORTER OPTION GOING DIRECTLY TO THE VISITORS' CENTRE: turn left on this dirt road **C***, over the bridge, with the picnic area below you on the left. Continue on past a fork sharply up to the right, until you arrive at the footpath marked 'Airone 1',* **a***, also to the right. Follow this path, which comes out into a field and there joins to a track* **G** *(you are actually converging with another path called 'Airone 1' here) that quickly becomes a small path passing between some cottages. From here, pick up directions from* **G** *on p. 189 – to finish the walk.*

Go right on this dirt road, which leads to the Botanical

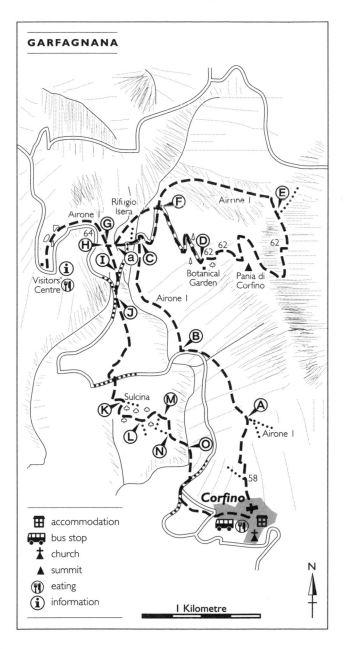

GARFAGNANA

Airone I

Rifugio
Isera

F

E

Airone I

G

64

H

I

a

C

D

62

62

62

n

Botanical
Garden

Pania di
Corfino

Visitors'
Centre

Airone I

J

B

Sulcina

M

A

K

Airone I

L

N

O

58

Corfino

accommodation
bus stop
church
summit
eating
information

1 Kilometre

N

Garden in about 45 minutes. The garden is in process of development, but worth a look.

LEAVING THE BOTANICAL GARDEN

The sheer cliff face to your left as you face the Botanical Garden is where we're going.

Standing outside the Botanical Garden and facing it, before reaching the treetrunk which is on display there, turn left. There's a little area with wooden benches and some big boulders (one of which is marked CAI 62), and also a wooden sign on a tree seeming to point to this sitting area. As you face this area (but before entering it), there's a small footpath, unmarked, to the left of it, going uphill. Take this **D**. (If in doubt, ask someone who works at the gardens where CAI 62 is. There is another way of getting there, but rangers recommend this way.)

There's a tiny wooden sign in the ground – on the right side of the path, near the bottom, barely visible, which says 'Pania n. 62'. As you climb, you'll see in about 20 m another CAI wooden marker with '62'.

Soon you reach a hillside completely covered in scree. Begin climbing up along the edge of this, going straight up to where the scree ends and the big rocks begin, where the path turns right.

It takes about 45 minutes to climb this hillside. The ascent is fairly tough going, and though it's marked, the marks are not always obvious. Just keep going along towards the peak you see in front of you; it's pretty clear which direction you want to head in. As you climb this hillside, you can see the Alpi Apuane behind you; the scenery is stunning.

Just below the main peak is a saddle. It's grassy here, and the path is trodden into the grass. Take this grassy track to the right as it leads to the top of the hill, Pania di Corfino.

At the top of the hill, pick up the Airone trail down the back of the hill to the edge of the woods, where there's a T-junction; go right (still Airone).

Follow this Airone trail down behind the hill, through alpine meadows with beautiful scenery and lots of butterflies.

About ½ hour's walk from the summit of Pania di Corfino there's a big wooden cross on a hillside. CAI 64 goes on ahead, re-entering the woods; Airone 1, the path you want, turns left downhill **E**.

In another ½ hour or so, coming out on the road to the Botanical Garden **F**, turn right. In a few metres you'll come to the Airone 1 trail on your right; take this.

Follow this Airone trail towards the Visitors' Centre, watching for a right turn at the corner of a stone wall (off what looks like a bigger path) that crosses a stream.

The shorter walk joins the longer one here **G**. Pass between some cottages (the path has been tarmacked here); the path comes out on a small asphalt road with a large stone monument to Bruno Segre **H** to the left. Turn right here.

Follow this small asphalt road. About 15–20 m before this little road comes out on a bigger asphalt road, there's a track forking off to the right towards a little wood cabin; take it.

About an hour's walk from the summit of Pania di Corfino, you'll arrive at Ristorante Orecchiella and the Visitors' Centre near by.

RETURN FROM VISITORS' CENTRE TO CORFINO

Go back the way you came as far as the stone monument to Bruno Segre **H**. The Airone 1 trail on which you came turns left here. Don't take that. Instead take the unmarked (ATW) path that leads straight ahead, past the monument (which is to your right as you pass it). It is the bigger, downhill path that you want here, not the smaller uphill footpath to the right of it.

Follow this until it comes out on asphalt **I**. Turn right. When you come to the intersection with the main asphalt road, take the first (unmarked) left **J** – about 10 m from the intersection – a fairly wide, grassy track.

Keep on this main path, descending towards Corfino, ignoring any smaller paths.

The path gets quite rocky, and then comes out on an asphalt road. Cross the road and continue on the path on the other side of the road. This path comes immediately to a small asphalt path; turn right.

Follow this asphalt path through the little farm hamlet of Sulcina, passing the Bar Ristorante Luisa on your right. Just beyond here, on the left, is a fountain (working) and a chapel. Instead of following the asphalt road – which turns to the right here – go straight ahead, downhill on a cement track between houses. This leads to a T-junction with the little tarmac road; turn left.

Follow this road as it winds downhill, making first a right-hand bend (maybe 40 m ahead) and then, just before it makes a left-hand bend, look for a gravel track off it to the right **K**, which looks like a driveway leading to a white (ATW) house with red tile roof. Take this.

This 'driveway' goes past the back of a newish house. Follow it to the right, where it becomes a dirt track, curving sharply left towards Corfino after 100 m. Beautiful old chestnuts line the path.

At the first fork (another 100 m), go left **L**. The path gets a little rougher here. It crosses a stream, and in about 150 m, where the main path bends round to the right, a slightly smaller path goes off to the left, effectively forming a T; (ATW there's a large wood pile here). Go left **M**.

The path bends to descend parallel to and to the left

of some telegraph poles. This is a beautiful secluded valley, though the path is somewhat overgrown. In 5–10 minutes the path converges with a better-maintained path coming from the right **N**. Continue straight on, going steeply down to the bottom of the valley, where you cross a stream on a little raised walkway **O** and begin to climb. Look out for the forlorn little abandoned house below you on your right as you climb. (Ignore the downhill fork that takes you down there unless you want to examine it more closely.)

In 2 more minutes you come out on the asphalt. Turn right, and go into Corfino. (Go left after passing Hotel California to get to the centre.) It is about 40 minutes from Sulcina.

SOUTH TUSCANY

Less frequented by tourists than Chianti but every bit as beautiful, and in fact superior in terms of its towns and buildings, the area below Siena, stretching from the monastery at Monte Oliveto south to Montalcino and east to Montepulciano, concentrates some of the most rewarding walks to be had in Tuscany.

Three quite distinct landscapes are linked by the itineraries in this section. Most dramatic is the region of eroded clay hills known as the *crete*, stretching intermittently between Siena, Monte Oliveto and Buonconvento. These strange, pale, barren-looking slopes, with their bare cliffs, broken gullies and white Jurassic limestone, look altogether more lunar than terrestrial. A number of elegantly austere farms nevertheless seem to be eking out a living here, grazing sheep and growing crops in the scoops and patches of fertile land. Nature, rather than man, is largely responsible for these eerie monuments to erosion. During the Pliocene age (between seven and three million years ago) much of Italy sank below sea level, creating marine basins where quantities of sand and clay were deposited on the land that subsequently emerged. The *crete* never acquired a protective layer of vegetation, and have been quietly disintegrating ever since.

Much of the rest of this area was later covered with lava from the volcanoes at Radicofani and Monte Amiata. The lava cooled into a layer of permeable black

rock known as trachyte, which helped create the fertile farmland around Montalcino and further east around Pienza and Montepulciano. These regions, like Chianti, though with a slightly wilder flavour, constitute what we think of as the classic Tuscan landscape of terraced vineyards, olive groves, fields of wheat and sunflowers, little orchards, hedges of dwarf maple and small oaks and cypresses planted for their silhouette effects by landowners uniquely conscious of the visual possibilities of their domains. And, as in Chianti, the peculiar qualities of this landscape are a direct result of human choice, namely the rejection of the 'industrial option' which presented itself as a possible avenue of development as early as the eighteenth century. Instead of pursuing what in the English Midlands, say, resulted in slum-filled cities with belching factories and vast mills, the Tuscan ruling class, guided by the Accademia dei Georgofili ('friends of agriculture'), made a conscious decision to adopt sharecropping as the best way of exploiting their properties. Whether the rural poor would have been better off as urban wage slaves than under this semi-feudal system whereby a large share of all their labour went to their landlord is debatable, but the countryside itself certainly benefited. Even today, over twenty years after the sharecropping system was legislated out of existence (and with it many of the small farms), the overall impression you get as you walk through the hills is of an extraordinarily rich and harmonious relation between human beings and their environment.

Between Sant'Antimo and Pienza, the itinerary passes along the Val d'Orcia, a rugged green stretch of Mediterranean *macchia* (scrub), gorges and the blue shallows of the Orcia river itself. There are few roads here, and few settlements apart from the surrounding hilltop castles and fortified towns such as Ripa d'Orcia and Rocca d'Orcia, some of them dating back as far as the eighth century.

At one time the route through the valley formed part of the Via Francigena, the chief route linking Rome with the north (hence the number of castles standing sentinel over it). Nowadays the only part of the region receiving visitors in any serious quantity is the little spa town of Bagno Vignoni, though, considering its charms, even this town manages to maintain a surprisingly low profile. The delightful spring-fed pools here belong to a geo-thermal system that more or less encircles Monte Amiata, producing an abundance of natural springs. Monte Amiata itself, the only real mountain in southern Tus cany, has plenty of walks and a well-developed trail system. But unless you're planning on going deep into the woods and camping out, you can expect big crowds and the type of establishments that cater to them. Still, if it's midsummer and too hot to walk elsewhere, at least you can be assured of cooler temperatures.

Culturally, almost every one of these walks has something of outstanding interest to offer. The fine Renaissance monastery of Monte Oliveto with its amazing fresco cycle and intarsia choir stalls, the walled medieval town of Buonconvento, the great hill towns of Montalcino and Montepulciano, the unfinished 'Utopian' city of Pienza, the abbey of Sant'Antimo (surely one of the loveliest Romanesque buildings in all of Italy); with such a quantity of gems, all of them set in gorgeous countryside, it would be hard to imagine a more pleasant or fascinating set of walks.

The Walks

The first eight walks in this section are connected in a single itinerary which you can join or leave by public transport at any juncture except Ripa d'Orcia (to or from which you must walk or hitch, but it's quite close to Bagno Vignoni, so even if you don't want to stay overnight at Ripa, you can easily walk on to Bagno Vignoni the same day; see notes to walk 4). The only place that doesn't offer accommodation is Sant'Antimo, so you'd either need to return to Montalcino by bus (buses do this 10-minute trip several times a day) or else bus (or hitch) to Sant'Antimo in the morning and walk on to Ripa d'Orcia or Bagno Vignoni.

Some of the walks are fairly long, but few are especially strenuous. The country on the whole is unshaded, which makes these low-altitude walks best in spring and autumn.

The last walk, from Stazione Murlo (La Befa) to Murlo/Vescovado, is offered primarily for anyone who thinks they would enjoy a short ride on a small branch-line train which looks gleefully toy-like, a country walk and a visit to the Etruscan museum. The museum is just small enough to be completely absorbing without being overwhelming. The walk to Murlo, with wide views and pretty fields, passes through an area rich in wildlife (a wild boar trotted straight across our path when we were there), and there's an *osteria* (and nothing else) in La Befa which is reputed to be excellent; but otherwise, this is a very low-key walk. The addendum to it, from Buonconvento to Stazione Murlo, is given in case you want to start the walk in Buonconvento; there is no way back to Siena from Stazione Murlo, however (the only train is early in the morning), so you must walk all the way to Murlo/Vescovado.

Food

The clay hills of the *crete* produce excellent white truffles. Montalcino and Montepulciano are of course chiefly known for their wines (respectively Brunello and Vino Nobile di Montepulciano), but Montalcino also has quite a substantial sideline in good-quality honey, while the hand-rolled eggless pasta, or *pici*, of Montepulciano and

Pienza forms the basis for a number of simple, tasty dishes. Superb pecorino and other sheep cheeses are also a particular speciality of Pienza.

Restaurants in the area are generally good, keeping for the most part to the traditional Tuscan standards – *ribollita*, *panzanella*, *pappa al pomodoro* (a bread-based tomato soup), grilled meats, roast game. For gourmets with cash to spare, there's La Chiusa near Montepulciano, reckoned by some to be south Tuscany's best restaurant.

LOGISTICS

SIENA

(Ψ❶) Eating
⊞ Accommodation
🚌 Transport
ⓘ Miscellaneous info

(Ψ❶)
Rosticceria Monti
Via Calzoleria, 12
Tel. 0577-289010
Open at lunch and dinner, a great (and inexpensive) place to drop in for a quick bite. You can sit at a small counter and watch the kitchen through a big plate-glass window. They also do takeaway, a great source for picnics: prepared dishes, salads, cheeses and salami, as well as bread and wine. They run a restaurant upstairs, serving the same good food as downstairs, but in a more relaxed environment. A

nice, inexpensive wine they were serving when we were there was the Casa Nova, Vino da Tavola Rosato della Toscana '93, L.8500.

La Finestra
Piazza del Mercato, 14
Tel. 0577-42093
Gnocchi with spinach and mascarpone is a dish encountered here and there throughout Tuscany, but to taste it as it should taste, go to La Finestra in the Piazza del Mercato. It's quite a rich dish, but with a full fresh flavour of spinach coming through the mascarpone. Excellent pasta with *porcini* and rocket (*arugula*) seems to be a house speciality.

Good food, appetizing place, moderate price.

Osteria Castelvecchio
Via Castelvecchio, 65
Tel. 0577-49586
Closing day: Tuesday
Largely vegetarian, serving specialities such as couscous, though they also have meat dishes. Interesting *crostini*. Slow service. Good pork with apple.

Osteria Numero Uno
Via dei Pispini, 25
Tel. 0577-221250
For an extremely cheap meal in a tiny place away from the tourist beat, try Osteria Numero Uno.

A perfect *pasta arrabbiata* (a spicy tomato sauce – ask for it hot and garlicky), good salads, *porchetta* and other hearty meat dishes, and an extremely substantial *ribollita*. No menu, really a locals-only joint. Prices seem to vary according to the whim of the proprietor, but are always low.

Bar Pasticceria Brogi
Via Rinaldini, 17
Just at the corner of the Campo, this was definitely the best place for breakfast, as they have delicious warm home-made pastries in the morning (try the ones filled with *riso*) and superb coffee.

Nuova Grotta del Gallo Nero
Via del Porrione, 65/67
Another inexpensive choice.

PICNICS

See Rosticceria Monti, above.

Morbidi, Via Banchi di Sopra, 73/75; tel. 0577-280268
Closed: Wednesday afternoons

PALIO DINNERS

The city of Siena is divided into districts, or *contrade*, and all of these neighbourhood associations periodically hold dinners, most of which are connected in some way with the Palio, Siena's famous bareback horse race. These dinners occur throughout the year, however, not just at the times of the Palio. Long tables are set out in the street, and the area is festooned with the flags of the district. It's possible to buy tickets for these dinners. If you're interested, contact the Siena Tourist Office.

⊞

Tre Donzelle
Via Donzelle, 5
Tel. 0577-280358
A huge, rambling, fairly inexpensive place; they are good about letting you leave bags. They have a room where they put them though the security of this room seems not to be of the tightest.

AFFITTACAMERE

The Siena tourist office has a good list of rooms for rent.

🚌

BUS

The main bus line in this region is TRA-IN (tel. 0577-204111). The bus station (San Domenico) has a computer set-up that gives bus info in English and can print out schedules (both 'to' and 'from') for any specific destination.

TRAIN

The station is a short distance out of town (regularly served by local buses). Train information, tel.: 0577-280115; from April to October there is usually someone there who speaks English. Twenty-four-hour left-luggage facilities.

ⓘ

Maps and guidebooks: can be bought at Feltrinelli (0577-44009). English spoken.
Tourist office: Piazza del Campo, 56; tel. 0577-280551
Local CAI: Via Mazzini, 95; tel. 0577-270666. Hours: Mon., Wed., Fri., 6–7.30 p.m. You can also contact CAI member Gianfranco Muschietti. Via Caffarini, 7, 53100 Siena; tel. and fax 0577-52739
Xerox and fax service: Media, at Banchi di Sotto, 37, is great. The owner is incredibly helpful; while you're sending and receiving faxes, you can get a useful update in his beautiful English on the weather, politics, the ins and outs of the Palio, or anything else that the language barrier had previously obscured.

14 | MONTE OLIVETO MAGGIORE TO BUONCONVENTO

A long but mostly downhill walk through the mysterious landscape of the *crete*, connecting one of the great monastic buildings of early Renaissance Italy, with the walled medieval town (albeit thoroughly modern in its outskirts) of Buonconvento. The eroded clay and limestone hills of the *crete*, at their most bizarrely lunar on the way from Siena to Monte Oliveto, merge with forest and arable land here to form a dramatic scenery of gullies, rolling hills, thick copses and meadows ending in sudden precipices. A number of handsome farmhouses punctuate the route (which in May and June, when we were there, was a feast of flowers), most of which goes along small paths and little-used dirt roads.

The Abbey of Monte Oliveto stands on the ridge of a hill in a glade of tall black cypresses. A splendid, asymmetrical gatehouse with a Della Robbia terracotta leads into the wooded grounds, where the simple, beautifully proportioned brick structures of the abbey itself stand in all their original seclusion and tranquillity. Two great treasures are housed in the abbey: lining the main cloister is a fresco cycle of the life of St Benedict by Signorelli and Il Sodoma (who seems intent on imparting as much camp and general homoerotic insinuation into the cycle as he can get away with, including a louche-looking portrait of himself in white gloves, and a couple of glimpses of his pet badgers). Less famous, less sensational, but perhaps of finer quality, are the wooden intarsia choir stalls by Fra Giovanni da Verona, masterpieces of wooden inlay with stunning pictorial detail of musical instruments, landscapes and geometric forms.

The monastery was founded by a group of wealthy Sienese merchants, among them Giovanni Tolomei, who started having visions of the Virgin after losing his sight. The group retired here in 1313 with the aim of reviving the plainness and austerity of the original Benedictine rule. Within six years their Olivetan Order had been officially recognized by the Pope. An ambitious building programme began, and the monastery grew into one of the most powerful in Italy, a measure of which was the visit paid by Emperor Charles V in 1536 with a retinue of two thousand soldiers. Napoleon suppressed the monastery in 1810, but it was re-established after the last war, and is now home to a couple of dozen white-robed monks who specialize in restoring old books, and making wine, honey, olive oil and Flora di Monte Oliveto, a herbal tonic which they sell in the monastery shop.

Contrary to what you might expect from its somewhat unprepossessing approach, Buonconvento turns out to be an exquisite little town, enclosed in the rectangular walls built by the Sienese in 1371. There isn't much to it, but the medieval brick buildings, ornate gateways (the monumental northern gate opens towards the capital of the province), the squint little alleys and pretty four-teenth-century parish church (altarpiece by Matteo di Giovanni) have an unusual delicacy. There's a small but very select museum of Sienese religious art, the Museo d'Arte Sacra, with paintings by Matteo, Bartolo di Fredi, Sano di Pietro and others. Buonconvento has been the seat of a *podestà* (head of the *comune*, or 'mayor') since 1270, and the coats-of-arms of twenty-five *podestà*s from the old days can still be distinguished on the facade of the fine town hall.

Food

There's a pleasant little restaurant, La Torre, in the monastery grounds at Monte Oliveto. The food is simple but well prepared and inexpensive: good salads, plain but appetizing pasta dishes such as ravioli with butter and sage. Decent sandwiches and plates of cheese, *prosciutto* or salami, as well as fresh fruit, are available from the bar, which keeps longer opening hours than the restaurant.

Both restaurants in the old part of Buonconvento seem to be popular with the locals. The fare is good, if basic, at the *rosticceria*. As you'd expect, roast meats are the best things, and if the idea of a plain but well-cooked piece of rabbit or guinea-fowl or roast beef appeals, then this is the place to go. As always in such places, it's worth asking what specials they have, as many dishes (particularly vegetables) don't appear on the menu. For something a little fancier (and a wider selection of pasta dishes), try the *trattoria* in the Hotel Roma down the street.

LOGISTICS

MONTE OLIVETO MAGGIORE TO BUONCONVENTO,
4 hours

🚌 Transport
🍴 Eating
🏨 Accommodation
ⓘ Miscellaneous info

🚌

FROM SIENA
By bus: TRA-IN (tel. 0577-204111/204245) to Chiusure (route 109)
Length of journey: about 45 minutes, plus another 15 minutes to walk the 2 km to the monastery.
Frequency: one bus daily, ATW 2 p.m.
The bus should say 'Castelmuzio' on the front, though you'll only be going as far as Chiusure.

NOTE. Double-check bus time; the drivers gave us incorrect information. If your Italian isn't very good, you might want to check at the tourist office. Once on the bus, tell the driver that you're going to Monte Oliveto, as they don't actually stop at the monastery, they just let you off at an intersection **B**, from which you have to walk for about 15 minutes to the monastery itself.
By train: to Asciano-M. Oliveto Maggiore. Note: this station comes *before* Asciano station.
Length of journey: 25 minutes, plus walking or hitching to monastery, about 10 km
Frequency: about every 2 hours
Train info: tel. 0577-280115

RETURN FROM BUONCONVENTO TO SIENA

By train: for information phone (Siena) 0577-280115 or (Buonconvento) 0577-806104; also left-luggage facility
Length of journey: about ½ hour
Frequency: every 2 hours or so. In the afternoon, ATW, there are trains at 3, 4, 4.45, 6, 7 and 8.45
By bus: TRA-IN bus (tel. 0577-204111/204245) from Buonconvento town centre and also at the railway station
Length of journey: 30–40 minutes

Frequency: fairly frequent. Check in *tabacchi* in town.

🍴 MONTE OLIVETO

La Torre
(at the monastery gate)
Tel. 0577-707022.
Hours: lunch and dinner
Closing day: Tuesday
Note: the bar attached to La Torre is pretty much open all the time, including Tuesdays, with a good snack selection, including fresh juice, desserts, sandwiches.

BUONCONVENTO

Ristorante Da Mario (the *rosticceria*)
Via Soccini, 60
Tel. 0577-806157

Albergo Roma
Via Soccini, 14
Tel. 0577 806021; fax 0577-807284

🏨 MONTE OLIVETO

Abbazia di Monte Oliveto Maggiore
53020 Siena
Tel. 0577-707017
The monastery is a very nice place to stay, albeit extremely simple. Very peaceful. They're not exactly forthcoming about

having rooms available, though are more so if they know you're on foot. It really just seems to depend on whether they're full or not. (When we were there in June, the place was virtually empty, but apparently this can change very quickly.) You can write ahead to reserve, or call. There's someone at the monastery who speaks English; alternatively, you could ask someone in the Siena tourist office to call for you.

Agricola Mocine (*agriturismo*)
Chiusure
Tel. 0577-707105
We didn't actually stay here, but we list it because of the limited overnight options here.

BUONCONVENTO

Albergo Roma
Via Soccini, 14
53022 Buonconvento (Si)
Tel. 0577-806021; fax
0577-807284

ⓘ

Tourist office: Comune di Buonconvento, Via Soccini, 32; tel. 0577-806012/806016; fax 0577-807212

There are weekend dance evenings in the Palazzo del Popolo in Piazza Gramsci, Buonconvento.

Directions

Leaving the monastery gate **A**, follow signs for Asciano and then Chiusure, walking towards Chiusure, which you can see above on a hill. Specifically, after passing through the monastery gate, bear right at the first fork and follow this road out to the main road, on which you turn right. Reaching an intersection (which is also the bus drop-off point), go right round the intersection, a hairpin turn **B**. This road leads to Chiusure.

As you approach Chiusure, bear to the right (rather than following the road around its hairpin left turn), entering the village on Via Porta Senese, almost immediately passing the PT (post office) on your right.

Bear right again as the road forks, and you'll soon see above you on the left a bell tower. Shortly after this, a dirt road leads off the asphalt road to the right. Take it.

Reaching a T-junction (near a line of cypress trees) turn right **C**. Here you get good views on either side of rolling hills with sudden precipices. An interesting mix of forest, farmland and the beautiful clay *crete*, with a good view of the monastery thrown in.

Keeping to the main path, you'll pass the driveway of the homestead Fornacino, (a newer-looking house with large pine trees growing all round it). The road curves left round Fornacino's perimeter where, near the back of the house, there is a smaller dirt track forking to the left. Take this. (CAI's red and white signs here.)

Soon the road forks (with a green gate on the left fork), and you should bear right here **D**.

Where a new track appears on the left, leading up to the crown of a hill, take either side – they rejoin in 50 m or so.

This path comes out on a slightly more major-looking dirt road of a mauvish-colour (as opposed to the beige-white-grey sand colour of the path we've been on), overlooking valleys and long vistas ahead and behind. Turn left here **E**; 10 minutes later the road winds to the left of the gated villa of Podere S. Carlo.

In another half hour the road goes up a hill past the farm buildings of Podere Olimena, and then begins descending.

Take the lower fork past Villa Casale.

About 15 minutes later, the road comes out on a T-junction with another road. Go left **F**.

In another 5–10 minutes, this road comes to an asphalt road leading to Buonconvento. Turn left here **G**. (You may want to hitch the last kilometre from here to town.) In another kilometre you'll come to a T-junction **H** where you can go left to reach the railway station, or enter Buonconvento through the city wall.

MONTE OLIVETO MAGGIORE TO BUONCONVENTO

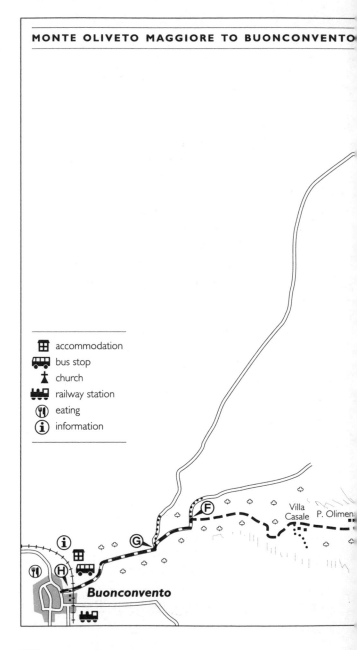

accommodation
bus stop
church
railway station
eating
information

F

G

Villa
Casale   P. Olimen

H

Buonconvento

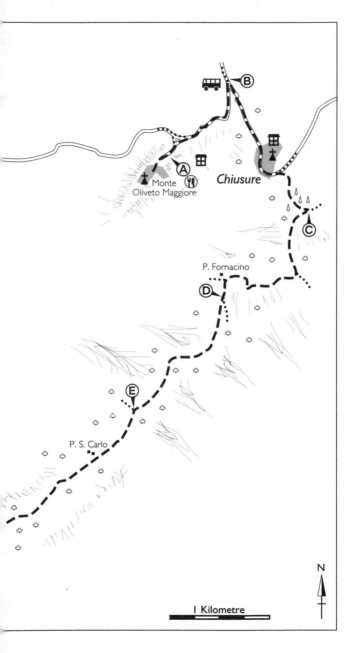

15 | BUONCONVENTO TO MONTALCINO

Apart from the steep final climb to Montalcino at the end, this is a fairly gentle walk through pretty rolling farmland with sunflowers and grain crops giving way to vineyards as you approach the valuable (and correspondingly well-tended) wine-growing country of Montalcino, where Italy's most highly rated/priced wine, Brunello, is produced. You may catch sight of deer, boar or hares, as much of the walk passes through the wildlife protection zone of Podere S. Anna.

This is a long walk, mostly along mule tracks, but there is also a long stretch along a little-used dirt road. Because of this, if you are doing only one walk in the area, you may want to pick one of the shorter ones.

Coming at the end of a fairly long walk, the final approach to Montalcino high on its hilltop does look rather daunting, but it's actually less brutal than it seems, and with its stunning views and avoidance of the usual sprawl surrounding these old towns, it makes an exceptionally pleasant entrance.

The walled town with its impregnable-looking fortress hasn't changed much since the sixteenth century, when it offered the besieged Sienese republicans a last refuge from the imperial army of Charles V, earning itself the title of the 'Republic of Siena at Montalcino' and the honour (still observed) of leading the parade every year at the Sienese Palio.

It's a quiet, affluent, attractive town, with pretty buildings and flower-filled squares, and a number of excellent shops selling (of course) Brunello, as well as the high-grade honey the region also produces.

Food

There's a pizzeria/pub/spaghetteria with some tables outside, called L'Europeo on the outskirts of Bibbiano, an hour or so into the walk.

In Montalcino, if you have transport, or if you're staying at the nearby agriturism farm of La Croce (see 'Logistics' below), there's an excellent restaurant outside the town at the Fattoria dei Barbi. The setting is pleasant – an old farmhouse with a vast fireplace – and the food, imaginative variations on traditional Tuscan dishes, is worth the higher than usual prices. Highlights include an intensely flavoured polenta with *porcini* mushrooms, beautiful fresh vegetables from the garden, the local version of *ribollita* (distinguished from the Florentine version by the absence of black cabbage), fresh ravioli stuffed to bursting with spinach and ricotta, guinea-fowl cooked in *vin santo secco*, rabbit with Brunello, and for dessert a wonderful *crema di ricotta*.

LOGISTICS

BUONCONVENTO TO MONTALCINO, 4–5 hours

🚌 Transport
🍴 Eating
🎱 Accommodation
ⓘ Miscellaneous info

🚌
SIENA TO BUONCONVENTO
By train: (Siena) 0577-280115

or (Buonconvento) 0577-806104; left-luggage facility
Length of journey: about ¹/₂ hour
Frequency: every 2 hours or so; ATW morning trains are at 6, 6.15 and 8.04
By bus: TRA-IN bus (tel. 0577-204111/204245
Length of journey: 30–40 minutes
Frequency: fairly frequent

**RETURN FROM
MONTALCINO**
TRA-IN bus to Siena
Frequency: about ten a day
Length of journey: 75 minutes

🍴

BIBBIANO
Pub-Pizzeria L'Europeo
Tel. 0577-807077

MONTALCINO
Fattoria dei Barbi
Tel. 0577-849357
Closing day: Wednesday
This restaurant isn't actually in
Montalcino, it's a few miles
south. Take the road to
Sant'Antimo, and watch for the
sign to the restaurant on the left,
just past the hamlet of La Croce.

⊞

Centro Agrituristico 'La Croce'
(3 km from Montalcino)
Via La Croce, 9
53024 Montalcino (Si)
Tel. 0577-849463; in winter,
0564-491731
Price: double room from L.
40,000–50,000 in low season;
single from L. 30,000–40,000;
also, the whole apartment is
available on weekly or monthly
basis

The house dates back to 1290,
has 4 double rooms, 2 bathrooms,
sitting-room and open kitchen.
Garden to have dinner under the
pergola, where there is a
barbecue and tables and chairs;
or eat with the family, which is a
blast. They have great food, and
their own home-made,
extremely enjoyable, wine. This
place is excellent, and good value
too.

There are two *agriturismo*
establishments along this route,
Casa Colsereno (tel. 0577-
847030) and Piampetrucci (tel.
0577-808304). Both are marked
on the map. We didn't stay at
either of them, but you might
want to – it would break up a
rather long itinerary. You could
inquire at the Siena tourist office
for more information.

ⓘ

Tourist office: Ufficio Turistico
Comunale, Costa del Municipio,
8, 53024 Montalcino (Si); tel.
0577-849331/849321. Closed
Mondays.

Castiglione del Bosco has the
oldest cellar in the area (tel. 0577-
807078).

Directions

From the front of the railway station **A**, cross the main street and follow the street straight ahead of the station.

Take the first right, and then the first left (the road to Bibbiano), which crosses the Ombrone river by some distinct maritime pines.

After the bridge, take the first left **B**, a dirt road leading to a farmhouse, Pian delle Noci.

Just before reaching the house, just before the stacks of wood and the small brick animal pen, you take a right along a farm track heading towards the trees. Where you reach the trees, a cement platform bridge crosses the Stile river.

As you pass the castle tower on your right, watch at the end of a line of hedges for a less-used track on the right **C**. Take that, uphill, towards a brick castellated lodge. Reaching that, go left on the gravel road which runs in front of it.

When the road bends right, with a slightly more minor fork carrying on to the left (which is actually straight ahead), take this left fork **D**.

When the road forks by a small pond, take the right branch. About 40 m past the fork, at the end of the hedge, the path is intersected by a slightly smaller track. Go left here (there's a CAI marker on a pine tree to the right just as you turn) **E**. (Note: make sure to take the *track*, which is about 5 m in front of the pine tree, rather than the entrance to a field which is directly in front of the tree.)

Follow this track, crossing through a line of trees between two fields. Keep on straight; when the path seems to give out, just in front of the beginning of a hedge (and where another track leads down into a lower field), keep on straight ahead, keeping to the edge of the field, alongside this row of bushes and olive trees (just

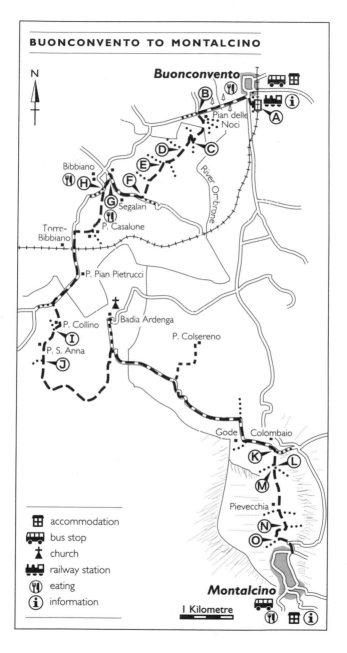

BUONCONVENTO TO MONTALCINO

N

Buonconvento

B

Pian delle
Noci

D

C

E

River Ombrone

Bibbiano

H

F

G Segalari

P. Casalone

Torre-
Bibbiano

P. Pian Pietrucci

P. Collino

Badia Ardenga

I

P. Colsereno

P. S. Anna

J

Gode   Colombaio

K

L

M

Pievecchia

N

O

Montalcino

1 Kilometre

accommodation
bus stop
church
railway station
eating
information

to your right). The track reappears almost immediately alongside this hedge.

Follow the path out on to the gravel road which runs along the edge of the cypress trees, and go right on it **F**. Follow this road directly into Segalari, which is visible ahead of you on the right.

Bear right on the asphalt through the little hamlet of Segalari, passing the pizzeria/pub/spaghetteria L'Europeo on your left. At the intersection near a building with a small bell tower, go left on the asphalt road (signed towards Montalcino) **G**.

The road turns to gravel right outside the village. Soon after this it bends around to the right, and you'll see a smaller dirt track on the left side (but actually leading straight ahead). Take this **H**.

When this path comes directly in front of the farmhouse of Podere Casalone (in a sort of T–junction – as if it ends there), bear right and you'll find the path in the far right-hand corner of the farmyard (between the farmyard and 'garage'), that leads down to the main dirt road. Take this, and at the dirt road go left.

Cross the railway tracks (by Stazione Torre–Bibbiano, about an hour and a half after leaving Buonconvento). Just after this is Agriturismo Piampetrucci.

Cross the Ombrone again (here it's a real river, as opposed to the tiny stream it was when we first met it just outside Buonconvento). Take the first left, (about 200 m after the river), a farm road winding uphill. Gaining the hill and the farmhouse, Podere Collino (not to be confused with Capanno del Collino), the path winds round behind the house, and then drops down and passes alongside four big metal storage silos.

Follow the path until it meets the main dirt road. Turn left there **I**. This begins a wide circle that will bring you towards Badia Ardenga.

A little more than ½ km from where you turned left

on to this road, there's a fork, just beyond the farmhouse of Podere S. Anna. Keep left here **J**, staying on the main road (unless you want to go to Castiglione del Bosco, about 2 km away).

Stay on the main dirt road, passing through vineyards of Brunello. This is a no-hunting zone, with more boar, deer and hare than pleases the local farmers. The Montalcino tower is visible on a distant hilltop. When the road comes out at an intersection with another road (about 3½ km from where you got on it at Podere Collino), go right, unless you're interested in seeing Badia Ardenga, formerly an abbey, now a rather ramshackle *agriturismo* (about ½ km), in which case go left.

Soon you'll cross a small bridge over a stream, where you'll see a sign to Casa Colsereno, which is about 1 km away on the left. Ignore this left turn unless you are going to the agriturism farm here.

Continue on the main path, a little-used dirt road that winds in a more or less south-easterly direction through open farmland. From early on you get views of Montalcino on its high hill.

About 3½–4 km past the Badia Ardenga turning, there's a signed right-hand turning, the entrance to Gode. The road makes a sharp left turn here; stay on it. About 300 m further on, you'll pass a house, Colombaio, on the left. Just after this, the left side of the road is lined with cypresses. About 50 m after they end, there's a big solitary oak tree on the left, and a few metres beyond that a gravel road turns off to the right (signed to 'Az. agr. Capanna, Pertinali and Paradiso'). Take this **K**.

Follow this for about 300 m, ignoring deviations, until you come to a similar-sized left-hand turn where the road is signed right to 'Paradiso, Pertinali and Capanna'. Take the left-hand turn **L**. This immediately crosses a small cement platform bridge over a stream, and then bends to the right **M**. (Ignore the left fork here.)

Continue along this road, passing after nearly 1 km an old house on the left, and then in about 100 m or so, one on the right, Pievecchia. The road turns left here, and then bends right. (Ignore a left fork up to an old house.)

Passing a beautifully made stone wall with an arched drinking-fountain recessed into it, follow the main path as it bends sharply to the right **N**, ignoring a fork off to the left.

After another 300 m or so, you come out at another gravel road **O**, which you take uphill to the left, passing a little stone chapel (ignoring a fork back to the right, just before the chapel, and another fork down to the left 50 m after it).

Soon after this, you see the stone arch of Porta Burelli, through which you enter the town of Montalcino.

16 | MONTALCINO TO SANT'ANTIMO

A pleasant walk through farmland and Brunello country, passing some old farmsteads and hamlets that appear completely untouched by the centuries. Villa a Tolli especially is a solitary, strange and serene hamlet, with its fountain and tall cypresses, crumbling walls, little houses, minuscule cemetery and wooden cross at the fork in the road. The slight discomfort of an unavoidable (but brief) stretch on the asphalt road is more than made up for by the prettiness of the rest of the walk, above all the stunning sight of the Romanesque abbey of Sant'Antimo lying below you in the olive groves and pastures full of white heifers as you come over the ridge of the Starcia valley. Though the abbey is best seen from the other

side, even from here it would be hard to imagine a more sympathetic combination of architectural grace and natural setting.

Begun in 1118, the abbey was once home to a prominent Benedictine community. Few of the monastic buildings remain (the chapter house and refectory are now used as barns) but the abbey itself, with its rounded apse and perfectly proportioned tower, survives in all its glory. Creamy stone bricks, luminous Volterran alabaster, playful carvings and frescoes of animals (copulating pigs in the sacristy) give it a peculiarly sunny air. Note the apse with its little radiating chapels, and the women's gallery, an unexpected borrowing from Byzantine architecture.

A group of French Cistercian monks now run the abbey, celebrating Mass with Gregorian chants several times a day.

Food

Up the road from the abbey, towards the village of Castelnuovo dell'Abate, is a little restaurant called Basso-mondo; an extremely pleasant place frequented by local farmers and the (surprisingly few) tourists who visit the abbey. The menu offers the basic repertoire, but the cooking is above average: delicious home-made ravioli and an aromatic casserole of wild boar cooked with garlic and rosemary, among the best we ate in Tuscany. Wild boar tastes something like a cross between pork and beef, with a definite fruit flavour which reflects the animal's sweet tooth (a lot of cherries, judging by the little piles of cherry stones you see all over the woods).

You can also get sandwiches here if you don't want a full meal.

LOGISTICS

MONTALCINO TO SANT'ANTIMO, 3 hours

🚌 Transport
🍽 Eating
🎫 Accommodation
ⓘ Miscellaneous info

🚌

FROM SIENA

TRA-IN bus (tel. 0577-204111/ 204245) to Montalcino
Length of journey: 75 minutes
Frequency: about ten a day

RETURN FROM SANT'ANTIMO TO MONTALCINO

The TRA-IN bus picks up on the road to Montalcino, across the street from the Ristorante

Bassomondo; you must walk up to there from the abbey.
Length of journey: 15 minutes
Frequency: four or so a day

🍽

Osteria Bassomondo (at the top of the road that leads down to the abbey itself)
Tel. 0577-835619
Hours: lunch and dinner
Closing day: Monday
Price: inexpensive

🎫

There's no accommodation for the general public at Sant'Antimo, so you can either return to Montalcino by bus (buses run this 15-minute trip several times a day, see above) or else bus to

Sant'Antimo in the morning and walk on to Ripa d'Orcia or Bagno Vignoni. (See Montalcino, Ripa d'Orcia or Bagno Vignoni sections.) There is *agriturismo* accommodation at Il Cocco (tel. 0577-285086), but we have not stayed there. Ask at the tourist office in Siena about *agriturismo* options in the area.

Comunale, Costa del Municipio, 8, 53024 Montalcino (Si); tel. 0577-849331/849321
Sant'Antimo abbey: tel. 0577-835659. Gregorian Mass at 9 a.m. daily; on Sundays it's also at 11. Vespers every day at 6.30 p.m. The abbey is open 9–7 in summer, 10–7 in winter.

(i)
Tourist office: Ufficio Turistico

Directions

Start at the large intersection by the south-west tip of the Fortezza wall, where the car road signed to Sant'Antimo begins. Cross over the intersection, heading for the bar (A T W, Le Terrazze) on the hill in front of you and on the right. Immediately past here the first street on the right is called Via del Poggiolo. Take this **A**. (Note: this is not the road signed to Sant'Antimo. Also, ignore the first right off Via del Poggiolo, the Traversa del Poggiolo.)

The asphalt soon gives way to gravel, and the road descends. At the bottom of this hill the road forks; take the right fork, going downhill **B**. Follow this path (ignoring a downhill fork to the right).

About 10–20 minutes after leaving the main intersection by the fortress, the road makes a sharp bend to the right **C** and you'll see an old stone water conduit or drainage system in the corner of the bend (on the left-hand side) channelling water under the road. From here, follow alongside an old tall stone wall on your left, passing a turning to the left where the wall curves around.

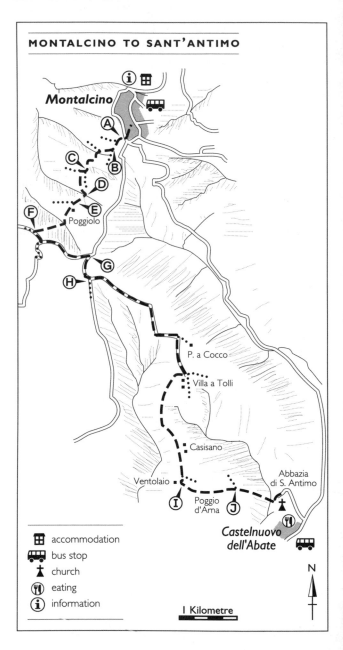

MONTALCINO TO SANT'ANTIMO

Montalcino

A

C

B

D

E

Poggiolo

F

G

H

P. a Cocco

Villa a Tolli

Casisano

Ventolaio

I

Poggio d'Arna

J

Abbazia di S. Antimo

Castelnuovo dell'Abate

N

⊞ accommodation

🚌 bus stop

⛪ church

🍴 eating

ⓘ information

I Kilometre

Continuing downhill, you'll soon pick up another stone wall on your left; take the next left-hand turn (where the wall curves round) along a slightly more minor track with a private property sign, and with olive trees on the right.

This path leads uphill, passing to the left of an old stone farmhouse and continuing to follow along an old stone wall on the left. Keep on along this track, passing above a garden and fruit trees on the right, and ignoring a more minor deviation up to the left where the stone wall ends.

After this, the path descends into woods and soon crosses a tiny stream bed **D**. Following along the left side of a ravine, the path emerges into the open again, with a wide panorama across the valley, before re-entering a short stretch of woods. Just after this, the path forks. Take the left uphill branch **E**.

Passing through another stretch of panoramic views, you'll soon come to a stone farmhouse, Poggiolo. (This is perhaps 40 minutes out of Montalcino.) Continue on along the track.

The path comes out on a T-junction with a bigger gravel road. Turn left here **F**.

The road soon becomes asphalt, but it's mostly used by farm traffic. Continue straight along it (don't take the right turn for Tavernelle).

About 1 km past the turning for Tavernelle, you'll reach a T-junction with another asphalt road **G**. Turn right, towards Grosseto. This road is not pleasant to walk along, but fortunately you leave it in about 5 minutes. When you come to the first left, a gravel road for Villa a Tolli, take it **H**.

Stay on this main gravel road, through pretty country-side with good views of Monte Amiata along it. There's no traffic on it.

After a little more than 2 km you pass the entrance

for Podere al Cocco on the left, and in less than 1 km more you reach Villa a Tolli.

After passing the first house of Villa a Tolli, the road makes a pretty good case for a fork, the right branch wrapping round the back of the house, the left branch heading towards the bell tower of the little church. Take the right, but first you may want to look around this archaic and forgotten little place.

In about 20 minutes (a little more than 1 km after Villa a Tolli), you'll pass a farmhouse on the left, Casisano. (Ignore a slightly more minor fork up to the left soon after it.) Keeping to the main track, on the right along here you have a view to the village of San Angelo in Colle.

Just under ⅔ km past Casisano (5–10 minutes), at the farmstead of Ventolaio, where the main dirt road swings around to the left, go instead straight ahead (as though entering the property), passing to the left of a solitary oak, after which you'll see a smaller dirt road to your left, which leads towards the wooded hilltop of Poggio d'Arna. Take this **I**.

Keep to the main path, which is easy. In 10–15 minutes it ends at a gate, with a fenced water pump (and a fantastic aerial view of Castelnuovo dell'Abate to your right).

On the right of the gate, a gap allows you to follow down the right-hand side of the fence. At the bottom of the fence you'll see a long, straight strip of grass leading between the trees. This is the line of the aquifer; follow it.

After 200 m you converge with another path coming from the left, and continue on to the right **J**. The views from this ridge path become steadily more impressive. The path soon begins to descend steeply, and after a couple of minutes you get your first glimpse of the Abbey of Sant'Antimo, and shortly after that you come out on a full view of the building. Watch your footing on this steep descent, especially if wet. It's easy to trip over the drainage channels cut across it.

In 20 minutes you reach the bottom, cross the stream on the cement bridge and turn left up to the abbey.

17 | SANT'ANTIMO TO RIPA D'ORCIA

This is a gorgeous and varied stretch of country, the rolling contours of the Starcia valley giving way to the more dramatic scenery of the Val d'Orcia with its knolls, streams, gorges and castle-topped promontories. The view of Sant'Antimo to the left as you set off is magical. The abbey with its agglomeration of slopes and terraces sits like a small stylized hill on a background of fields, cypresses and Braille-like arrangements of olive trees that manage to look decorative without showing the fanatical orderliness of over-exploited farmland. Meanwhile the colours and contours of the town of Castelnuovo dell'Abate blend almost indistinguishably into its own real hill, forming an unusually harmonious meeting of man and nature.

As you reach the River Orcia (where a small amount of wading may be necessary, depending on recent rainfall), and move into the Val d'Orcia, the pervading atmosphere begins to feel more remote. There are few asphalt roads around here, and the silence is impressive. Little pathways lead through a characteristically Mediterranean scrub of holm oaks (leaves like a cross between hollies and regular oaks), arbutus and broom, sufficiently dense and abundant to shelter animals such as boars, foxes, porcupines (a good spot for finding quills), hares, roe deer and badgers. Coming out of woods you'll see

the splendid central keep of Ripa d'Orcia ahead of you, with the fortress of Rocca d'Orcia behind it. The castle and tiny hamlet of Ripa d'Orcia belonged to Siena in the medieval period, later passing into the hands of the Carli branch of the Piccolomini family, who own it today, and have turned it into what must be one of the most peaceful hotels (complete with its own restaurant) in the country.

LOGISTICS

SANT'ANTIMO TO RIPA D'ORCIA, 3 hours

🚌 Transport
🍴 Eating
🏨 Accommodation

🚌

FROM MONTALCINO

It's pretty easy to hitch to Sant'Antimo, as it's just one road straight from Montalcino to Sant'Antimo.

By bus: the TRA-IN bus (0577-204111/204245) drops off near Osteria Bassomondo, above the abbey itself. This is where the itinerary departs from.

Length of journey: about 15 minutes

Frequency: about 5 per day

You have to walk or hitch, either to Bagno Vignoni or back to the abbey (Bagno Vignoni being closer) to get a bus.

🍴

The hotel Ripa d'Orcia has a restaurant, serving full à la carte dinners to guests (L. 25,000– 50,000). Even if you're not staying the night at Ripa, you can enjoy a light lunch at the bar from 12 to 1. Best to reserve (tel. 0577-897376).

▦

Castello di Ripa d'Orcia
53023 Castiglione d'Orcia (Si)
Tel. 0577-897376/897317; fax
0577-898038

Open 1 March to 7 January. They have a two-night minimum, but will waive it for readers of this book. *Price:* (1996) L.135,000–160,000 double room; includes breakfast for two, tax and service.

Directions

Coming from the Abbey of Sant'Antimo take the steep road up to the intersection with the main road from Montalcino **A**. Turn right towards Castelnuovo, but instead of continuing on into town, take an immediate hairpin left, up past the Osteria Bassomondo, passing it on your right and carrying on along that road, a small gravel road with nobody on it.

There's a wonderful view to the valley on the left of the abbey set amidst patchwork fields punctuated by cypresses.

After about 20 minutes, you'll pass Podere La Fornace on the right. Wide views on the right out to Monte Amiata.

After passing the two farmhouses of Podere Loreto– S. Pio on the right, the road begins to descend, and you'll soon see the glitter of the River Orcia.

About 15–20 minutes past Loreto–S. Pio, you'll pass Podere Casata on the left (a relatively new stone farmhouse). Bear to the left after passing the house, and

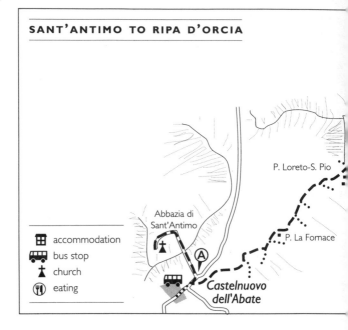

SANT'ANTIMO TO RIPA D'ORCIA

P. Loreto-S. Pio

Abbazia di
Sant'Antimo

🏨 accommodation
🚌 bus stop
✝ church
🍴 eating

P. La Fornace

Ⓐ

*Castelnuovo
dell'Abate*

then continue descending, passing over the railway line
B. The path becomes rougher and stonier here.

Down near to the river and the railway tracks, there
are several different paths (one leads under the railway,
one leads down to the river, etc.), with the main path
bending round to the left. This main path is fenced off
about 20 m from here, so don't take it. Instead, take the
path just to the right of it **C**, a more minor path which
runs alongside the river, first as a grassy path, and then
very soon as a more open track (where you turn right)
a little bit further from the river. In 30 m or so this track
crosses a stream.

On the other side of the stream, at a three-way intersection, go left **D**. This path comes immediately into a
field where it turns left, running along the bottom edge
of the field, and then bends right, still running alongside
the field (which is on your right) and next to trees on

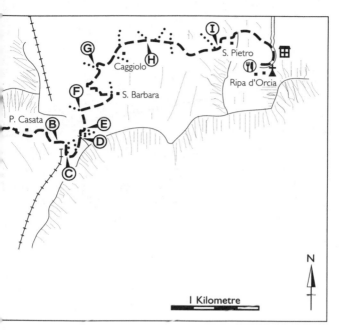

your left. On this edge of the field, about halfway along, the path bends left and enters a break in the trees and begins to climb **E**.

About 10 minutes later, when this path comes out on a T-junction with another similar path, go right **F**.

Just before reaching a newish farmstead, Santa Barbara (with ΛTW, a sign 'Il Poggio, località agrituristica S. Barbara'), there is a slightly smaller but still good-sized fork sharply to the left and back, uphill. Take this.

Stay on this until you reach, in about 5 minutes, a path of about the same size on the right. Turn right here (CAI signed) **G**. Stay on this until you come out (another 5 minutes) at the farmstead of Caggiolo.

Bear left past the house and, where the road forks just beyond it, take the right fork. The path soon forks again; go right again **H**.

You'll come to an open space which looks as if it

might have been mined or quarried. See on the right the CAI red and white mark, and a smaller branch of path off to the right. Take that. (There are two more CAI marks in the first few minutes of this branch, in case you are in any doubt.)

This is a very nice, mostly wooded path, well marked by CAI. Ripa d'Orcia, and Rocca d'Orcia behind it, appear on the right; and of course Monte Amiata.

Coming to a fork – to the left of an olive grove, through which there's a good view of Ripa – take the downhill right (essentially straight ahead) branch (see CAI marks there) **I**. You shouldn't have a problem if you follow the CAI marks.

In about 5 minutes the path turns left and widens at the farmhouse (to the right and below), S. Pietro.

Reaching a T-junction in another 5 minutes, with a chapel on the left, turn right, and so into Ripa d'Orcia in another 5 minutes.

18 | RIPA D'ORCIA TO BAGNO VIGNONI

A pleasant, effortless walk along the Val d'Orcia, most of it downhill, with the bonus of a swim in a spring-fed pool at the end. A sharp descent from the castle of Ripa d'Orcia leads to the banks of the Orcia itself, a clear, shallow, boulder-strewn river at this point, with the ruins of a bridge that was swept away in the great floods of 1929. This was once an important crossing, connecting the castle of Ripa with those of Rocca and Castiglione d'Orcia. An abandoned mill across the river gives this forlornly picturesque area its name: La Mulina. The stones for the impressive pillars of the bridge were brought from a travertine quarry (now derelict) which you'll pass through just before reaching Bagno Vignoni. Shortly after it a clear, gushing, slightly sulphurous stream marks the beginning of the geothermal spring system on which the spa of Bagno Vignoni was built, and a little beyond this you'll reach the cliff below Bagno Vignoni itself, with its warm spring water splashing down into an extraordinary light opaque blue pool where you can bathe. Up at the top of the cliff you'll be greeted by the surprising sight of a long culvert with a number of generally rather overweight bodies lying in it, reading the newspapers while the curative waters gush over their limbs.

The waters of Bagno Vignoni have been popular since Etruscan times, its thirty-six springs gushing from 1000 m underground. St Catherine of Siena is said to have appreciated their therapeutic qualities, as is Lorenzo the Magnificent, whose family built the splendid arcaded *piscina* (swimming-pool) – a kind of flooded, bubbling piazza, famously used by Tarkovsky for some of the more surreal passages of his film *Nostalgia*. It is off limits for bathing these days, but in addition to the cliff pool you can bathe in the Posta Marcucci hotel, a converted Renaissance summer house built by Pius II, who also built the nearby town of Pienza. Most of the other buildings in this attractive little town were put up in the last century.

Food

Bagno Vignoni is little more than a hamlet centred on the curative waters. But as it caters to a tourist trade (mostly Italian, as the place has really not been developed), there are several places to eat, none of them spectacular, but all decent. We had a good pasta and pizza dinner on the back patio of our hotel, Le Terme, which is reputed to have better food than the more expensive hotel, the Posta Marcucci.

LOGISTICS

RIPA D'ORCIA TO BAGNO VIGNONI, 1 – 1 ½ hours

🚌 Transport
🍽 Eating
🏨 Accommodation
ⓘ Miscellaneous info

🚌

There's no public transport to Ripa d'Orcia, so this isn't really a good place to join the itinerary. If you particularly want to see Ripa, you can start from Sant'Antimo.

RETURN FROM BAGNO VIGNONI

There are no direct buses to Siena. You can take a bus from Bagno Vignoni to San Quirico d'Orcia, which is less than 10 km away, and then get a TRA-IN bus to Siena (about seven a day),

Pienza or Montepulciano. For bus schedules between San Quirico and Bagno Vignoni call the tourist office at San Quirico (0577-897211).

(🍴) (⊞)

Le Terme (on the main piazza in Bagno Vignoni).
Tel. 0577-87150

(ⓘ)

• Bike rental at 'Club Mountain Bike' in Piazza del Moretto.

• A splendid panorama can be seen from the Castle of Vignoni, about 1 1/2 km out of the village.

• 'From the Orcia Valley to the Slopes of Mount Amiata: Historical and nature itineraries in the area around Castiglione d'Orcia' – this useful booklet (in English) has a map and guided itineraries around Ripa d'Orcia and points south. The hotel had some copies when we were there; it's produced by the Comune of Castiglione d'Orcia.

Directions

From Ripa d'Orcia, follow the road out, soon passing on your left a chapel at a fork in the road (where you came in to Ripa if you walked from Sant'Antimo) **A**.

Bearing right past the chapel, you'll pass a driveway on the right (ATW, P. Casino), a track to the right at a stone house and then a third right which leads into a field. Immediately after the third right, there's a dirt road to the right, with a drinking fountain (not working) and across from it a low stone wall and some cypress trees. Take this right **B**.

The path winds steadily downhill for about 20 minutes, when it crosses a stream bed, and forks **C**. The right fork goes down to the river, which is very pretty – 50 m down to the right you can see the ruined travertine pillars of the old bridge.

To continue to Bagno Vignoni, take the left fork at **C**. Be alert here, as you will need to leave the main path

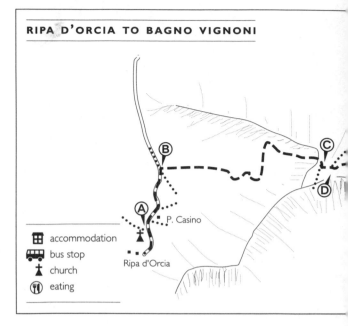

RIPA D'ORCIA TO BAGNO VIGNONI

P. Casino

Ripa d'Orcia

accommodation
bus stop
church
eating

quite soon, and the terrain isn't very clear at first. If you get lost, it might be helpful to know that from here to Bagno Vignoni you are essentially following the course of the river.

After climbing between small trees for about 100 m, the path comes to a field on the left. After about another 15 m or so, you'll see a narrow little track going down to the right (the first track to the right) **D**. This is your turning: take it, and ignore a fork to the left that you come to almost immediately.

The track more or less follows the course of the river, winding in and out of scrub.

When you reach a big field, turn right, following the path as it skirts first this edge of the field, and then, reaching the corner of the field, turns left and follows along this next edge about ⅔ or ¾ of the way, maybe 80−100 m from where you first entered the field; at this

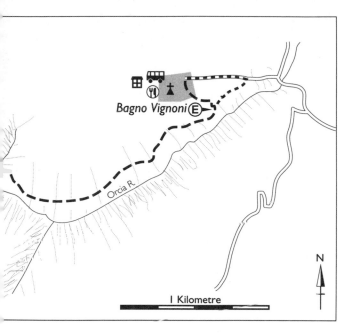

point there's a little gap in the hedges bordering the field on your right, and a path: take it.

Depending on the time of year (i.e., what's growing in the field), the path around the field might become invisible before you reach this gap, but just go on until you see it.

Shortly after this, the path widens as a number of other paths converge with it (including a bigger one soon after you leave the field, on the right, dropping down to the river itself).

About 15–20 minutes from the fork at the river **C**, you come to an abandoned travertine quarry with the old machinery rusting away in the buildings. Pass through it, bearing left.

In 10 minutes you cross a clear, gushing, slightly sulphurous stream, and soon after that you reach an eroded cliff face on your left, with water splashing down it. There is usually a car or two parked on the dirt road here, and there's a path leading up towards the cliff **E**. For a gentle approach to town, continue on the dirt road, and then turn left when you reach the asphalt. Otherwise, climb up the cliff path and you'll come to a light blue pool, very inviting – and you can jump right in. Go on climbing up to the top of the cliff, where you'll see the long culvert full of bathing beauties. This is Bagno Vignoni, a very pleasant place.

19 | BAGNO VIGNONI TO PIENZA

Old farm tracks, dirt roads and paths, still lined in places with the squared-off stones from the ancient medieval and Roman roads that once passed through this area, link the spa of Bagno Vignoni with Pienza, one of the great urban artefacts of the Renaissance; this is a peaceful walk through rolling fields of corn and wheat. Fortress-like stone farmhouses, many of them abandoned in the flight from the countryside that marked the end of the sharecropping system in the sixties and seventies, line the way. The fields and hedgerows are full of pheasants, partridges, rabbits and hares. After the summer harvest, when the farmers sometimes burn the stubble, the fields are contoured with black stripes against the gold. Black cypresses and large, scattered oaks provide a few choice verticals – this is the archetypal Tuscan landscape.

As you climb towards Pienza, you'll pass the eleventh-century Romanesque parish church, Pieve di Corsignano, with a cylindrical bell tower and two decorated portals. Carved sirens, dragons, a musician and dancer deck the entrance, a scene thought by some to disclose the existence of an ecstatic cult descended from ancient Dionysian ritual. With its beautiful little sculptures inside and out, and the peculiar intimate charm of its primitive interior, this is well worth a visit (ask in the house at the back for the key).

Pienza itself, visible on its hill with its needle-like tower for much of this walk, is monumental on a miniature scale. When the great humanist scholar Enea Silvio Piccolomini became Pope Pius II, he decided to transform his birth-place, Corsignano, into a Utopian city, renaming it Pienza after himself. He commissioned the architect Bernardo Rossellino, who had worked under the tutelage of the great Alberti, the theorist of early Renaissance art and architecture. In just three years, 1459–62, the cathedral, the papal and bishop's palaces, and the central blocks of the town itself, were completed. The intention was to extend the town across the hill, but the project ended as abruptly as it had begun: Pius died two years after the con-secration of the cathedral, and his successors showed little interest in bringing his plans to completion. What might have been a *città ideale* froze at little more than the size of a village. Its strange air of grandeur and folly has guaranteed its use as a stage set, most famously by Zeffirelli, who used it as a backdrop for his film of *Romeo and Juliet*.

In May the town hosts a flower show featuring extravagant floral displays inspired by Renaissance paint-ings. There's also a renowned cheese fair on the first Sunday in September.

Food

As you'll see from the shop windows, Pienza prides itself on its *pecorino* and other sheep's cheeses. Rightly so; the clayey grazing land around here is full of wild herbs and aromatic plants which give the milk a slightly perfumed flavour, producing exceptionally fine cheeses. Fresh or mature, rolled in herbs, crushed peppers or ashes, these have long been the basis for the local economy. The traditional Pienza *pecorino* is small and round, and at one time was used in a local ball game known as '*cacio al fuso*', which is still played at the cheese fair.

The large number of *fattorie* and *cantine* in Pienza make it an ideal place for assembling a gourmet picnic. Cantine Zazzeri at 6 Corso il Rossellino (the main street) has beautiful cheeses and prepared foods. Across from there, at 6 Via de Leone, Fior di Pienza makes good mozzarella and sells fresh fruits and vegetables. Further down the main street at no. 27, you can buy wild boar sausages and preserved mushrooms, jars of all kinds of preserved fruits, candied fruit and other delicacies.

Local specialities include the rustic, hand-rolled flour-and-water pasta known as '*pici*', *tagliatini* in broth, bread-based soups and *panzanella* (Tuscan bread salad), also called *salimbecca*, as well as sweet desserts and cakes such as *serpe* and *ricciarelli di Pienza*.

A good place to sample the local cuisine is Il Prato, where robust, well-prepared dishes are served in a relaxed atmosphere, indoors or outside. Notable productions from the kitchen included a fine chick-pea soup flavoured with rosemary and delicious home-made herbed rolls.

LOGISTICS

BAGNO VIGNONI TO PIENZA, 4 hours

 Transport
🍴 Eating
⊞ Accommodation
ⓘ Miscellaneous info

🚌
FROM SIENA

There are no direct buses from Siena to Bagno Vignoni. You can take a TRA-IN bus (tel. 0577-204111/204245) from Siena to San Quirico d'Orcia (there are about seven a day) and from there get a bus to Bagno Vignoni, which is less than 10 km away. For bus schedules between San Quirico and Bagno Vignoni, call the San Quirico tourist office at 0577-897211. (TRA IN buses also run the San Quirico–Pienza–Montepulciano route; see below.)

RETURN FROM PIENZA

There are occasional TRA-IN buses from Pienza to Chiusi where you can get a train to Florence or Siena. TRA-IN buses run a regular Siena–Buonconvento–San Quirico–Pienza–Montepulciano service.

🍴
Il Prato
Viale S. Caterina, 1/3
Pienza
Tel. 0578-748601
Closing day: Wednesday

PICNICS
See introduction above.

⊞
Camere Il Falco
Piazza Dante Alighieri, 7 (across from bus-stop)
Pienza
Tel. 0578-748551
Clean, basic rooms.

ⓘ
Tourist office: Ufficio Turistico Comunale, Piazza Pio II, 53026 Pienza (Si); tel. 0578-748502. Hours 10–1 and 4–7. They have a useful handout 'From the Orcia Valley to the Slopes of Mount Amiata: Historical and Nature Itineraries in the Area around Castiglione d'Orcia'. This

booklet (in English) has a map and guided itineraries, not in the immediate area, but around Ripa d'Orcia and points south.

Directions

Standing in front of the Albergo Le Terme, facing the central piazza (the old pool), turn right. Walk to the end of the street (the corner of the pool) and turn right (heading east) **A**.

Walking along a dirt track with a stone wall on your left, you come very shortly to an intersection where you meet with five paths. Ignoring the rightmost (which leads to asphalt), the two leftmost (each closed by a big metal gate), and turning your attention to the remaining two in the middle, take the leftmost of these two, the path which climbs a hill (towards the north) and follows along the left side of a stone wall.

The path soon becomes a single track and a bit overgrown, but still recognizable. Just keep climbing up straight ahead; the path soon levels off and reaches a T-junction with a dirt road **B**. Go left here.

Follow this road uphill about 5 minutes, until you come to the first (an old) house on the right, Tassinaie. Just past it, beginning in front of their driveway gate (and following a very short distance along a stone wall connected to the front gate), is a path on the right **C**. Take this, bearing left where the stone wall turns a corner to the right.

When the path forks **D**, ignore the right fork going towards an old farmhouse with a big electric power pylon next to it, and take the left fork (actually straight ahead) going into a field.

In a few metres you reach the field. Turn right and walk along the edge of it. At the corner of the field you come to a T-junction with another farm track; turn right, towards a house about 20 m in front of you (Cerrolungo).

Follow the track past the house and beyond, as it curves around to the left and downhill, passing under the electric line. Continue following this track until it soon comes out on to another track **E**. Take this downhill to the right.

Follow this straight down to the asphalt road; cross over and almost directly across the road find a farm track that leads into a field. The path goes left and then immediately right, crossing down towards trees. Follow it into the trees, where it bends round to the right, crossing a little stream, and then climbs across a field to the farmhouse of Casellona.

Bending left between the abandoned buildings of the farm, the track then starts to descend. Watch for a small fork to the left 50 m after the buildings, and take it.

In another 50 m you come to a stone and gravel path, where you go left **F**. (This is perhaps an hour's walk from Bagno Vignoni.)

Here, as in many places along this track, you can see the vestiges of the old Roman road, the squarish stones laid in straight lines.

When this path comes out on a T-junction **G** with another dirt road, go right, uphill, towards a file of cypresses on the hillside just ahead. Continue on this road, passing a new house on the right **H**.

Pass through Marciana, an old stone and brick farmstead, going to the right of its two main, old buildings, and taking a smaller farm track just beyond. The town of San Quirico d'Orcia is visible to your left in the distance. Ahead on a distant hillside is the silhouette of the Pienza tower.

Near the top of the first hill you climb, the main track turns left, but there is a slightly smaller track bending to the right, towards some trees. Take that **I**.

BAGNO VIGNONI TO PIENZA

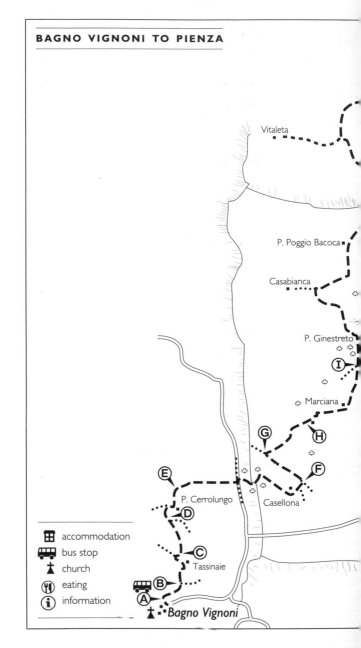

Vitaleta

P. Poggio Bacoca

Casabianca

P. Ginestreto

I

Marciana

G   H

F

E

P. Cerrolungo

D

Casellona

C

Tassinaie

B

A

Bagno Vignoní

accommodation
bus stop
church
eating
information

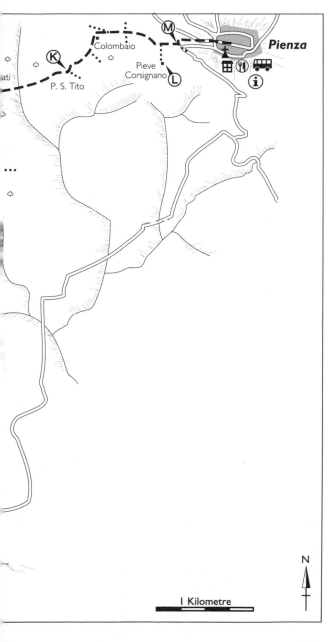

This track heads downhill through trees, to arrive at Podere Ginestreto, an abandoned house of red brick, with the external staircase to the upper level – a feature found in many of the old farmhouses of the region, the upper level housing the people of the farm, the ground level the animals. Pass to the left of the building.

The road drops down, and then climbs over a wild hillside. Cresting the hill, in the distance ahead, San Quirico is again visible, and more immediately, the agriturism farmstead of Casabianca. When you reach the gravel road (Casabianca is to the left here), turn right.

Pass the simply styled red-brick house of Poggio Bacoca.

(If you want to make the detour to Vitaleta, watch for the turning on the left about 1½ km from here. Vitaleta is a white travertine church, its façade extremely photogenic against the background of *crete* and cultivated fields.)

In ½ hour or so, you'll approach the next farmhouse, Costilati, on the right. Here, take a smaller branch forking off the main gravel road to the right of the farmhouse and going downhill **J**.

This farm track leads down into the valley between cultivated fields, and then up the other side towards Pienza, passing on your right the abandoned Podere S. Tito. Just past here, where the path forks, turn left **K**.

Pass a house on your left. Continue on the path, still climbing (not too steeply) towards Pienza.

Soon after this, you'll pass some vines on the right and two stone sheds with terracotta roofs; 20–30 m after this the path forks. Ignore the left fork, and continue straight ahead.

Pass 'Colombaio' on your right – there are some cypresses on the driveway – and then a new house closer to the road, also on the right.

The path comes out on asphalt by the Pieve Corsignano on your right **L**. After visiting the church, return to the asphalt road which led out from the dirt track we were on, and follow it straight on, uphill, soon coming to an old stone house on the right, and a smaller road to the left. Take this smaller road **M**, which leads uphill into Pienza.

20 | PIENZA TO MONTEPULCIANO
(or Montepulciano to Pienza)

Travelling on foot between these two great hill towns gives you a much better sense of their relationship to the landscapes they respectively overlook than the usual 20-minute bus or car ride could possibly do. The slow pace turns the rich arable and grazing land around Pienza and the steep green vineyards of Montepulciano from mere backdrop to intimately experienced context, making one's appreciation of the towns themselves incalculably more vivid and intense.

If you're following the itinerary described in this chapter, you'll be walking from Pienza to Montepulciano, but in case you want to do it the other way round, we've given the directions for both ways. It's too long to go there and back in one day, but there are buses in both directions if you want to return on the same day. Several attempts failed to yield a satisfactory ring walk for this itinerary, hence the duplication of the route – which, in the event, is merely the old (now apparently forgotten) dirt road connecting Pienza and Montepulciano.

The route passes near the pleasant walled village of Monticchiello, whose crooked watch-tower is visible from afar. There is the thirteenth-century parish church and a tavern-like restaurant with a small selection of Tuscan dishes. Every year in the last weeks of July and first week of August, the village presents its popular Teatro Povero, a dramatization of current issues related to the community's traditions, written and performed by the villagers.

Montepulciano

Montepulciano is one of the most attractive towns in Tuscany. Higher than Montalcino, and livelier too, with its many churches and handsome *palazzi*, its warren of steep cobbled alleys and vine-trailing stone bastions, it is essential viewing for anyone venturing south of Siena, and makes an excellent base for excursions into southern Tuscany. Tourism is well-established (aided by the various festivals the town hosts), but it's far from overwhelming, and the real base of the local economy is wine – the Vino Nobile di Montepulciano, internationally prized for over a thousand years.

On a clear day from the top of the town you can

see tremendous panoramic views over the countryside, stretching towards the Sibillini mountains, the high peaks of the Gran Sasso, Assisi's Monte Subasio, Monte Amiata, the Val d'Orcia, Pienza, and even the towers of Siena. It was up here that the idea for this book was conceived.

Food

As in Pienza, the speciality is the hand-rolled flour-and-water pasta called *pici* (from *appiciare*, to roll). *Panzanella, ribollita* and other Tuscan dishes are common, as is the olive-oil-based bread known as *caccia*. A soft cheese called *raveggiolo*, presented between two fern leaves, is one of the tastier local products, and there's also a local version of *crème caramel* known as *lattaiolo*. Capon, goose, rabbit, pheasant and guinea-fowl, as well as *nana* (chicken split down the middle), are served roast or stewed in the local Vino Nobile. And various special cakes such as *ciaccia dei morti* or *crogetti* are made for the Day of the Dead and other feast days. Between the many *cantine* (wine shops) and the excellent grocers (many of them nowadays well stocked with natural foods and organic produce), you should have no difficulty assembling an outstanding picnic.

There are several restaurants in town, all fairly simple and inexpensive. Porta di Bacco Pulcino (just inside the Porta al Prato) is as good a place as any, serving excellent *pici* and *ribollita*, good grilled sausages, and various pizzas. Up the road a bit, the Fattoria Pulcino serves food and wine from its own farm, including suckling pig and grilled meats. It's a pleasant place, but the service is extremely slow. You can get food to take away at the Rosticceria di Voltaia (closed Friday), or at the Thursday morning open-air market held in the gardens outside the Porta al Prato. For a more elaborate (and expensive) dining experience you could either drive or walk to La

Chiusa, one of Tuscany's most famous restaurants, in Montefollonico (see Montepulciano–Montefollonico itinerary).

LOGISTICS

PIENZA TO MONTEPULCIANO or Montepulciano to Pienza, about 4 hours

---

🚌 Transport
🍽 Eating
🏨 Accommodation
ⓘ Miscellaneous info

🚌

By train: Montepulciano station is 10 km out of town and the buses that link the station with the town are not always exact connections. If you're using the train, it's easier to use Chiusi station, which has more frequent main-line connections anyway, is served by a regular LFI bus service (more or less every half hour to Montepulciano) and is not much further away (about a 45-minute ride). There are also occasional buses from Chiusi station to Pienza. There is an LFI bus information kiosk outside the station at Chiusi.

By bus: Montepulciano is on the main bus route between Siena and Chiusi. Several TRA-IN buses a day go from Montepulciano to Pienza, San Quirico, Torrenieri (change for Montalcino) and Buonconvento; one each morning and afternoon continues to Siena. (SITA buses connect Siena with Florence.) There is a regular LFI bus service between Montepulciano and Chiusi station (see above).
Bus info: TRA-IN: 0577-204111/ 204245
LFI: 0575-370687
SITA: 055-214721

🍽

MONTEPULCIANO
Porta di Bacco Pulcino
Via di Gracciano nel Corso, 106
(just inside the Porto al Prato)
Tel. 0578-757948

Fattoria Pulcino
Via di Gracciano nel Corso, 146

PICNICS
Rosticceria di Voltaia, Via di

Voltaia nel Corso, 86 (closed
Friday)

🎫
Affittacamere Bella Vista
Via Ricci, 25
Tel. 0578-757348

ⓘ
Tourist office: Via Ricci, 9; tel.
0578–757442. Closed Monday.

Teatro Povero di Monticchiello: last
half of July and the first week of
August, every night at 9.30,
except Mondays.

Directions

Leaving Pienza through the south-eastern gate at the
bottom of Corso Rossellino (the far end of town), cross
over the main asphalt ring road, and take the small asphalt
road that leads downhill to the left **A**.

This road soon turns to gravel, taking you immediately
into rolling farmland, with views over the hills to the
Monticchiello tower.

After reaching the bottom of a valley and beginning
to climb (about 1 km), the road forks **B**; go right (signed
to Monticchiello).

Follow the road for about 2½ km, until you reach a
T-junction. Go left here **C**.

In another ⅔ km you come to a T-junction at a stone
farmstead; turn right **D**.

Soon you'll cross over a bridge and come to a fork
just after it; turn left **E**.

The road becomes asphalt; take a left at the intersection **F** where the stop sign is.

Follow the road, which at the next intersection goes
left for Monticchiello and right for Montepulciano. If
you're visiting Monticchiello, turn left.

Continuing on to Montepulciano, the road soon
changes to gravel. Just follow it (ignoring a fork to the
left just around the point where the gravel begins).

When you come out on the main asphalt road **G**

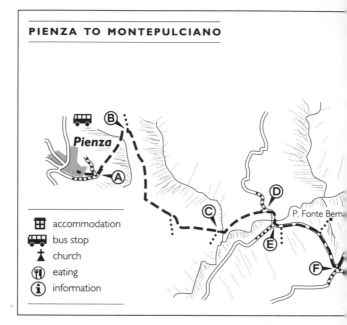

PIENZA TO MONTEPULCIANO

Pienza

⊞ accommodation
🚌 bus stop
✝ church
🍴 eating
ⓘ information

P. Fonte Bern

about 5½ km later, go right, and in about 200 m, at an intersection **H** with another main asphalt road, turn left (Viale della Rimembranza). You'll pass the church of San Biagio on your left after about ½ km. Bearing right past the church, proceed upward into Montepulciano.

MONTEPULCIANO TO PIENZA

Directions

From the entrance of San Biagio that faces towards town, head away from the church to the right (i.e., as you stand with your back to the church) along Viale della Rimembranza, an asphalt road lined with cypresses. Reaching the stop sign and intersection **H** at the end of this road, turn right on the main asphalt road.

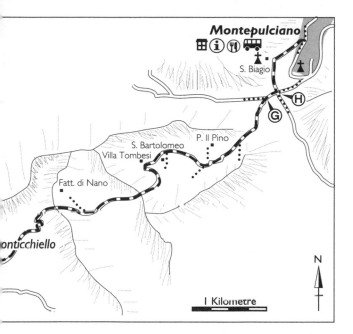

Take the first left-hand turn **G** (in about 150–200 m) off the main asphalt road. This narrow asphalt road climbs and after about 200 m the asphalt gives way to gravel.

When the road forks, with the gravel road, 'Via dell' Artigianato', to the left, take the right fork.

Stay on this main road (which ATW is mostly gravel, with a couple of would-be asphalt stretches), ignoring smaller deviations off it.

About 3 km from San Biagio, you'll pass the little abandoned church of San Bartolomeo, above the road on the left. There's a view behind it of forested hills merging into the *crete*.

In about another 2 km, you'll pass Fattoria di Nano (Villa Nano on IGM map) on the right (sales and tasting). There's a non-functioning fountain on the left side of the road here.

Monticchiello tower is visible on a hilltop ahead.

Reaching, after about 2 km more, a cemetery on the right near Monticchiello, the road becomes tarmac again (though empty), and winds along a stone wall for a while before reaching an intersection at Monticchiello. To visit Monticchiello go right (actually straight ahead). Go left to continue on to Pienza.

This asphalt road passes through a short stretch of modern houses until it reaches an intersection **F**. Pienza (and SS 2 Cassia) are signed straight ahead, but turn right here.

Along this stretch the tower at Pienza is visible on a hilltop out to the left. Tarmac soon gives way to gravel.

Continue along this road (ignoring a turning to the right after about ⅔ km). About 1½ km past the intersection at **F**, the road comes to a T-junction (there's a sign to Pienza). Turn right **E**, crossing a small bridge, after which the road bends around to the left (notice a small footbridge off to the right here). About 100 m past where the road bends round to the left, there's a left turn (smaller but same type of surface), signed for Pienza. Take this **D**.

When the road crosses another hardly noticeable bridge (the metal railings are nearly hidden in shrubbery), the road forks again. Turn right **C**.

Follow this road, which brings you to Pienza in about 3 km. (When the road reaches a T-junction **B** – which is really just our road turning left, but with a fairly good-sized track coming in to join it from the right – turn left, towards Pienza.)

The road becomes tarmac (but untravelled) 50–100 m or so before Pienza.

21 | MONTEPULCIANO TO MONTEFOLLONICO

La Chiusa, reputedly one of southern Tuscany's greatest restaurants, is located in the little walled town of Monte-follonico, a few miles from Montepulciano. The walk there happens to be a pleasant excursion in its own right (though unshaded), passing through exceptionally pretty vineyards and rolling fields with the usual poignantly attractive ruined farmhouses. The town has a thirteenth-century frescoed church and Palazzo Comunale as well as at least one other adventurous-looking (but far less expensive) restaurant, Ristorante 13 Gobbi, so it's worth coming here even if you choose not to lay out about £70 per head for a meal at La Chiusa. Unfortunately, the only way back that doesn't entail long stretches of busy road is the way you came, with the slight exception of the alternative routes available for entering or leaving Montefollonico itself.

The church of San Biagio, where this walk begins, is a handsome Renaissance building of porous travertine, located in a pretty, uncluttered setting below Montepulciano. Clap your hands underneath the dome to check out the splendid acoustics.

Food

La Chiusa works hard to reconcile its wish to remain faithful to the straightforward, farm-kitchen basis of Tuscan food with its ambition to be a glamorous and expensive establishment. The results are mixed, though for the most part impressive. Located in a lavishly restored farmhouse and olive press, the restaurant grows much of its own food (though sadly, the olive trees were wiped out by frost), and purchases most of the rest from local farmers, ensuring exceptionally high standards of freshness and general quality. Herb breads, pastas and excellent pastries are prepared every day on the premises, and an imaginative, seasonal menu regularly features the kinds of Tuscan specialities you might find in somebody's private home but not often in a restaurant – mousses (*sformati*) of home-grown spinach or chard; stuffed *zucchini* flowers, game roasted or stewed in a variety of sauces; beautiful little pies filled with local cheeses, home-made sorbets, and so on. For those unable to choose between the elaborate temptations of the menu, there's a seven-course *menu degustazione* of smallish portions, though this is a somewhat piecemeal experience and if you're more interested in satisfying your appetite than your curiosity you'll do better à la carte. We had, among other things, superb tortellini with garlicky hazelnut sauce and a succulent *stufato*, or stew, of spring lamb.

The down side is a certain unctuousness in the service and general tone: overdressed waiters, grandiose tablewear, a few too many private visits to your table from the various different kitchen departments – all of which seem designed to justify the inordinately high prices, and makes it hard to forget that the place exists principally to separate you from your money. Still, this is certainly a cut above most other supposedly high-class restaurants.

LOGISTICS

MONTEPULCIANO TO MONTEFOLLONICO,

2–3 hours

🚌 Transport
🍽 Eating
ⓘ Miscellaneous info

🚌

For trains and buses to Montepulciano see p. 246. There is no public transport between Montepulciano and Montefollonico. If you opt not to walk back you will have to arrange a car or taxi.

🍽

La Chiusa
Via della Madonnina, 88

53040 Montefollonico (Si)
Tel. 0577-669668; fax 0577-669593
Closing day: Tuesday, except in August and September; closed from January to March
Price: very expensive
Note: it's OK to wear shorts, etc., to lunch at La Chiusa.

Ristorante 13 Gobbi
Montefollonico
Price: much less expensive than La Chiusa

ⓘ

Tourist office: Montepulciano, tel. 0578-757442

Directions

From the entrance of San Biagio that faces town, and with your back to the church, turn right, and then take the first right, the road that circles the church.

Stay on this road, leaving the church behind and passing on the right the turning of Cimitero di Santa Chiara. The next left after the turning is Via delle Colombelle. Take this **A**.

Montefollonico is visible on the hill in the distance, and you stay on this dirt road heading towards it.

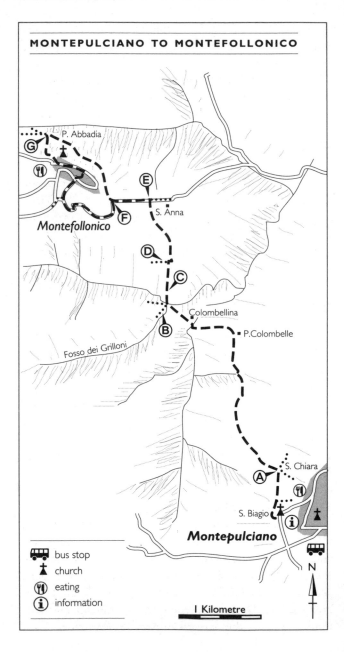

MONTEPULCIANO TO MONTEFOLLONICO

P. Abbadia

G

Montefollonico

F

E

S. Anna

D

C

Colombellina

B

P.Colombelle

Fosso dei Grilloni

A

S. Chiara

S. Biagio

Montepulciano

N

🚌 bus stop
✝ church
🍴 eating
ⓘ information

I Kilometre

About 2½ km from the beginning of Via Colombelle, you'll come to an abandoned farmstead on the right, Podere Colombelle.

From here the road slopes down, crosses an old stream bed, and reaches another abandoned farmhouse, Colombellina (not shown on the IGM map for this region).

The road continues to descend, and at the bottom of the hill crosses the stream, Fosso dei Grilloni **B**. After crossing this, take the path that leads to the right **C**, skirting round the outside of a large field. Keeping on this main track, you wind round the barn of a farm, coming to a T-junction with a larger path **D**. Turn right, towards an old farmhouse with solar panels.

Reaching this farmhouse, follow the main path up to the left, passing a little ruined outbuilding almost immediately on your right. The path climbs moderately and steadily, opening wide farmland panoramas to the right and left.

Ignoring a couple of minor deviations to the right, the path passes a farmhouse on the left, coming out at a T-junction with a white dirt road, and the ruined chapel of Santa Anna on the right. Turn left here **E**.

In about 400 m (5 minutes), the road forks **F**. From here two different routes are possible. (Note: a reader tells us there is a C A I route straight ahead at junction **F** (where our two routes diverge), which leads directly into Montefollonico.)

SHORTER ROUTE

Take the left fork, and follow it all the way into Montefollonico, a steepish climb of about 1 km, along gravel and then asphalt. Before a right bend into Montefollonico, you'll see a sign pointing left down Via della Madonnina, to La Chiusa. Otherwise, to see the town, go round to the right, keeping to the right (main road) until you reach the gardens under the old centre. Turn right, and then left through the arch. Immediately on your left is Ristorante 13 Gobbi.

LONGER BUT PRETTIER ROUTE

Take the right fork. Follow this quiet little farm road. In a little more than 1 km pass Podere Abbadia on the right; 100 m or so past here on the left is a farm track climbing uphill (there's also a track downhill on the right about 5–10 m ahead). Take the left, uphill, track **G**.

The track turns left into a field soon after (10–15 m) you begin it, but there is also a narrow footpath that continues straight ahead which you take.

This footpath climbs up to Montefollonico through woods. (At one point you reach a T-junction; turn left, which is obvious, as this is the direction of Montefollonico.)

The path forks when you come in sight of a stone house/tower and some stone walls. Carry on straight ahead, towards it, ignoring the right fork.

You'll immediately come out on a small asphalt road – turn left here, and follow the road, bearing left just after you pass through the stone wall here.

Pass a church on your left, then the PT (post office), a stone building with a bell tower and clock face.

Continue along this road until you reach the next possible right, at the little piazza. Take this, bearing right and passing through stone archway. (A restaurant, 13 Gobbi, is located here.) There's a fountain on the left just on far side of gate if you want to freshen up.

Turn right here (Via del Pianello), and take the next left, Via della Madonnina (signed to La Chiusa). Follow the road down to the restaurant.

22 | STAZIONE MURLO (LA BEFA) TO MURLO/ VESCOVADO

LOGISTICS

The walk takes, 3–4 hours

For information on Buonconvento, see p. 203–4.

The Osteria in La Befa is closed Wednesdays.

ATW the trains from Siena to Stazione Murlo (La Befa) are at 6.48, 12.49, and 13.55. This gives an idea of frequency, but check the schedule.

Comune Murlo, tourist information: tel. 0577-814213.

Antiquarium di Poggio Civitate (Etruscan Museum) is open every day except Monday, and closed in the middle of the day. Call the Comune for the opening hours if you're on a tight schedule.

Vescovado is where you get the bus back to Siena. It's about 2 km from Murlo, and easy to hitch if you don't feel like walking.

Directions

From Stazione Murlo, with the tracks to your left, follow the dirt road away from the station. At the T-junction turn left **A**. (Right leads in 5 minutes to La Befa – your only chance for provisions or coffee until Murlo. Closed Wednesday.)

Cross the railway and follow the road, ignoring minor deviations to the right and left; you soon pass between the two farmhouses of Podere Molinello. Continue along the road, ignoring a left-hand turn by a large, solitary oak about 100 m after the houses.

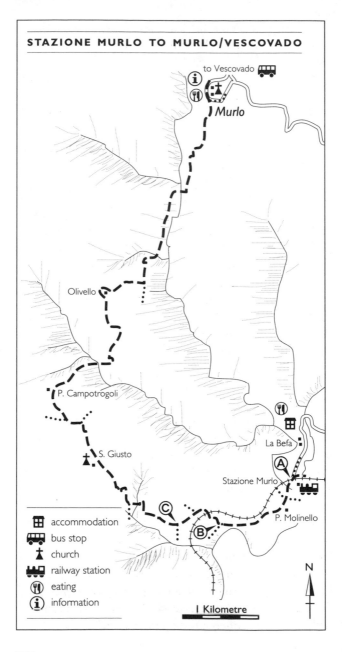

STAZIONE MURLO TO MURLO/VESCOVADO

to Vescovado

Murlo

Olivello

P. Campotrogoli

S. Giusto

La Befa

Ⓐ

Stazione Murlo

Ⓒ

Ⓑ

P. Molinello

accommodation
bus stop
church
railway station
eating
information

N

1 Kilometre

About 1 km after the farmhouses the road forks – take the right branch **B**, which crosses over the railway tracks.

When the road forks again shortly after crossing the tracks, take the downhill, left fork.

Shortly the road forks again. Take the right uphill fork **C**.

About an hour from the start, you'll pass through the ruined hamlet of San Giusto.

When you reach a T-junction about 10 minutes after San Giusto, go left.

In another 10 minutes or so, you'll come to an abandoned homestead (Podere Campotrogoli). The path forks; take the right branch, around the back of the house.

The road will begin to climb; stay on it, continuing to climb and ignoring deviations.

As you pass a little pond on your right at the approach to the hamlet of Olivello, there's a fork. Take a left. Wander up through the village, and then at the top turn right, passing under an old passage between two buildings over the road; a kind of arch. Then bear left past an old well with a pointed conical roof, staying on the main (dirt) road.

Coming downhill from Olivello, at a rather steep downhill section of the road, the main road curves to the left, while three somewhat smaller paths fork off to the right of it, signed 'CAI 6' on a telephone pole. Continue on the main road (unsurfaced here), bending to the left.

When you reach the new asphalt road of Miniere Murlo, follow it as it passes through the small village and leads out of it at the end, to the right.

After a fairly uninteresting uphill stretch – relieved, however, by the sound of tinkling sheep bells rising off the plain below – you'll reach Murlo, with beautiful wide views on either side as you approach.

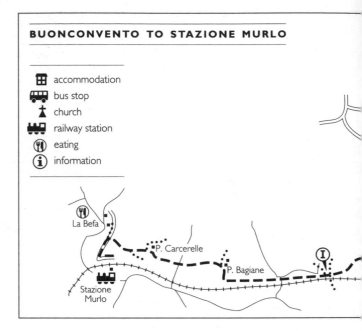

BUONCONVENTO TO STAZIONE MURLO

- ⊞ accommodation
- 🚌 bus stop
- ♱ church
- 🚂 railway station
- 🍴 eating
- ⓘ information

La Befa

P. Carcerelle

P. Bagiane

Stazione Murlo

Vescovado is about 2 km from here, easily hitched if you don't feel like walking.

ADDENDUM: BUONCONVENTO TO STAZIONE MURLO (LA BEFA)

Directions

From the front of the station **A**, cross the main street and follow the street straight ahead of the station.

Take the first right and then the first left (the road to Bibbiano), which crosses the Ombrone river **B** by some distinct maritime pines.

After the bridge, take the first left, a dirt road leading to a farmhouse, Pian delle Noci.

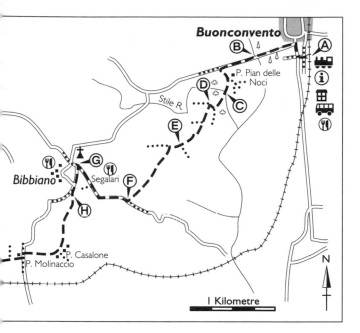

Before reaching the house, just before the stacks of wood and the small brick animal pen, you take a right along a farm track heading towards the trees. Where you reach the trees, a cement platform bridge crosses the Stile river **C**.

As you pass the castle tower on your right, watch at the end of a line of hedges for a less used track on the right. Take that, uphill, towards a brick castellated lodge. Reaching that, go left on the gravel road **D** which runs in front of it.

When the road bends right, take the slightly more minor fork carrying on to the left (which is actually straight ahead).

When the road forks by a small pond, take the right branch **E**. About 40 m past the fork, at the end of the hedge, the path is intersected by a slightly smaller track. Go left here (there's a CAI marker on a pine tree to the right just as you're turning). (Note: be sure to take the *track*, which is about 5 m in front of the pine tree, rather than the entrance to a field, which is directly in front of the tree.)

Follow this track, crossing through a border of trees between two fields. Keep on straight; when the path seems to give out, just in front of the beginning of a hedge (and where another track leads down into a lower field), keep straight on, along the edge of the field, beside this row of bushes and olive trees just to your right. The track reappears almost immediately alongside this hedge.

Follow the path out on to the gravel road which runs along the edge of the cypress trees, and go right on it **F**. Follow this road directly into the little hamlet of Segalari, which is visible ahead of you on the right.

Bear right on the asphalt through Segalari, passing the pizzeria/pub/spaghetteria L'Europeo on your left. At the intersection near a building with a small bell tower, go left on the asphalt road **G** (signed towards Montalcino).

The road turns to gravel right outside the village. Soon after this it bends round to the right and you'll see a smaller dirt track on the left side (but actually leading straight ahead). Take this **H**.

When this path comes directly in front of the farmhouse of Podere Casalone (in a sort of T-junction, as if it ends there), bear right and you'll find the path in the far right corner of the farmyard (between the farmyard and 'garage'), that leads down to the main dirt road. Take this, and at the dirt road go left and then immediately right (at farmhouse Molinaccio).

Bear left (actually straight on) at the first fork.

Follow along the road until you come to an intersection **I**, with a blue metal bridge on the left-hand turn. Do not go there, but continue straight ahead. The road forks again immediately, the left branch being a slightly more minor track. Take this.

This track goes parallel to the railway for about 15 minutes and then bends away from it, uphill to the right, towards Podere Bagiane. Reaching this farmstead in five minutes (good views of rolling fields and woods), you'll see a circular brick well with a red and white CAI sign on it.

Fork left off the main path here, passing to the right of a brick shed and going down into a field with a line of telegraph poles crossing it. Bear left across the field, ignoring a fork to the right that appears as soon as you enter it.

In another 10 minutes this peaceful farm track leads you through lovely open countryside to the abandoned farmhouse of Podere Carcerelle, where you bear left, downhill.

After 200 m the path forks; go right, staying on the main path until you come out on the asphalt road. La Befa is 5 minutes up to your right. To connect with the Murlo walk or go to the station, turn left instead.

Continue straight on this road until you reach the railway; turn left into the station here or, for the Murlo walk, cross the tracks and continue straight ahead. Pick up the La Befa to Murlo walk here.

WEST OF SIENA
SAN GIMIGNANO, MONTERIGGIONI
AND THE MONTAGNOLA

To the west of Siena, across the Val d'Elsa, lies the hilly, thickly wooded region known as the Montagnola Senese. Sparsely populated and, unlike neighbouring Chianti, not often visited by tourists, it retains a certain sombre flavour from the medieval period, when it was crossed by the Via Francigena, the great pilgrim route connecting Rome with northern Europe. Much of the landscape, dominated by the three peaks of Monte Maggio (671 m), is essentially a forest broken by occasional quarries and farms, many of them abandoned. Deer and wild boar roam through the stands of oak, chestnut, maple and hornbeam that roll on for miles. Dark woodland paths (comfortable walking even in summer) come out on clearings that might be filled with a dazzling crop of sunflowers, or might as easily be in the process of reverting to the scrub of broom, myrtle and blackberry that marks the first stage of reclamation by the forest itself.

The hand-hewn stonework of the Via Francigena and its subsidiaries survives for long passages on many of the numerous trails. Painstakingly squared-off, the sunken slabs of these little-known ancient roads (which exist all over Italy, and are generally referred to as 'Francigena', whether or not they formed part of the original route) are surely one of the most touching monuments of the medieval period. More prominent survivors of this

era are the Cistercian abbey, Abbadia a Isola, and the stunning thirteenth-century fortified hill town of Monteriggioni, which presides over the northern boundary of the Montagnola, its lovely ringed wall with fourteen sentry towers sitting slightly awry like a tilted crown.

Further up the Val d'Elsa, the landscape opens up into steep, dovetailing vineyards where San Gimignano's Vernaccia wine is produced; this is half the reason for the rejuvenation of the local economy. The other half is of course tourism, and as you get your first glimpse of the stone towers of San Gimignano bristling over the countryside like a kind of medieval Manhattan you will understand why this has become one of the most popular destinations for tourists in all of Tuscany. Needless to say few of these tourists ever venture beyond the town walls, so that walkers can be pretty sure of having the surrounding countryside, with its superb views of this photogenic landmark, more or less to themselves.

The Walks

CAI has recently published a 1:25,000 trail map for the Montagnola Senese. At the time we were researching this area, they were in the process of clearing and renumbering the mass of old woodland trails to conform with their map, so there was a certain amount of confusion. By now this should be cleared up, and the area, with its miles of gentle, extraordinarily peaceful walks, ought to be pleasant and easy to explore. Both of our Montagnola walks begin in Monteriggioni; one of them a ring walk via the Abbadia a Isola and an old pre-Etruscan site, the other ends at the little hamlet of Santa Colomba, where the *agriturismo* Gavina makes an ideal base for further explorations of the region.

We also have a ring walk from San Gimignano that goes deep into the surrounding countryside, and could be spread over two days, with a break for the night at the delightful agriturism farm of Voltrona.

Monteriggioni

About 11 km north of Siena, the little fortified hill town of Monteriggioni, built in 1219, is one of the prettiest sights in all of Tuscany. Though Dante compared the fourteen towers to giants in an abyss, the modern eye is likely to find them charming rather than forbidding. Both of the following walks have particularly splendid views of the town.

> Thitherward not long
> My head was raised, when many a lofty tower
> Methought I spied. 'Master,' said I, 'what land
> Is this?' He answer'd straight: 'Too long a space
> Of intervening darkness has thine eye
> To traverse: thou hast therefore widely err'd
> In thy imagining. Thither arrived
> Thou well shalt see how distance can delude
> The sense. A little therefore urge thee on.'
>
> Then tenderly he caught me by the hand;
> 'Yet know,' said he, 'ere further we advance,
> That it less strange may seem, these are not towers,
> But giants. In the pit they stand immersed,
> Each from his navel downward, round the bank.'
>
> As when a fog disperseth gradually,
> Our vision traces what the mist involves
> Condensed in air; so piercing through the gross
> And gloomy atmosphere, as more and more
> We near'd toward the brink, mine error fled
> And fear came o'er me. As with circling round
> Of turrets, Monteriggioni crowns his walls,
> E'en thus the shore, encompassing the abyss,
> Was turreted with giants, half their length
> Uprearing, horrible, whom Jove from heaven
> Yet threatens, when his muttering thunder rolls.

Inferno, xxxi, translated by the Revd Henry Francis Cary

23 | MONTERIGGIONI RING WALK
with Optional Spur to Montauto

This is a fairly gentle, varied walk through woods, farmland and old settlements rich in history.

Abbadia a Isola is a pleasant eleventh-century Cistercian abbey built on what was once an island (hence 'Isola') in the centre of marshes. To visit it, ask the caretaker (house to the left of the church). At the southwest angle there remains a little polygonal rampart surmounted by a circular turret with arrow slits at the summit.

The walk also passes a moving monument to partisan martyrs of the Val d'Elsa murdered by fascists during the last years of the war. At the Casa Giubileo, next to the monument, the spur trail to Montauto departs, passing through deep woods, the path shaded by old holm oaks bending over it like a continuous Gothic arch. Ruins of a pre-Etruscan castle and two medieval buildings lie in a state of rather indecipherable semi-excavation among the blackberry bushes up here, but the trip is worth making for the fantastic panorama it offers over the Val d'Elsa. A great place for a picnic.

Food

Tiny as it is, Monteriggioni has two restaurants and a fancy hotel, as well as a small store where a reasonable picnic can be purchased. Of the restaurants, Il Castello is the cheaper, but if you can afford to pay a little more, it's well worth eating at the excellent Il Pozzo. The food here is fresh, imaginative and beautifully prepared.

Among the lighter offerings are crisp mixed salads, delicate fried *zucchini* blossoms, ravioli stuffed with pumpkin, *tortellini* with truffles roasted in foil, and wonderful mixed cheese pastries. For something more substantial try the wild boar with polenta, or one of the many rich dishes of roast game. The dessert trolley – usually about as enticing as a morgue – is truly tempting here, offering exceptionally good *panna cotta*, *frutti di bosco* (wild berries) and plums in Chianti. The place is unpretentious and friendly; despite our walking boots and sweaty shirts, we were made to feel extremely welcome.

LOGISTICS

MONTERIGGIONI RING WALK, 4 hours (plus 45 minutes if doing Montauto spur)

For a much shorter walk, of about 1½ hours, you could go as far as Abbadia a Isola and take the bus back from there.

🚌 Transport
Ⓜ Maps, guidebooks and trail info
🍽 Eating
🏨 Accommodation
ⓘ Miscellaneous info

🚌

FROM SIENA, AND RETURN
The TRA-IN bus (tel. 0577-204111/204245) lets you off on the main road, which is below the actual village of Monteriggioni. If you want to visit the town before doing the walk, you'll have to walk up there (about 5 minutes); otherwise, you can pick up the route from where the bus lets you off.

For the return journey, the bus to Siena again picks up on main road, below the actual village.
Length of journey: under ½ hour
Frequency: buses are fairly frequent, and run on Sundays and holidays as well (though not so frequently)

Ⓜ

• CAI map, Carta Turistica e dei Sentieri, 'Itinerari nella Montagnola Senese', 1:25,000

MONTERIGGIONI RING WALK

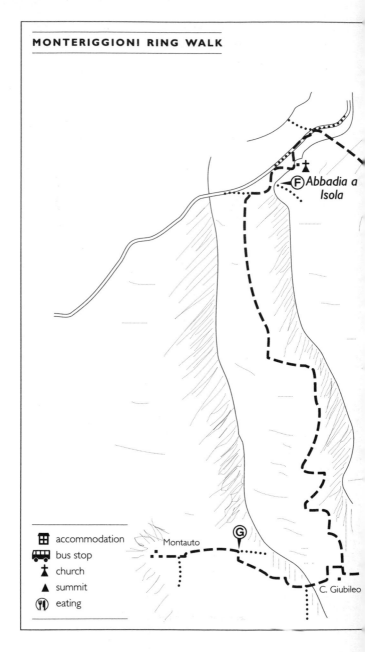

accommodation
bus stop
church
summit
eating

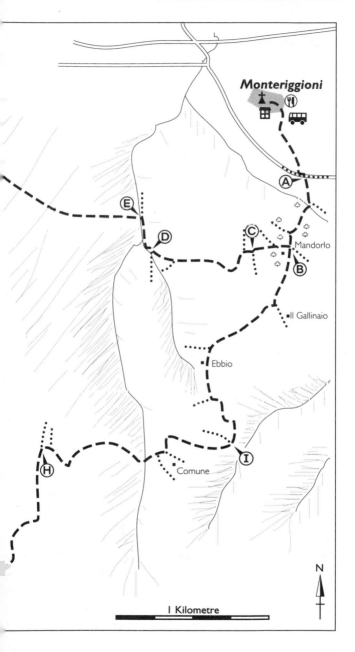

Monteriggioni

Mandorlo

Il Gallinaio

Ebbio

Comune

1 Kilometre

N

This map has many walks routed. The descriptions are in Italian, but if you've got a compass and some experience with maps, it's a good bet for additional walks in the area.

🍴

Il Pozzo
Piazza Roma, 2
53035 Monteriggioni (Si)
Tel. 0577-304127; fax 0577-304701
Closing day: Sunday evening and Monday; closed January and August

⊞

Monteriggioni has a four-star hotel and several *affittacamere*

options (get a copy of the excellent Siena APT pamphlet 'Hotel, Campeggi, Agriturismo, Affittacamere, Osteli' available at the Siena tourist offices) if you want to stay over rather than returning to Siena.

ⓘ

Local CAI: Siena CAI, Viale Mazzini, 95; tel. 0577-270666. Open Monday, Wednesday and Friday, 6–7:30 p.m.
Forest ranger station (Stazione Forestale): Corpo Forestale dello Stato, Comando Staz. Viale dei Mille, 8, Colle Val d'Elsa; tel. 0577-929554

Directions

Standing in the piazza with the church beside you to your left, go out through the gate facing you, turning right on the small asphalt road. Staying on the asphalt, walk about ½ km downhill to the main road. Here turn left for 20 m, and then take the dirt road to your right **A** signed to Il Mandorlo. This dirt road has a sign which says 'Strada privata', but it is a CAI trail and may be used by walkers.

After 150 m the road forks. Go right. A gentle climb then takes you to a wood where the road forks again. Take the left fork this time.

At the intersection 70 m from here **B**, take the right turn, signed to Il Mandorlo. (This is about 25 minutes from Monteriggioni.) The middle and left paths here are also CAI trails, so be sure you have the correct one.

Walk straight along this road, which turns into a well-defined grassy path at the rear of the big house on the left, and follows alongside the grounds. The path quickly becomes a dirt track and enters the woods. (This is *not* CAI 101.)

When the path forks **C**, very soon, go right, downhill, keeping straight along this path (ignoring a dubious-looking similar-sized path immediately on the right, uphill). This rugged stone path dates back to medieval times, and is well travelled today by porcupines, as the many quills along the way attest.

When the path comes out by a large cultivated field (planted with sunflowers when we were there) bear right along the edge of it (open field to the left, woods to the right). The path passes through the edge of the woods again, and then comes out at the end of the field.

At the end of the field, keep straight on, ignoring a left-hand grassy fork, and almost immediately meeting a dirt road, slightly larger, on to which you turn right **D**. (This is 50 minutes or so out of Monteriggioni.)

This path in turn comes out on another dirt road **E**. Go left here, between large expanses of field. Follow this road until you come to the asphalt road in about 2 km. Turn left there and, in 100 m or so, come to the Romanesque church of Abbadia a Isola. (The woman in the house to the left of the church is the caretaker and will let you in with a very large key. A small tip is appreciated.)

Leaving the abbey, turn left on to the same asphalt road, and immediately take the dirt road forking off it to the left.

Pass the old polygonal chapel, continuing up the road about 20 m until you come to a junction **F**; bear right here, picking up red and white CAI signs.

Very shortly, the road forks again. Go left. Again, there are CAI red and white markings here.

Follow this stony road, ascending, for about 3 km (about an hour), always staying on the principal track, until you reach Casa Giubileo, a large old homestead on the right (with a green sign, '*Punto di sosta*' on the corner of it). There is a monument to the partisan martyrs of Val d'Elsa on the left side of the road here and also, behind the stone wall on the right side of the road, the burial sites of two of them, who were gunned down by the fascists when sleeping here.

The spur to Montauto departs from here.

MONTAUTO SPUR (about 45 minutes round trip). From the road, before actually reaching Casa Giubileo, you can see a gap between the right rear corner of the house and the stone wall behind it. On the stone wall there's a very visible CAI red and white mark which says '105'. Pass through this gap.

Go down alongside the house and you'll see a circular well. Pass round the left side of the well, and you'll find a track leading down to the right. Take this.

After 30 m it comes out at a flat area of scrub. The path is a little hard to find here. Look ahead to the right and you should see a red and white CAI sign on a tree 50 m off. Then look for a thin trail through the rather thorny scrub that leads to it. Once there, the path becomes clearer, bearing left towards the wood, with more CAI signs to help you navigate. In the woods the path is easy: a deep-shaded route, the trees arching over the path.

*Follow the main path straight ahead, ignoring a right fork after about ⅔ km **G**. In another 300–400 m you'll come to a junction with CAI 105. Go right. A short climb brings you to the ruins and panorama of Montauto.*

On the way back, watch you don't take a fork to the right (marked with old CAI sign) after 1 km that you might not have noticed on the way.

Continuing on along the road past Casa Giubileo (ignore two lesser forks to the right), you come after about 15 minutes to a right fork **H** almost the size of the main path. It's marked '105 B' and crosses diagonally over the main path. Take it to the right. In 50 m it joins a similar road coming from the left; follow on round to the right.

After 15 minutes you approach the house, Comune. The owner keeps hounds in a large pen. Just before this pen, take the lesser path that forks down to the left. This is CAI 102.

This path follows a pleasant wooded hillside with occasional views towards the delicate, uneven crown of Monteriggioni.

At a fork after 5–10 minutes, go right **I**. The path goes through abandoned olive groves, with a lovely view of Monteriggioni. In 100 m it re-enters woods. BE ALERT HERE: the path zigzags and forks, but it's well signed, despite being overgrown and narrow in places, so you simply follow the CAI signs – they're never far from any juncture.

In 10–15 minutes you come down on to a wider, level path where you turn right. This takes you alongside the organic gardens of Ebbio (see the next walk), and

down past the garden buildings, where you come on to a white gravel road. Proceed on this, ignoring a similar white gravel fork to the left, 100 m past the main house.

About ½ km down the main path you'll come to a T-junction with Il Gallinaio on your right (this is about an hour past Casa Giubileo). Go left. After a few minutes you come to an intersection **B** with CAI 101. Go across, staying on the main gravel road.

A splendid view of Monteriggioni comes soon, on your left.

The gravel road winds down to asphalt (and the bus back to Siena). To return to Monteriggioni, go left on the main asphalt road and then immediately up to the right.

24 | MONTERIGGIONI TO SANTA COLOMBA

This is a perfect day walk from Siena; alternatively, you could stay overnight at the lovely *agriturismo* of La Gavina, taking the bus back to Siena the next day, or taking your chances with the CAI map to do a loop back to Monteriggioni.

It is a long but not too strenuous walk, much of it through deep woods, making it an appealing prospect even in summer. There are one or two hauntingly beautiful abandoned farms along the way, and some fine samples of the old stone Via Francigena.

Early on you pass through the organic gardens and meditation centre of Ebbio, one of the region's more interestingly offbeat *agriturismo* establishments. A little over an hour later you reach the road to the pretty little hamlet of Colle a Ciupe, worth the brief detour to have a look at the little Romanesque church with its fine views over the surrounding landscape. The last part of the walk is a little tricky as the trails no longer conform precisely to the CAI map, though you're never far from houses, and if you get lost, anyone will be able to direct you to Santa Colomba. The Villa di Baldassare Peruzzi, at Santa Colomba, was transformed in the seventeenth century into the vast, weirdly disproportionate monument that broods over the distinctly unmonumental landscape today. It's an extraordinary sight, not exactly beautiful, but impressive. It's private, but the American owner holds an art festival and general *festa* in the grounds every year in late June.

There's a small bar in the village, and you can either get a bus back into Siena (check on times), or stay in the *agriturismo* of La Gavina, about a mile away (the owner will pick you up from Santa Colomba).

Food

Il Pozzo in Monteriggioni (see Monteriggioni ring walk). The bar in Santa Colomba allegedly functions as a *trattoria*, though by reservation only, which probably means they will require a minimum number of guests. La Gavina, the nearby *agriturismo*, prepares delicious food for people staying there, much of it from its own organic gardens. Excellent salads and vegetables, as might be expected, a subtly flavoured risotto with wild mushrooms, good local wines, and all of it in abundance, as is usually the case in these establishments.

LOGISTICS

MONTERIGGIONI TO SANTA COLOMBA,

4 hours

🚌 Transport
Ⓜ Maps, guidebooks and
trail info
🍴 Eating
⊞ Accommodation
ⓘ Miscellaneous info

🚌

FROM SIENA

See p. 268.

RETURN TO SIENA

TRA-IN bus 37 (0577-204111/
204245) from Santa Colomba
Frequency: about 4 a day
Length of journey: 30 minutes

Ⓜ

See pp. 269–72. This walk
follows CAI 102; partially/
imperfectly signed.

🍴

MONTERIGGIONI

See p. 272.

SANTA COLOMBA

The *trattoria* in Santa Colomba,

by prior reservation only;
tel. 0577-317105.
Closing day: Monday.

⊞

La Gavina (*agriturismo* near Santa
Colomba)
Az. Agr. Papini Sergio
Loc. Gavina di Sopra
Santa Colomba
53100 Monteriggioni (Si)
Tel. 0577-317046.
Very pretty and peaceful location,
a really nice change and contrast
from the city. Delicious food
from the organic garden. Horses
stabled. English spoken. Local
trails.

Podere Ebbio OMC
53035 Monteriggioni (Si)
Tel. 0577-304037
Meditation centre; *agriturismo*,
sculpture, horses, organic
vegetarian food; Rajneesh
element. Very peaceful little
spot. English spoken.

ⓘ

See p. 272.

Directions

Standing in the piazza in Monteriggioni with the church beside you to your left, go out through the gate facing you, turning right on the small asphalt road as you leave the gate. Staying on the asphalt, walk about ½ km downhill to the main road. Here turn left for 20 m, and take the dirt road to your right **A**, signed Il Mandorlo. This dirt road has a sign which says '*Strada privata*', but is a CAI trail and may be used for walking.

After 150 m the road forks. Go right. A gentle climb then takes you to a wood where the road forks again. Take the left fork.

At the intersection 70 m from here **B**, keep to the main path that curves round to the left (signed to Gallinaio), ignoring a sharp left and a right. (CAI trails go down each of these forks, so be sure you have the correct one.)

The path winds gently up, in and out of woods, and after 5 minutes you come to another fork. The left-hand path goes to Il Gallinaio. Take the right, always keeping to the main white stone path. Ignoring a minor fork down to the right after 5 minutes, follow the main path up to the left past the houses of the Ebbio *agriturismo* and meditation centre.

Go on through the property. The white stone road becomes a smaller path; 100 m past the house it enters a wood. BE ALERT HERE: the path forks and zigzags numerous times as it climbs through the wood, though on the whole it is very well signed by CAI, and you shouldn't have to look far at any intersection before you find the red and white markers. The following instructions are probably not necessary, but here they are just in case.

About 70 m after entering the wood, there's a narrow fork up to the left off the main path. Take this, and keep

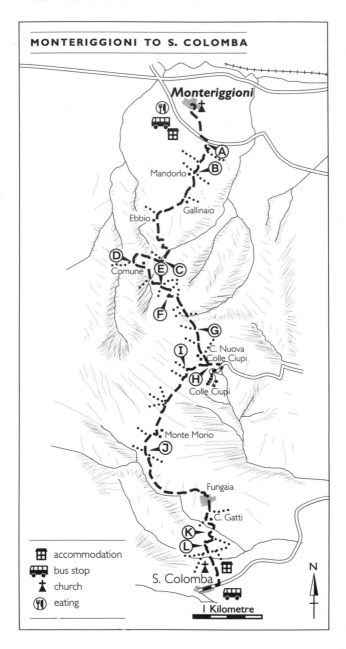

MONTERIGGIONI TO S. COLOMBA

Monteriggioni

(A)
(B)
Mandorlo
Gallinaio
Ebbio
(D) (E) (C)
Comune
(F)
(G)
C. Nuova
(I) Colle Ciupi
(H)
Colle Ciupi
Monte Morio
(J)
Fungaia
C. Gatti
(K)
(L)
S. Colomba

▦ accommodation
🚌 bus stop
✝ church
🍽 eating

N

I Kilometre

left at the fork that comes in another 20 m. The path is narrow and somewhat overgrown here, but well signed. At the next fork (70 m) go left; 30 m after this, take the right fork (you'll see the sign once you've taken it). After another 70 m a sign like this ⌐ on a stone points you to the right, off what seems to be the main path. After 100 m of winding and climbing, the path bends round to the left and passes under a telephone wire. In another 100 m you come to a tiny clearing where you go straight across, bending round to the right at the junction that comes a few metres later. The path widens a little, goes along to the left of an old stone wall and comes out of the woods.

Go straight ahead, ignoring a fork to the left. Ignore also the entrance to an overgrown olive grove a few metres ahead to the right. Climb straight ahead on a reddish dirt track (there are fewer CAI signs here), with wide panoramas opening behind you. Ignore a branch that goes down sharply to your right after 100 m **C**, and follow the main path for another ½ km to a T-junction **D**, where CAI 102 (your trail) joins CAI 105b. Go left, and then, a few metres later, left again, past the house marked Comune, and straight on out by their drive

Proceed along the white stone road in and out of woods, ignoring a wide reddish track up to the right after 5 minutes. In another 5 minutes you come to a clearing with an intersection **E** where a wide road branches backward to the right. Look for a narrow path that branches *forward* to the right, and take this (this is where CAI 102 branches off from CAI 105b). After 50 m you come out on a wide dirt road, where you turn right for 50 m and then take the path **F** that forks sharply left into the woods.

Ignoring a fork back down to the left after 70 m, you come out of the woods and go straight on, ignoring a steep path up to the right and 50 m later a second similar path up to the right. After another 30 m, as you re-enter the woods, the path forks at a gap in an old stone wall. Take the right fork and keep to the main path, ignoring smaller digressions to the left and right. After 10–15 minutes you come out at a T-junction **G** with another little path. Turn left. After 5 minutes, at another wide fork, go left again. In a couple of minutes you'll come to a house (Casa Nuova Colle Ciupi) where you bend round to the right, ignoring a sharp left at the house itself.

At the intersection 70 m past the house **H**, either continue straight on to visit Colle Ciupi (a hamlet and chapel with deteriorating Trecento frescoes inside and good panoramic views), turning right at the T-junction; or, if bypassing Colle Ciupi, take the sharp right here, a farm track. CAI 102 joins CAI 107 here; (ATW, neither trail is marked, but will be soon, apparently).

The track enters a field and bends round to the left, following a deep ditch and passing a pond. A little past the pond you'll see that the deep ditch has turned into a pleasant little sunken path; however, it hasn't been maintained for very far, so keep above it, entering another field and forking left **I** at the far left corner, on to a stony path. Ignore a right fork after 50 m.

Climbing gently you'll come after 10 minutes to a little clearing with three paths off to the right (one of them is CAI 107). Go straight on along the main path, passing through an opening in an old stone wall and following the path as it bends to the left, ignoring a fork to the right 30 m past the wall.

Crossing a narrow meadow and re-entering the woods you'll pass the back of the abandoned, pinkish stone house of Monte Morio, home to a few sheep at present. Go round the pond and take the left fork. After 5–10 minutes you come to an intersection **J**, where you go straight on.

After 25 minutes you enter the pretty stone-built hamlet of Fungaia. Bending left past the church for 20 m, take the little path that goes right along the side of the first house. The path winds through open country-side, with a view ahead to the oversized villa of Santa Colomba. Ignore a left turn that comes after 150 m, and pass to the right of the abandoned house (Casa Gatti) just beyond this. At the fork, turn left (a gentler descent than CAI, who go steeply down with the telephone poles).

At the bottom of the hill take a sharp left **K**. Then, a few metres after, fork right, uphill, coming out at the beginning of a larger dirt road. In 200 m you reach a T-junction **L** with an asphalt road. Cross straight over, taking the middle one of the three paths that enter the wood here.

In 10 minutes the path brings you out on an asphalt road where you turn right, into Santa Colomba.

25 | SAN GIMIGNANO RING WALK
via San Donato

A leisurely, attractive walk through farmland, Vernaccia vineyards and wooded hills. This takes you deep into the countryside, most of it unspoiled and extraordinarily peaceful, with only the occasional pretty farmstead or sleepy hamlet to remind you what century you're in. You're unlikely to find anyone in San Donato (which in 1833 was home to 151 inhabitants) unless you pass through at lunchtime, when the one remaining family

will be at home. There's a thirteenth-century church there though, well conserved. (Note: a reader tells us that there is now farm accommodation at the winery at San Donato.)

If you have the time, it's worth making a two-day excursion of this, staying at the Fattoria Voltrona, where you can sample *agriturismo* at its most easygoing. There's a swimming pond here, pleasant, clean rooms, and delicious food from the farm, where they produce every-thing from the wine to their own ham.

The wooded section of this walk is difficult to follow, so we strongly recommend you get the IGM map, which you can buy at the San Gimignano Comune 'Ufficio Tecnico', for about L. 5000, or the guidebook listed below, generally available in the San Gimignano stores.

Food

There are numerous restaurants in San Gimignano. Standards are generally quite good, and prices not exorb-itant. Il Pino at Via San Matteo 102 has good truffle dishes. Near by, at no. 77, is the reliable, straightforward Trattoria La Stella, serving Tuscan standards such as *ribollita* and *stracotto*, with vegetables from its own farm. For something a little more adventurous, you might try Ris-torante Dorando at Vicolo dell'Oro 2, which takes an archaeological approach to cooking, allegedly recreating dishes from both the Renaissance and the Etruscan periods of Tuscan gastronomic history.

Osteria Antiche Terre Rosse, near San Donato, is a pleasant place to stop for lunch. Robust home cooking, specialities such as *tortelli maremmani alle noci* (pasta with a sauce of walnuts and garlic), a spicy *penne* with olives, roast guinea-hen with garlicky potatoes.

If you're staying at Fattoria Voltrona, expect to eat abundantly and well. Guests and the family who run the farm all dine together at long tables on the terrace. Home-cured olives, fresh salads, bowls of pasta, bottles of wine, plates of *prosciutto*, dishes of grilled chicken or home-made sausages, appear in steady succession from the kitchen. It's an extremely satisfying way to finish a day of serious hiking.

LOGISTICS

SAN GIMIGNANO RING WALK VIA SAN DONATO, 6–7 hours

🚌 Transport

Ⓜ Maps, guidebooks and trail info

🍴 Eating

🏨 Accommodation

ⓘ Miscellaneous info

🚌

FROM SIENA

TRA-IN bus (tel. 0577-204111/ 204245) to San Gimignano

Length of journey: about 45 minutes

Frequency: very frequent; less frequent on Sundays and holidays

Ⓜ

- IGM map 113 III NO ('San Gimignano')
- Guidebook: *Dolce campagna, antiche mura* (in Italian)

🍴

Osteria Antiche Terre Rosse
San Donato
Tel. 0577-940540
Hours: 12–2 and 7.30–9.30
Closing day: Monday

🏨

There are several hotels in San Gimignano, and many *affittacamere*; outside the town there are many *agriturismo* establishments. For listings, check in with the San Gimignano tourist office, or get a copy of the excellent guide offered at the Siena tourist office, 'Hotel, Campeggi, Ostelli, Agriturismo, Affittacamere'.

AGRITURISMO

Fattoria Voltrona (1500 m past San Donato on our route)
Loc. San Donato
53037 San Gimignano (Si)
Tel. 0577-941447; fax 0577-923538

An excellent *agriturismo*. If you decide to make a two-day trip of this itinerary, staying overnight at Voltrona, you'll get a good lunch at Voltrona. Swimming pond. Organic farm, their own organic wine. Cheese from local neighbour. Their own olives, deliciously cured, the best we've had. Home-cured *prosciutto*. Can stable horses here if you reserve (but they don't hire out horses).

ⓘ
Tourist office: Ufficio Informazioni
Associazione Pro Loco, Piazza del

Duomo 1, 53037 San Gimignano
(Si); tel. 0577-940008; fax
0577-940903. Closed Mondays.

Directions

Leaving through the southernmost exit from San Gimignano, turn right, passing a round tower and coming to
a parking lot in front of you. Take the road **A** downhill
to the left of the parking lot, passing the Carabinieri
headquarters on your left.

Just past here, the asphalt leaves off, and the road
brings you very soon into pretty countryside. Passing a
turning to the left **B**, follow the road straight ahead,
crossing a small bridge at the bottom of the valley, and
then beginning to climb.

Keep following the road, climbing fairly steadily and
coming about 50 minutes after leaving San Gimignano
to a farm (Vineyard Montenidoli **C**, whose proprietor is
very friendly towards walkers) with a big new building.
The path winds in front of this new building and to the
left, and ends on a T-junction. Go right here, passing a
small pond immediately on the left, and climb towards a
wood. On the edge of the wood the path turns to the left.

Ignore a branch off to the left just past here, climbing
straight ahead and coming almost immediately to a gate;
turn right, climbing into a wood of oak and pine, where
the path is somewhat reduced and rougher.

Soon the path comes to a fence, turns right and then
right again, becoming wider. For a couple of minutes,
the path is more in the open again. The calcareous limestone rocks here on the path are full of shell fossils, which
you can find by breaking the bigger rocks.

The path then enters the wood again for about 20 m,
before coming to a semi-cleared area where it bends to

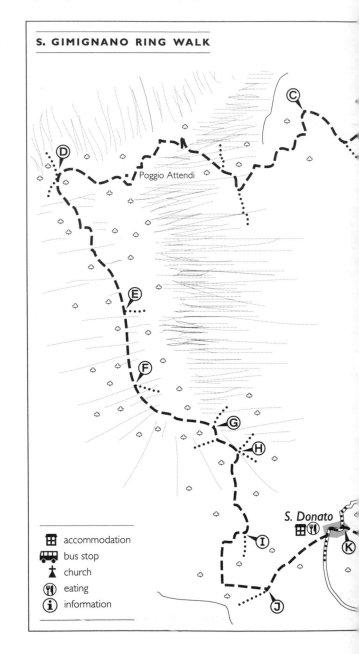

S. GIMIGNANO RING WALK

Poggio Attendi

S. Donato

accommodation

bus stop

church

eating

information

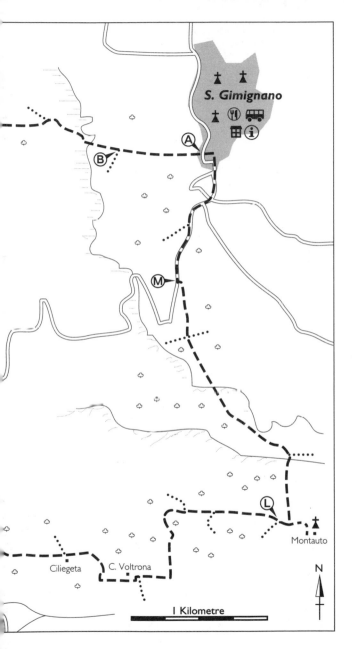

S. Gimignano

B

A

M

L

Montauto

Ciliegeta   C. Voltrona

N

1 Kilometre

the left (this is only about 10 minutes past Montenidoli). But instead of following the path left, take another path going to the right.

From this crossroads, go about 60 paces until you come to a much smaller path forking uphill to the left of the main path. ATW it is fairly well-marked with bright reddish-orange paint marks. Go up here.

It's a very narrow but well-defined path, marked by the reddish-orange paint. Stay on this path, going straight on at a junction where two of these little paths cross. ATW there is an orange (rather than orangish-red) mark on a tree here on the right, and just ahead the usual bright orange-red sign on trees to the left. Follow these markers.

The path continues to climb, at one point taking a sharp right near a blue paint mark. Stick to the main path; there are paint marks all the way.

The path comes to an area of pine trees notable for their symmetrical, linear planting. (There's a blue paint splotch on a tree just in front of you.) This is about 40 minutes past Montenidoli. The path winds to the left here. Follow it as it winds along. Soon the path runs in between two stone walls. Follow along between the walls until reaching the homestead of Poggio Attendi, about an hour past Montenidoli.

Passing around Poggio Attendi on your right, come out in front of the house on to the dirt road there (their driveway). Follow this. Don't turn off to the left at the intersection with the power-line track. Just after this there is a major intersection **D** where our path crosses another wide path, about 10 minutes past Poggio Attendi; go left here. (On a tree to the right there's a wooden first aid box.)

After 10 minutes or so, reaching the corner of a large field on the left (with tracks down to it), bear to the right, skirting the field on your left. The path narrows here.

Follow this little path through the woods. It's small

but clear enough. At one point, around 5–10 minutes after you made the turn at the large field, there's a similar-sized path to the left **E**, which should be ignored. (This track to the left fizzles out soon anyway, while the path straight on becomes a bit more distinct and begins to go noticeably downhill.) Continue straight ahead. ATW this section is marked with plastic strips of pink and white stripes — it may be about to be waymarked as a trail.

About 20 minutes after passing the large field above, the path begins to follow along the left side of a little moss-covered stone wall. This wall starts to break up and then turns right, and about 10 paces beyond that the path forks **F**. Go right.

Always follow the most worn bit of this tiny path, passing through some tiny clearings. The route is vaguely marked, by 'Oasi di Protezione' signs.

In another 15 minutes past the little moss-covered stone wall, the path comes out on a wider dirt track **G**; go right.

In about 5 minutes you will pass a similar-sized path making a sharp right from our path; ignore it. Our path bends gracefully to the left.

Very soon you'll come to an intersection **H** with a similar-sized path going left and right, and a smaller one carrying on ahead (and bending to the right). Take the right turn.

In about 10 m, this path turns left, and then right again. Follow this main path as it descends lightly, soon passing the skeleton of an old car.

The path then comes out on a junction **I** with a bigger path and a '*Pronto soccorso*' (first aid) box on a tree. Go right. (The plastic strips lead to the left here.)

Descend for about 20 minutes until the path comes out on a T-junction **J**; go left. San Donato soon comes into view ahead.

Meet the main asphalt road. Cross over to the smaller

asphalt road just below the main road to San Donato, unless you're going to Trattoria Franco to eat, in which case, instead of crossing over down to the smaller road, go right on the main road, and the restaurant is on the right, just across from where the little road to San Donato forks off.

FROM SAN DONATO

Passing through the hamlet on the little asphalt road, you'll come to a right-hand downhill turn **K** – a dirt road about 30 m before a 'give-way' sign (which is in turn about 40–50 m before the intersection with the main road). The road is marked with the red and white CAI bands (path TR 18–19) and there is also, ATW, a sign for Fattoria Voltrona *agriturismo*.

Walk down this road, passing through (after about 1 km) the farmstead of Ciliegeta and, in another 500 m or so, the Fattoria Voltrona.

Follow the road, passing a house at the top of the hill. Continuing on downhill, the road bends left and passes another house on the right. Keep going straight on past the house, enter on to a farm track straight ahead (the road simply diminishes into farm track).

After a brief stretch through the woods, the path comes out on a T-junction at a vineyard. Go left.

The path winds up between two houses, a new brick one on the left, an old stone one on the right. Pass through here, continuing straight ahead.

Keep on, passing between two more houses, again on the crest of a small hill.

Keep on the road until it ends at a T-junction **L**. Go left.

In another 20 m or so, the road forks again; take the left. (This is all gravel road.) The right goes to Montauto.

Arrive at an asphalt road after about 2 km **M**. Turn right here, reaching San Gimignano in another kilometre.

UMBRIA

NORTHERN UMBRIA

26 | GUBBIO RING WALK

Backing up against the windy slopes of the Umbrian Apennines the hill town of Gubbio with its steep stone alleys and tightly clustered medieval buildings has an austere splendour all its own. Legend and history agree on a certain quality of wildness and stony independence about the town, and a trace of this survives. Local folklore holds that it was one of the first five towns built after Noah's flood, and it's certainly true that the foundations go back to pre-Etruscan times. In the twelfth century the Emperor Frederick Barbarossa had a league of twelve towns poised to attack Gubbio. The town's bishop, Ubaldo, managed to persuade the emperor to restrain them, for which the good bishop was subsequently adopted as the town's patron saint. This act of diplomacy was echoed in the next century by no less a figure than St Francis. This time it was wolves rather than the imperial league plaguing the town. One in particular was terrorizing the local populace, and the story goes that the saint simply went out into the countryside, found the animal, spoke to it and worked out a settlement whereby in return for regular meals it would stop preying on the townsfolk. The deal was ratified by a shake of the paw, memorialized by a bas-relief over the door of a church in Via Maestro Giorgio. Recently, for what it's worth, the skeleton of a large wolf was discovered buried under a slab of stone by workmen repairing another church.

More recently the town was a centre of resistance to the Nazis; tragically so: forty partisans were executed in the square at the entrance to the town, now named 'Piazza Quaranta Martiri' in their memory.

Traditions from the Middle Ages survive in two important festivals. The Palio della Balestra is a crossbow competition held on the last Sunday in May, providing a nice occasion for the national civic obsession with dressing up in medieval costume. A larger event, held earlier in the same month (15 May), is the Festival of the *Ceri* (large wax candles used in churches), in which teams of men race through the streets and up the extremely steep lower slopes of Monte Ingino to the Basilica of San Ubaldo above the town, carrying colossal constructions that look something like vast and ornate wooden egg-timers, each topped by a wax saint. These *ceri* are kept on display at the basilica, as is the body of San Ubaldo himself, minus three fingers which were lopped off by his servant for a lucky charm.

This is an exceptionally beautiful walk through the high pastures, woods and old farmsteads in the mountains above Gubbio. The beginning is certainly the most dramatic of any in this book; a ride up Monte Ingino to the Basilica of San Ubaldo on the *funivia*, something between a ski chair and a cable car, with stunning, wobbly, vertiginous views to the town and the plain below. From the basilica, the walk continues along old farm tracks through increasingly remote and attractive countryside: meadows full of wild flowers and butterflies, thick hedgerows of blackberry bushes, rolling hills covered with yellow broom, white Chianina cattle grazing in the fields, and behind them the rugged mountains of the Umbrian Apennines. There's a particularly lovely old farm on the way that looks like something from a seventeenth-century painting, complete with

pitched haystacks and bundles of twigs tied with strips of bark.

The last 20 minutes of one of the two possible routes back is along asphalt road, but there are buses every 20 minutes (except Sundays) which you can get before you reach the main road, so you don't have to walk this stretch if you prefer not to.

The Food

High-quality white truffles grow in the fields above Gubbio, and feature prominently on the local restaurant menus. If you've never tried them, probably the best way to appreciate their amazing (to some tastes rather overwhelming) flavour is in a simple dish of scrambled eggs sprinkled with truffle shavings. The Taverna del Lupo does this exceptionally well, though the restaurant is one of the more expensive ones in town. Another somewhat fancy place, with a perhaps more innovative menu, though a rather stiff atmosphere (and the surreal practice of giving a lady's menu, from which the prices have discreetly absented themselves) is Maestro Giorgio, where there are set menus for L.35,000 and L.65,000.

Dishes include marinaded hare, grilled vegetables, fresh *fusilli* with a sweet pepper sauce, *strangozzi* (hand-rolled pasta) with a delicious buttery sauce of pigeon stock flavoured with truffles, duck with green olives, *sformato* (a kind of soufflé) of potato and snail with a *porcini* mushroom sauce, and an excellent creamy risotto with mascarpone and *zucchini* flowers. The food is presented hospital-style, under a china bonnet, by buttoned-up waiters, who use a spoon and fork just to move your napkin. The wine list includes a Marchesi Antinori, Borro della Sala 1992/Castello della Sala; an excellent bottle, reasonably priced at L. 22,000.

For a cheaper meal (and a less solemn atmosphere), try the Bargello. The best thing here is the self-service *antipasto* buffet, where you can sample local specialities such as onion *agrodolce* (sweet and sour), grilled aubergine and courgettes, deep-fried olives, potato and ham croquettes, and puréed cauliflower.

Down the street from the Bargello, there's a little café in the Piazza di Signoria where you might like to sit outside before dinner, sipping a Bellini, made of *prosecco* (similar to champagne) and raspberry juice, and contemplating the exquisite Palazzo dei Consoli.

Finally, if you've been in Italy long enough to feel like a break from Italian food, Gubbio has a great Chinese restaurant, Chang Cheng, which compares well with anything in Chinatown or London's Soho, serving beautifully cooked and inexpensive dishes, and incidentally using a much wider variety of vegetables than most of the Italian restaurants in town.

(Note: a reader who reports that prices at Maestro Giorgio have become 'stratospheric', recommends the restaurant Frederico da Montefeltro, at 35 Via della Republica. Tel: 075-9273949.)

LOGISTICS

GUBBIO RING WALK,
4–5 hours

🚌 Transport
Ⓜ Maps, guidebooks and
   trail info
🍽 Eating
🏨 Accommodation
ⓘ Miscellaneous info

🚌
FROM PERUGIA

By train: the nearest station is at
Fossato di Vico, about 20 km
from Gubbio; ASP buses
connect to Gubbio
By bus: ASP (tel. 075-9271544);
there is a bus and train information office in Gubbio at Via
della Repubblica, 13. Gubbio bus
station is in Via San Lazzaro (tel.
075-9273927); most buses also
stop in Piazza Quaranta Martiri
Length of journey: 1 hour
Frequency: 9–12 per day
Buses also connect from Fossato
di Vico, Gualdo Tadino,
Umbertide, Città di Castello, and
daily to Florence and Rome.

Ⓜ
• Centro Nazionale di
   Speleologia, map 'Carta dei

Sentieri Massiccio del Monte
   Cucco', 1:16,000
Good for walks in the area, but
doesn't extend all the way to
Gubbio.
   For Gubbio, there's only the
Kompass, sheet 664, 'Gubbio–
Fabriano', 1:50,000, not as
detailed. You can always walk
up to the Comune office and
ask them to xerox their IGM
map for you.

🍽
Chang Cheng
Corso Garibaldi, 84/86
Tel. 075-9221326

Del Bargello
Via dei Consoli, 37
Tel. 075-9273724

Alla Fornace di Maestro Giorgio
Via Maestro Giorgio, 2
Tel. 075-9275740
Closing day: Monday

Taverna del Lupo
Via Ansidei, 21a
Tel. 075-9274368
Closing day: Monday

🏨
Albergo Galletti
Via Piccardi, 1
Tel. 075-9277753

Cheap good rooms, easy access by car (you can drive up to it and drop stuff off, and then go and park in the nearby public car park as you can't drive in the centre) or bus (just steps away from Piazza Quaranta Martiri where the bus-stop is).

ⓘ

Tourist office: Piazza Oderisi, 6 (off Corso Garibaldi); tel. 075-9273693

CAI: Via Galeazzi, 6, 06021 Costacciaro (Pg); tel. 075-9170236
Gubbio's local CAI section can be contacted through its president. Ask also at the tourist office; they have a handout from CAI that has phone numbers of several of the local members, including Fiorucci, Giulio, 075-9273560/9291573.

Directions

Take the funicular (*funivia*) from Porta Romana on the east side of Gubbio. From the top, walk up the hill to visit Basilica di San Ubaldo.

Standing in front of the basilica, with your back to it, turn right down the road, passing the intersection with the path back down to the *funivia*.

Follow this asphalt (but untrafficked) road, winding around, ignoring a left–hand turn **A** (also asphalt) after about 5 minutes.

The road winds through a little park/picnic area and passes the bar Tre Ceri, after which the asphalt gives way to unsurfaced track.

Pass to the side of a metal gate blocking the road to cars.

When the road forks **B** (the left fork actually goes straight ahead and has a private property sign; the right fork goes more steeply downhill), take the left fork.

When the road forks again **C**, take the lower, downhill right fork. Continue downhill, always staying on the main path.

When you come to a left bend in the road, where a house (Casa Sasso) sits off to the right on a bit of a ledge, and the road forks into an upper and lower branch, the junction **D** is signed by CAI. CAI 1 is where we came from; CAI 12/a is the upper, left-hand fork signed to Scheggia and Costacciaro: take this. (There's a drinking fountain here at the turn.)

NOTE: If you want to do only the first loop (though the second is beautiful, and we don't recommend missing it), do not take this fork signed to Scheggia and Costacciaro. Instead, skip to the end of these directions, where we describe the return to Gubbio from Casa Sasso.

Pass Casa Barca I, an abandoned farmstead on the right side of the road. (There's also an abandoned structure on the left side of the road here.)

About 5 minutes later, after passing a mining excavation on the right, you'll reach another house, Barca II, on the right side of the road. The road forks here; take the left, upper fork (signed CAI 12).

When you come to the next old farmhouse, inhabited and working **E**, go to the right of the house. (The path turns left here; do not take the right-hand turn downhill.) The path begins to climb past the outbuildings of the farm.

About 200 m past the farm, ignore a smaller fork **F** to the right off the main path (CAI signed 12/a).

Staying on the main path for the next 3 km or so, you pass through some of the prettiest unspoilt countryside in Umbria.

When you reach a T-junction with a similar road, go left.

In about 15 minutes more, the path reaches a T-junction (at a stone picnic table, suitable for 15–20 people) and turns left **G**, and then continues bending left, going back in approximately the direction we just

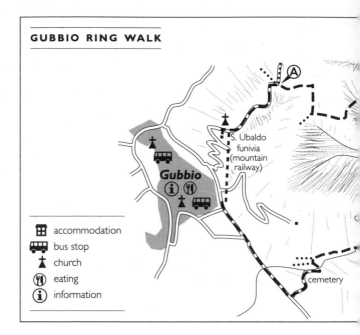

GUBBIO RING WALK

S. Ubaldo
funivia
(mountain
railway)

Gubbio

accommodation
bus stop
church
eating
information

cemetery

came from; 10–20 minutes later the path comes out on to another gravel road and joins it, bearing right.

When the path forks **C** (that is, there's a path going off to the left, downhill), you have the choice of either going right, back the way you came, to the *funivia*, OR going left, retracing your steps for about 1 km to Casa Sasso, and then taking the following route back to town.

FROM CASA SASSO

Standing at the intersection, and facing the house (looking down into the gorge), take the lower fork **H**, downhill (the fork we *didn't* take before); DON'T take 12/a signed to Scheggia.

In about ½ hour, when the path comes out at a T-junction across from a big white stone cemetery/chapel, turn left.

From here you can either walk out to the big asphalt

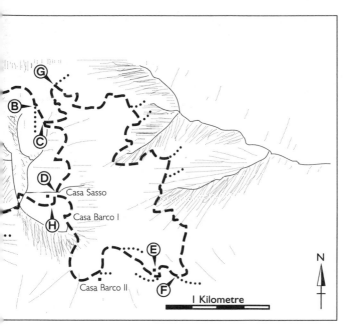

road and follow it into town or, to avoid an unpleasant asphalt walk, wait at the intersection for the bus, which runs between the cemetery and town every 20 minutes, except on Sundays, when it doesn't run at all.

27 | ASSISI
Monte Subasio and the Eremo delle Carceri

Given that St Francis has been unofficially adopted as the patron saint of the environmental movement, it seems only proper to offer a walk on the mountain sacred to his memory. We do so, however, with some reservations. Like much of the northern part of Umbria, the area around Assisi has been badly mauled by unsightly development, including a motorway running past the town of Spello, directly beneath Monte Subasio. You can hear the roar of traffic for some distance up the mountain on the Spello side, and you can see the suburban sprawl spreading for miles on the plain below you. The mountain has been a National Park since 1983, when an American priest and ornithologist, Bert Schwarzchild, appalled by the sight of so many hunting cartridges on the ground, and the corresponding absence of birds, launched an international campaign to protect the mountain from further devastation. Things may be better than they were, but there are still a number of matters the saint would not have approved of. An unpleasant cluster of radio antennae greets you at the rounded summit, and some of the pathways around the hermitage are appallingly littered. Most of the old trees on the slopes have been cut down and replaced by conifer plantations, while on the other hand the dense, ancient ilex forest around the hermitage itself – a source of pride to the present-day Franciscans – has, according to the naturalist Gary Paul Nabhan, been *over*-protected by fire suppression and other static preservation methods, to the point where it has stopped regenerating itself, and is in fact dying. For Nabhan the thousand-year-old tree in the hermitage, said to have shaded St Francis while he preached to the birds, and now held up by cables and iron stakes, is less a symbol of Franciscan solicitude for nature than of misplaced reverence and underlying neglect.

That said, the higher parts of the walk go through very pretty areas of grassy downland, and offer enormous views over the surrounding countryside. Then, too, the little hermitage itself is still quite lovely. This was where St Francis used to come on retreat and to commune with the birds. His cell, the 'Oratorio Primitivo' is still intact, and his pillow is allegedly among the relics held in the chapel. A few Franciscans still occupy the hermitage today, living off alms from visitors. This walk takes you within view of the summit of Monte Subasio, which you can continue on to if you choose, though it's not a particularly charming spot.

LOGISTICS

ASSISI RING WALK,
3¹/₂−4¹/₂ hours

🚌 Transport
Ⓜ Maps, guidebooks and
trail info
ⓘ Miscellaneous info

🚌

TO ASSISI AND RETURN
By train: the railway station for Assisi is at Santa Maria degli Angeli, 4 km from the centre of Assisi, with a bus link every 30 minutes
By bus: ASP (tel. 075-61807). Buses from Perugia and Foligno

arrive at the Piazza Matteotti; buses from Rome and Florence at the Piazzale dell'Unita d'Italia
Frequency: eight per day to Perugia

Ⓜ
The tourist office has a map of the area.

ⓘ
Tourist office: Piazza del Comune, 12; tel. 075-812534
Local CAI: Via della Gabbia, 9, Perugia; tel. 075-5730334. Open Tuesday and Friday evenings, 6.30−8.

Directions

From Piazza Matteotti (now a car park) at the top of Assisi, go to the upper left corner of the piazza, and walk up the road (Via Santuario delle Carceri) to the old city gate, the Porta Cappuccini. Just outside, take the cypress-lined stone track that leads to the left (trail

marked 50 and 51), a steep climb. Bear right past the
ruins of a fort (Roccacciola) after 200 m.

After about 20 minutes (a little more than ½ km), the
road forks **A**. Take the middle prong (signed 50, also
signed to the Eremo). The path narrows and begins to
seem a little less tame here.

Views open on to the vast plain below, which is fairly
built up. The sound from the major road is constant.

Continue on up past a truffle reservation.

The path levels off, and is joined **B** by path 53 and
another smaller path, both coming from the left. Go
straight on. In 15 minutes, passing a horribly littered
picnic site, you come out at the wide gravel road. Turn
right **C**. (Now signed 60.)

In a few minutes the Eremo (Santuario delle Carceri)
comes into sight – snugly situated in its wooded hollow.
The road forks **D**; if not visiting the Eremo, take the
left fork 50 m before the stone gateway, following the
sign for San Benedetto – an asphalt road (also signed
50). To visit the Eremo, go right. There's a surprisingly
modest kiosk at the gate, after which the peacefulness of
a real sanctuary has been well preserved. Notices asking
for silence are respected. A tiny stone staircase leads you
to St Francis's own minute stone cell, the doorway of
which is not much bigger than a cat-flap. Squeeze out
through this, and follow the *uscita* (exit) signs, passing
the little dovecote with its white doves. Note the wall
with ilex trees growing in and out of it.

Fork up to the left 30 m past a WC. The path is
marked 'Sentiero Sole e Luna'.

The path crosses the ravine. After about 30 m there's
a sharp left **E** leading uphill to the road; take this.

When you reach the road, in about 50 m, turn left
for a few metres and at the crook of the hairpin turn
you'll see a yellow sign indicating the trail to Vallonica
to the right **F**. Take this (it's also marked 50). The

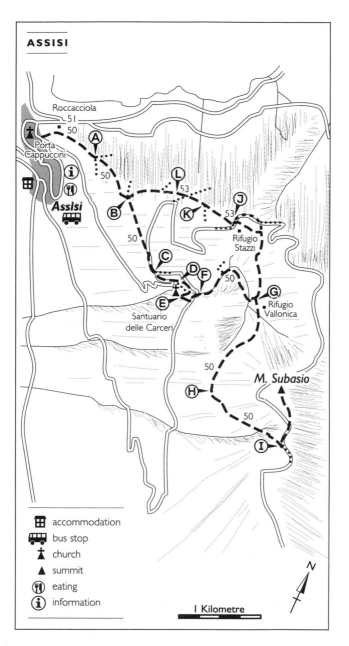

ASSISI

Roccacciola
51
50
Porta
Cappuccini
Assisi
A
50
L
53
B
K
J
53
50
Rifugio
Stazzi
C
D F
50
E
G
Santuario
delle Carceri
Rifugio
Vallonica
50
H
M. Subasio
50
I

⊞ accommodation
🚌 bus stop
✝ church
▲ summit
🍴 eating
ⓘ information

N

I Kilometre

entrance of this path is horribly littered, but things soon improve. The path narrows, climbs steadily through trees and bushes, and finally loses the traffic sounds.

Follow the main path 50, watching for where it turns right at a fork after about 10 minutes. The path rises through pleasantly shady woods, crosses a stream bed and soon after emerges into the grassy upper slopes of Monte Subasio. The path winds up to the pretty little Rifugio Vallonica – actually just an abandoned farm building. Just before the *rifugio* you come to a T-junction with a larger track **G**. Turn right, towards the *rifugio*, which is a good place for a picnic.

The path soon gets narrow and rather vague as it circles the summit – keep an eye out for the trail signs (red and white, 50). If in doubt, simply follow the central hollow. One rather ambivalent sign seems to suggest a turning to the right, but simply go straight ahead, keeping the long Subasio summit to your left. It might not be easy to navigate here in bad weather.

Over the first rise, the path becomes clearer, bringing you to a vast panorama just before it turns to the left. In a few metres you come to a fence with a stile. On the other side of the fence is a cross **H**. This is a great panoramic spot, and good place to end the walk. You can proceed from here to the top if you like; just keep following the path (it has a tendency to divide: keep to the upper level). You'll soon see a cluster of radio antennae. The path leads you to them, stopping at a fence, beyond which is a gravel road. Turn right at the fence until you come to a gap with a 'CA1 50' sign on it. Go left on the road **I** for a couple of hundred metres and you'll see the summit on your right across the grass. It's very desolate up here, and in July it's swarming with flies. Frankly, it's not worth the effort, except perhaps for the view, which is impressive on a clear day. Go back to the cross **H** the way you came.

From the cross, go back to the Rifugio Vallonica. A little beyond it, you'll reach the junction **G**. Instead of turning left the way you came, go straight on. In about 1 km, you'll see a road ahead of you, and the Rifugio Stazzi above you to the left. Either go to the road and turn left or else cut left across the grass to the right-hand side of the clump of trees at the right bend in the road. Just before the bend, you'll see a small sign marked 53 pointing down to the right **J**. There's no actual path at first, but follow the brow of the hill about 40 m above (and parallel with) the wooded hollow to your left and you'll soon find a stony track. Keep on this; after 200–300 m the path enters the woods, meeting a larger stone track where you turn right **K** (trail mark).

In 5–10 minutes from where you just turned right, the path is joined by another path coming from behind and right, and a few metres later it forks. Take the right fork **L** (marked 53 to Assisi).

Ignore a path off to the right after 250 m. But look for a sign (53) pointing down to the right about 300 m beyond that, and follow this.

Coming out at a T-junction **B** where trails 50 and 53 intersect, turn right (ignoring the smaller path immediately to your right). This is the way you came: trail 50.

In 20 minutes you'll reach Roccacciola. Continue on past here, returning the way you came, into Assisi through the Cappuccini gate.

This isn't one of the wildest or loveliest of the walks. You seldom feel very remote from civilization – whether in the form of traffic noises wafting up from the motorway, or the sight of the suburban/industrial sprawl on the plain below, or worst of all, the litter on parts of the path. But it's worth it for the lovely Eremo (you can drive there, but it feels more appropriately Franciscan to walk), for the pretty area up near the Rifugio Vallonica and for the sheer scale of the views up there.

SOUTH-EAST UMBRIA

Eastward from Spoleto to the border of the Marches lies some of the wildest and most ravishing countryside in Umbria. The two most adventurous walks in this book are to be found in this little-known region, and the gastronomic pleasures are also among the most varied and interesting.

The hill town of Spoleto with its magnificent fort, viaduct, medieval buildings and Roman amphitheatre has become one of the liveliest international cultural centres in Europe since the composer Giancarlo Menotti established his 'Festival dei Due Mondi' there in the 1950s, and it makes an excellent base for exploring the region.

Immediately east of the town lies the Valnerina, an upland valley running for about 40 km between steep limestone ridges with superb views, flower-filled meadows, and beech woods where wild boar are common and even the Apennine wolf makes an occasional appearance. The quick, clear Nera river is one of the main tributaries of the Tiber, flowing down from the Sibillini mountains in the east. Fortified villages, hermitages, abbeys and churches in a variety of styles including Lombardian (San Pietro in Valle), Romanesque (San Felice di Narco) and Renaissance (Santa Maria della Neve) dot the valley in a beguilingly picturesque manner. In the last century a railway built by a Swiss financier

ran from Norcia, zigzagging up the Valnerina through long tunnels and over dramatic viaducts, crossing the ridge into Spoleto. Abandoned now, this must have been one of the loveliest train rides in Italy. Today its trackless route forms the trail for an unusual and spectacular hike.

East of the Valnerina, winding above the pleasant town of Norcia (one of the great gastronomic centres of Italy), a small road climbs through the foothills of an austere, wild range of mountains called the Sibillini to a vast Alpine plateau known as the Piano Grande. In June this 16 km^2 meadow blooms with a myriad of brilliantly coloured wild flowers. Perched on a hill at the end of the plateau is the little farming village of Castelluccio, the highest – and probably the most isolated – settlement in peninsular Italy. Though a few visitors do trickle here, mainly for the superb hang-gliding, the atmosphere is one of wild remoteness, extremely unusual in modern Europe. It's easy to understand why the popes (who once ruled this area) used to ban travelling across the plain in winter; even today, when the fogs come down the bells of Castelluccio are rung to guide shepherds through the deceptively vast distances.

Rising high above the hilltop of Castelluccio are the great peaks of the Sibillini themselves, forming a natural amphitheatre around the Piano Grande. Named for the three ancient sibyls, one of whom is supposed to have delivered her oracular prophecies here (the sibyls were prophetesses, who foretold, among other things, the coming of Christ), these stark mountains retain a hieratic and slightly sinister aura. On the far side of Monte Vettore (at 2476 m the third-highest peak on the Italian peninsula and providing, along with its neighbours, wonderful opportunities for long ridge walks) is a curious bright blue lake called the Lago di Pilato. Allegedly the body of Pontius Pilate was buried here when the oxen transporting his body from Rome to his birthplace refused to go any further. There's evidence that the ancient Norcians used to sacrifice animals and possibly humans too up here. Between them – Pilate, the sibyls, and a large crag of rock with a distinctly diabolic profile – the area has not surprisingly acquired some notoriety as a place of devil worship. Judging from one or two of the individuals we saw drifting around this strange, desolately beautiful spot, the practice continues.

Food

Apart from Perugia (where the heavy suburban sprawl makes walking rather unsatisfactory), this is gastronomically the most rewarding part of Umbria, in terms of both quality and variety.

Like most mountainous areas, where there is more pasturage than cultivatable land, the cuisine is built around meat. According to Waverley Root the Umbrians eat more meat than any other Italian region; beef and lamb around Perugia, mainly pork and its multitudinous by-products here in the south-east, where thick oak woods provide the acorns that give the meat its rich flavour.

Simple cooking methods prevail: charcoal grilling, spit-roasting (the local *porchetta* is often spiced with fennel), and stewing with wine and herbs in the form of a *salmi*. A local roasting technique known as *pilottati* involves wrapping lard in oiled paper and letting it melt over the meat as it cooks. Lamb is sometimes seasoned with salt, pepper and a little vinegar, and cooked *all'arrabiata*, 'angry' – i.e. over an intensely hot flame.

But what truly distinguishes Umbrian cooking, and this region in particular, is the black truffle (*tartufo nero*), which grows in the hills above Spoleto and Norcia, and is probably the best in Europe. These two towns are the joint truffle capitals of Italy, and certainly the places to visit if you want to indulge in the peculiar gastronomic luxury of consuming your dishes – everything from simple pasta, to cheese, roast lamb, pâté, liqueurs and even chocolate – flavoured with sprinklings of this intense and aromatic fungus. Norcia holds an annual truffle festival in November. This is the beginning of the season, which extends to April, though there are some rare varieties that mature later in the year. Truffles can be preserved reasonably well in oil, or in the form of a paste, so don't despair if you miss the season. A measure of the high quality of the Umbrian truffle is the use of the Umbrian dialect word for truffle, *trifole* (rather than the Italian *tartufo*), to describe a kind of cooking – *trifolati* – whereby other foods such as kidneys, mushrooms and pasta are prepared so richly as to suggest truffles, particularly the Umbrian variety.

The chalky soil that plays its part in the delicate alchemy of the truffle also helps create an olive oil low in acids and rich in flavour, and the Spoleto olive oil is rightly considered to be one of the best in Italy. Excellent mushrooms such as the milky and orange agarics, honey mushrooms and *porcini* grow in the beech and chestnut woods. For the sweet-toothed, local specialities include *attorta* (a kind of apple strudel), a sweet *gnocchi* prepared around Christmas, various fried pastries such as *frappe* and *castagnole*, and a chocolate cake known as *crescionda* served during the February carnival.

Moving east, the Valnerina has exploited its resource of clean, fast-flowing water to farm not only trout, but also a particular kind of crayfish found otherwise only in Turkey, and most recently sturgeon. Meanwhile Norcia's reputation for gastronomic excellence, especially in the area of sausages, hams and other pork products, is such that high-quality pork butchers all over Italy refer to themselves as *norcini*. Unshaven boar hams, salami, fresh and cured sausage, rolled pig cheeks, cervelat, brawn made from the heads of hogs fed on horse chestnuts, *mazzafegati* (liver sausage seasoned with garlic, pepper and coriander), as well as a variety of sheep's cheeses and cone-shaped, rich ricotta cheeses, eaten fresh or mature (the mature ones, being much harder, are used for grating, like Parmesan), and often rolled in bran – fill the windows of the amazing *norcinerie* (charcuteries) of Norcia.

Two dishes described by Root, which you may have

better luck finding than we did, are *testina di vitello alla norcina* — pieces of calf's head coated with a mixture of ham, pork fat, mushrooms, butter, parsley and bread, wrapped in pig's membrane, rolled in breadcrumbs and fried in olive oil — and *fagiano alla norcese* — pheasant stuffed with truffles a day before being roasted and served with a *grappa*-flavoured gravy.

Even tiny Castelluccio has its claim to culinary distinction, in the form of the appropriately tiny Castelluccio lentil, grown exclusively around the Piano Grande, and richly flavoured. It's usually served in the form of a thick soup, or stewed with sausages, both of which make an extremely hearty and satisfying meal.

Finally the ancient grain known as spelt is still grown in this region, and forms the basis for a delicious savoury porridge-like mush called *farro*, served in many restaurants and well worth trying.

The Valnerina

The Comunità Montana della Valnerina puts out a pamphlet (in Italian, but it has maps) of walks in the Valnerina area: '20 sentieri ragionati in Valnerina', available free at tourist offices and hotels, and recommended for anyone interested in exploring the whole region on foot. Pretty woodland paths, old mule tracks and dirt roads connect most of the little hill villages, almost all of which have a church or old fortification worth visiting.

The railway walk begins at Sant'Anatolia di Narco, but we suggest staying the night a little down the valley at Scheggino where the accommodation, food and setting are altogether more salubrious. If you like the area, Scheggino would make a good base for a few days' walking in the valley. Castel San Felice, Vallo di Nera, Monte Coscerno, Muccafiora, are all in easy reach, and with the efficient bus service up and down the valley you should also be able to do a one-day or two-day walk as far afield as Preci and Monte Moricone.

28 | RAILWAY WALK
Sant'Anatolia di Narco to Spoleto

This is one of the great walking adventures in Italy, a day walk (two days if you decide to camp) that follows the old railway line (now minus the tracks) as it zigzags up through the Valnerina and over the mountains into Spoleto. Gorgeous countryside and in late spring and summer a pervasive smell of wild marjoram and mint make this a delight.

The track goes over some spectacular viaducts (these can be a little dizzying if you suffer from vertigo), as well as through tunnels bored straight through the mountains. The longest of these is 2 km; it's chilly, somewhat spooky and very dark, so unless you fancy groping your way along by touch, be sure to bring a powerful flashlight.

Towards Spoleto our route deviates from the old track for several stretches. This is to avoid fenced-off property (a problem that other routes conveniently ignore), and also a part of the track that has become overgrown and full of litter. The entrance to Spoleto is dazzling; approaching the city along the wooded ravine of the Tessino river, and over the magnificent fourteenth-century bridge and aqueduct, the Ponte delle Torri (designed by Gattapone, from Gubbio). With its ten superbly elegant arches rising over the 80 m ravine and leading to the impressive fortress known as the Rocca (also built by Gattapone, as was Gubbio's Palazzo dei Consoli), this is one of the great engineering feats of the medieval period, and surely one of the most fabulous approaches to any city.

Notes

- On no account lean on the metal railings along the viaducts; they aren't safe. Some of the tunnels are marked 'danger' or 'private property', but this is a CAI trail, and according to CAI they are safe (other than the first one, which is barred, and which all routes bypass).
- Wear strong-soled boots; the stony surface of the old track bed is too rough for sneakers. Remember to bring a flashlight and something warm to wear in the long tunnel.
- Rooms are difficult to come by in Spoleto during the festival (which runs for two weeks beginning in late June), so try to book ahead.

Food

Scheggino, where we recommend you stay (you can get an early bus to Sant'Anatolia di Narco in the morning), is an attractive stone village with some small canals stocked with trout and a species of crayfish imported from Turkey. Iron ore was mined here in the Renaissance, and used in both the Pantheon and the Vatican Basilica. Today the village is home to the Urbani family, Italy's truffle tycoons, which might account for the high quality of the local food. Of the two restaurants, Il Grottino is the prettier, while the Del Ponte (attached to the Albergo of that name) has slightly better food. Both specialize in crayfish, truffles and freshwater fish. The Del Ponte makes a better version of crayfish in *salsa verde*, and also does a superb (and reasonably priced) fresh sturgeon *storione*, albeit in a rather crude pink sauce (they'll grill it plain if you prefer, but it's less succulent that way). Their vegetarian *tagliatelle Porto Fino* is less impressive: the sauce is a lacklustre mixture of chopped vegetables.

The menu at Il Grottino is perhaps more ambitious, but the cooking is somewhat hit and miss. The best dishes are the *risotto al gorgonzola*, fresh trout with *salsa verde*, a darkly fishy *lumachini* (small stuffed pasta) with trout and truffles, and excellent fresh *tortellini* with a creamy nut sauce. They also do pizzas.

There's nowhere to buy food on the walk itself, so bring supplies. The Albergo del Ponte does its own baking, and have great morning pastries and cakes (try the *torta* if they have it). They'll also make sandwiches on request. Otherwise you can buy snacks at the bar at the beginning of the route in Sant'Anatolia di Narco, which opens early.

Among the numerous restaurants in Spoleto (some of them striving a little too hard to be original in a bid to catch the festival crowds), one that stands out is Pentagramma, where you can get a wonderful chick-pea soup (in an edible bowl). They also make a very good sauce of rocket, fresh tomato and the *guanciale* (hog cheeks) that hang in the windows of every *norcineria* like little hams. It tastes like a rather fatty bacon, with a sweet, intense flavour. Exceptionally good *porchetta* is sold in the Piazza Mercato, where there are a number of fine delicatessens.

There are wonderful cherries (in the season) all over Umbria, but for the hard-core cherry fan, there's an annual cherry festival at the village of Bazzano in mid-June.

LOGISTICS

RAILWAY WALK,
6–7 hours

🚌 Transport
Ⓜ Maps, guidebooks and
    trail info
🅨 Eating
🈸 Accommodation
ⓘ Miscellaneous info

🚌

TO CASTEL SAN FELICE, SANT'ANATOLIA DI NARCO, OR SCHEGGINO

From Spoleto: the SSIT bus (tel. 0743-212211) from Spoleto railway station goes to Castel San Felice and Scheggino; it also stops at Sant'Anatolia, between them. There are a couple of direct buses each day, and these take about 30 minutes. There are other buses which involve a change midway, however, so be sure the ticket agent knows you're going through to Scheggino so that you don't get stuck waiting for some terrible connection; buses are infrequent.

    The walk begins at Sant'Anatolia. The bus (in either direction) stops on the main road outside the village and some of

the buses then go on into the village itself; you want the main-road stop.

From Norcia: SSIT bus to Castel San Felice or Scheggino
Length of journey: 50 minutes
Frequency: about three per day
We suggest taking the SSIT bus from either Spoleto or Norcia to Castel San Felice, seeing the church there, and then walking down the Valnerina 1 ½ hours (quite flat) to Scheggino, a pretty village with the nice Albergo del Ponte (see addendum to this walk for directions). If you're staying in Scheggino the night before you do this walk, and taking the bus to Sant'Anatolia in the morning, try to buy your ticket the night before, in the *tabacchi* in Scheggino. If this isn't possible, you can run into the Bar Alberto in Sant'Anatolia where the bus lets you off in the morning and buy your ticket there, returning to the bus to have it stamped. In Scheggino, wait for the bus on the *main road, not* in the piazza. Finally, make sure to check the time of the morning bus that does the short trip from Scheggino to Sant'Anatolia: there is only one.

RETURN FROM SPOLETO

Spoleto is well connected to other towns by bus and train. Check in the tourist office for schedules.

From Spoleto to Florence by train, there are two routes, one through Foligno (with two changes of train), one through Orte (one change of train). Most of the routes take about 4½ hours, but by selecting carefully you can do it in 3½ hours with the Orte route.
Train info: Spoleto, tel. 0743-48516

Ⓜ

CAI Spoleto has a map of the area but, at 1:50,000, it's of limited use.

The Azienda di Promozione Turistica della Valnerina–Cascia has a pamphlet '20 sentieri ragionati in Valnerina' (in Italian, but has maps) that gives 20 walks in the region. It's available at tourist offices and some hotels.

🍽

SCHEGGINO

Albergo/Ristorante del Ponte
Tel. 0743-61131

Il Grottino
Tel. 0743-61142

SPOLETO

Pentagramma
Via Martani, 4
(just off Piazza della Libertà)
Tel. 0743-223141

🏨

SCHEGGINO

Albergo del Ponte
Tel. 0743-61131

SANT'ANATOLIA DI NARCO

Albergo Tre Valli
Tel. 0743-613118

SPOLETO

Rooms are difficult to come by in Spoleto during the festival, so try to reserve ahead if you are going in late June or early July. The tourist office can supply a list of *affittacamere* as well.

Dell'Angelo
Via Arco del Druso, 25
Tel. 0743-222385

ⓘ

Tourist office: Piazza della Libertà, 7 Spoleto; tel. 0743-220311/220435

Azienda di Promozione Turistica della Valnerina–Cascia, Piazza Garibaldi, 1, Cascia; tel. 0743-71147
Local CAI: CAI Spoleto, Vicolo Pianciani, 4, Spoleto; tel. 0743-220433. Open Friday

evenings, 5.30–7.30. They have excursions every Sunday.

Notes: 1. A new car tunnel from Sant'Anatolia to Spoleto is in the process of being built; this means that in the future, at the part of the path leading to the first tunnel, there will be a road – probably a fairly major road – below you to the left.

2. Across the bridge from Spoleto (Ponte delle Torri) you can take the right fork of the path for a nice, shaded walk to the church of San Pietro. The facade has some twelfth-century sculptures which are among the finest Romanesque carving in Umbria. Inside the church is a magical, very twentieth-century diorama about the Nativity.

Directions

The Bar Alberto (next to the Albergo Tre Valli) sits on the corner of the main highway (route 209) and a less-travelled asphalt road that goes into the village of Sant'Anatolia di Narco. Across this secondary road (i.e. directly across from the front of the bar) there's a dirt road running parallel to the main road. At the beginning of this dirt road, a small path leads off to the left between trees. Take this.

Soon this path turns right and crosses a bridge **A** over the road. Continue along the path, crossing in about 15 minutes a small asphalt road **B**. A few minutes past the asphalt road, the path converges with another path coming in from the left. There's also a path here making a sharp turn to the right. Ignore these **C**.

Continue along the principal track until, after crossing a small bridge, you approach the first tunnel. About 15 m before the tunnel, there is a path on the right, which you should take **D**.

After about 100 m, the path more or less dies out at a stream **E**. There's a track forking off to the right, on the other side of the stream and slightly uphill, but *don't* take it. Instead, see to your left a small vineyard. Go uphill along the far side of the vineyard, with the vineyard on your left. The vineyard then gives way to an orchard. At the top of the orchard, the path continues up into the woods, turning left just as you enter the woods.

Continue climbing up along this narrow path. After 5–10 minutes of climbing there's a small intersection of paths, with a somewhat wider one downhill to the left. Keep climbing up straight. Just after this point, the path bends sharply round to the right and climbs up to a T-junction with a bigger track, which is the railway bed. (This is only a minute or two from the small intersection of paths mentioned in the beginning of this paragraph.) Turn right on this **F**.

From here, follow the path of the railway line, which loops over itself several times as it climbs.

After the long (2 km) tunnel, the path is more in the nature of a dirt track. Keep to the main path, passing a first intersection near a house (on the right). At the next intersection go right. (If you pass the old Caprareccia station on your right, you've gone too far; the intersection is about 20 m before it.)

Reaching the main road in about 30 m, turn left on to it **G**. The reason for this digression is that the railway track passes through private property at this point, which is very overgrown and also full of rubbish.

After 100–150 m, the road makes a hairpin left turn. At the sharp point of this turn, there are two dirt tracks off the right side of the road; take the one on the left, downhill **H**.

In a few minutes, the path goes downhill and left, while to the right on the same level is something more like a little clearing. Ignore this clearing and follow the downhill left. Descending steeply, ignore a more minor turning which you'll pass on your right.

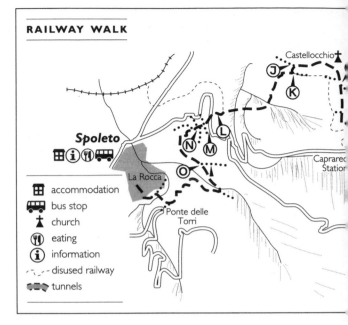

The path becomes narrower and forks soon after a sharp right bend. Take the right downhill fork, ignoring the left uphill one.

The path widens soon after this, and carries along comfortably until meeting a T-junction with another similar-size path. Go left here **I**.

In another few minutes there's a fork; take the rightish, level, flat path, not the left-hand uphill one.

Soon the path comes out above the town of Eggi. You can see a bell tower (Castellochio) close by – ahead and to the right – and beyond that the bell tower of Eggi.

Bear right downhill here, and very soon on the left, before reaching the bottom, is an old brick and mortar structure with a CAI paint sign on it, near the debris of what looks as if it might have been a quarry. Go left here.

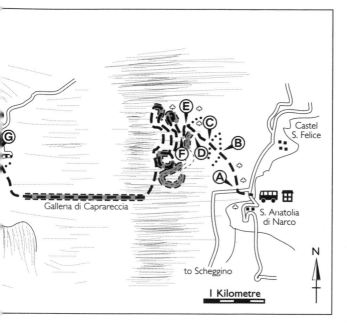

Castel
S. Felice

Gallena di Caprareccia

S. Anatolia
di Narco

to Scheggino

N

I Kilometre

The path gives almost immediately a view of Eggi on your right and then leads on into the woods. Climbing here, the path is marked with CAI signs, and passes above an olive grove on your right. ATTENTION: on this part of the path (a little before the halfway point of the olive grove), watch out on the right for a small boulder with a red/orange/red CAI waymark (rather than the usual red/white/red). About 4 m beyond it there's a pine tree on the left of the path, which ATW has a metal CAI sign with black letters 'SU' on it. (But you never know for sure if, in the future, the CAI sign will still be there.) There is a smaller path to the left here in front of the tree – not easily seen if you're not watching for it. Take it **J**.

This is a narrow path that climbs rather steeply uphill to rejoin the railway track, about a 5 minute climb, the last section of which is provided with a metal cable alongside to help you pull yourself up if you should be so inclined. At the top of this cable, meet a T-junction and turn right **K**.

This path, still narrow and climbing, brings you out in another 5–10 minutes on the railway path. Go right.

After passing through two short tunnels and crossing the long viaduct between them, you'll soon see an abandoned *casello* (railway house) on the left **L**. As you approach it, you'll see a path on the left, passing just to the side of the house. Take this.

The path almost immediately begins bending to the left. As it does so, watch on the right for a short, square structure made of bricks with a cement top. From here it is about 35 paces to a very small path up to the right (if you reach the field, you've gone too far). Take this path. It passes under an electric line. Climb up along the electric line towards the road, aiming to meet the road about 30 m to the right of where the line meets it.

Gaining the asphalt road, turn left. About 50 m beyond the power line, on the right side of the road, are two brick pillars (signed 'Villa S. Giovanni'). Turn right through here (passing a 'Beware of dog' sign) **M**.

Following this road, ignore both CAI 5 tracks crossing our path, and then a hairpin left turn. Beyond this, when the road forks, bear left uphill **N**. Follow the main path through this property (the house of the estate is on the right, its bell tower visible from various points of the path) climbing up and over a tiny hill after which Spoleto appears. Drop down here, following the path still, curving around an outbuilding on your right and then bearing left at the fork which immediately follows. Pass a paddock on the right.

Along this stretch you get good views of the castle (La Rocca), the viaduct (Ponte delle Torri), town and the church of San Pietro in the distance behind the viaduct.

Reaching a stone barn and stone house, the path divides. Ignoring the fork that leads down to the house, and the other, larger fork that continues on along the olive grove, take the path that leads to the right, towards the cliffs and mountains **O**.

This soon passes by a wooden gate and picnic table. Stay on the main path; there are some deviations (including one almost as big leading off downhill to the right), but it's clear which is the main path.

After great views of the viaduct, the path enters woods again. There's a break in the metal gate on the right, and some stone steps leading down. Ignore this, staying on the upper path.

Reaching the tower above the viaduct, you can drop down steeply or keep on the path, which descends (steeply enough) by a series of hairpin turns. Crossing the stunning Ponte delle Torri brings you into Spoleto.

ADDENDUM TO RAILWAY WALK: CASTEL SAN FELICE TO SANT'ANATOLIA DI NARCO OR SCHEGGINO

If you're going to Sant'Anatolia or Scheggino in the afternoon in order to begin the railway walk early the next morning, you might want to get off the bus at Castel San Felice and take this leisurely 1–2 hour walk to Sant'Anatolia or Scheggino. See p. 320 for logistics.

As you face the front of the church of San Narco in Castel San Felice **A**, take the dirt road along the left side of the church winding round behind it. Follow the path as it crosses a little bridge over the Nera, and take the right fork **B** at the end of the bridge. This path

ADDENDUM TO RAILWAY WALK

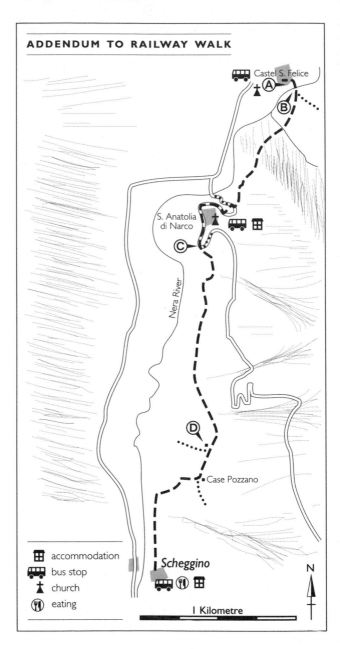

Castel S. Felice

(A)

(B)

S. Anatolia
di Narco

(C)

Nera River

(D)

Case Pozzano

Scheggino

accommodation
bus stop
church
eating

N

I Kilometre

is a pleasant valley walk – about 1 km – leading to Sant'Anatolia.

At the end of the dirt road you come to an intersection with asphalt. Cross straight over, and climb until you reconnect with asphalt. Turn right on this, following the walls of Sant'Anatolia, with lovely views of the valley to your right.

After a few hundred yards, where the road makes a hairpin turn to the left **C**, turn to the right on the dirt road that leads up to the left behind some new houses. Passing the houses, the dirt road continues towards Scheggino.

After about a mile you pass a cemetery on your right **D**. Ignoring the right turn directly after this, take the next right, about 250 m past the cemetery. Follow this road (which will gradually make a 90° left-hand turn) which brings you in about 1 km to Scheggino.

29 | NORCIA RING WALK

The handsome town of Norcia lies on a sloping, earthquake-prone plain under the Sibillini mountains. With its low, tiled buildings and flowery balconies, it has a curious Spanish air, and one half expects to see bulls being run through its circular piazza. What one does in fact see is a statue of St Benedict, who was born here in 480 (as was his twin sister St Scholastica), a fine church and Comune building, and several *norcinerie* – the fabulous butcher/delicatessens, whose mouth-watering merchandise is the main reason why the Italians visit this town and is the basis for the local economy.

The walk takes you into the hills above the town, to the tiny hamlet of Ospedaletto, an eerily quiet little farming village. Splendid views of the Umbrian countryside

– part wooded, part cultivated – with wild almonds and juniper, pretty hedgerows of dwarf maples, and high mountain sheep pastures in the region just past Ospedaletto itself, make this a perfect excuse for a gourmet picnic, for which Norcia is of course the ideal place to shop. (There are no stores in Ospedaletto anyway; so make sure to bring whatever you need, including water, with you.)

Just outside Norcia, the route passes some water meadows, *le marcite* – an area of tiny canals running between willows and cypresses, with meadows that remain green throughout the year and allegedly yield up to ten harvests. This is because the spring water in the canals never falls below 10°C, thus creating an artificially warm microclimate. You can wander around here, but watch out for the little sluices in the canals: several are overgrown by weeds, and you could twist your ankle in them.

The way back down from Ospedaletto is short but steep, and rather a scramble; certainly too rugged for sneakers. The CAI have marked the trail, but rather half-heartedly; you're unlikely to get seriously lost. Still, it might be easier to go back the way you came.

Food

In Norcia there are almost as many *norcinerie* as churches, a happy circumstance as it's in these that you'll find some of the best food in town. Also not to be missed are the truffle shops on the main street, one of which resembles a high-tech laboratory more than a food shop, such is its appropriately reverent attitude towards its merchandise. The restaurants can be a little hit and miss, though the hits comprise some of the best meals to be had in either Tuscany or Umbria. The *Cadogan Guide* lists Dal Francese as one of the ten best restaurants in either province. It's still possible to eat well there, though clearly it has seen better days. The home-made *panna cotta*, with its sweet custardy cream set off by a slightly tart sauce of wine, honey and hazelnuts, was sensational. On most counts though, the place is outclassed by the restaurant in the pleasant hotel called the Grotta Azzura. Here you can splurge on an entire *tartufato* menu featuring, among other things, a sublime roast lamb with truffles, or you can sample such things as *pappardelle alla norceria rossa* – thick ribbons of pasta with local hams and mushrooms in a creamy tomato sauce – or cannelloni stuffed with

spinach and ricotta in an unusually tasty tomato sauce, followed by very fresh grilled trout with chard sautéed in lemon, or sausages served in a bowl of delicious Castelluccio lentils, rounding it off with a *tiramisu* that ranged from terrible to sublime over the course of our stay there. The service is exceptionally friendly despite the large numbers of people eating here. Try to get a seat in the dungeon-like restaurant proper, where the grill is, rather than in one of the large-scale banqueting rooms.

LOGISTICS

NORCIA RING WALK,
4–5 hours
This walk is virtually walk 4 in the APT Valnerina (see 'Maps' section below) '20 sentieri' pamphlet. It's hard to cross a few yards of the *marcite*, so we've altered the beginning of the walk.

🚌 Transport
Ⓜ Maps, guidebooks and trail info
🍴 Eating
🏨 Accommodation
ⓘ Miscellaneous info

🚌

FROM FLORENCE
From Florence to Spoleto by train, there are two routes, one through Foligno via Arezzo (with two changes of train), one through Orte (one change of train). Most of the routes take about 4¹/2 hours, but by selecting carefully you can do it in 3¹/2 hours (to Spoleto) with the Orte route. For information on schedules, check in the Spoleto tourist office. Spoleto train info, tel. 0743-48516.

At Spoleto, buy your bus ticket to Norcia from the newsagent in the railway-station lobby. (You can also leave your bags with the *capo di stazione* if you want to take the local shuttle bus up into Spoleto for a few hours.) Norcia is well served by SSIT bus (tel. 0743-45815) from Spoleto (about five a day), Perugia, Assisi, Terni and Foligno.

Ⓜ

The Azienda di Promozione
Turistica della Valnerina – Cascia
has a pamphlet '20 sentieri
ragionati in Valnerina' (in Italian,
but it has maps) that gives twenty
walks in the region. It's available
at tourist offices and some hotels.

In Norcia, the *tabaccaio* in the
south-eastern corner of the Piazza
San Benedetto sells walking maps
and guides, as does the Cartoleria/
Edicola outside the Porta Massari.

🍴

Grotta Azzurra: see hotels

Dal Francese
Via Riguardati, 16
Tel. 0743-816290
Closing day: Friday

PICNICS

Try the *pizza* (the *ripieno* with
tomato) at the place on Via
Legnano in Norcia, also
accessible from outside the city
wall: as you face the gate of Porta
Massari it's on your left, next to
the bar.

Also good is the *ciambelloni* –
the sweet breakfast cake, a bit
like brioche – at Grotta Azzurra.

🏢

Always try to book ahead,
especially mid-July to

mid-September.
Hotel Grotta Azzurra
Via Alfieri, 12
06046 Norcia (Pg)
Tel. 0743-816513; fax
0743-817342.
Incredibly friendly, even though
incredibly busy, owners. Very nice
about storing bags for a few days,
convenient if you're going up to
Castelluccio. They will also
arrange rides up to Castelluccio
with the postman.

Pensione Benedettine Monastero
S. Antonio
Via delle Vergini, 13
Tel. 0743-816657
If you want a very peaceful, very
different place to stay (all the
rooms have desks), run by nuns,
it's a working convent with pigs,
bees, rabbits, an orchard and a
garden. The nuns make their
own *pesto* (from basil,
mushrooms, and anchovies),
honey, and various other
sundries. The monastery is in a
very nice area outside the main
part of town. Note: they had a
three-night minimum stay when
we were there, so check about
that.

ⓘ

Tourist office: Piazza della Libertà, 7, Spoleto; tel. 0743-22031l/ 220435

Azienda Promozione Turistica della Valnerina – Cascia, Piazza Garibaldi, 1 (tel. 0743-71147) or

Via G. da Chiavano, 2 (tel. 0743-71401) – both in Cascia.

Local CAI: Vicolo Pianciani, 4, Spoleto; tel. 0743-220433. Open Friday evenings 5.30 – 7.30.

Forest ranger station (Stazione Forestale): tel. 0743-816489

Directions

Leaving Norcia through the Porta Massari (sometimes called Porta Ascolana) on the south-east side of town, make a right outside the gate and follow the road as it winds round the outside of the city wall.

At the first intersection (marked with a stop sign), cross over the road and take the road directly ahead, leading downhill **A**. This road forks immediately; take the right fork.

This asphalt road (running parallel to the old railway tracks that are the beginning of the old Norcia – Spoleto line) will reach an old stone chapel on your left (the Madonna di Cascia). Just beyond this, the asphalt road makes a 90° bend to the right (at which point the asphalt gives way to gravel), while a dirt road leads straight ahead. If you want to have a look at *le marcite* (see introduction), take the bend to the right, following the road a short distance until you reach the poplar and cypress trees. From there two paths on the right lead into this green, watery area, with its old mill. Watch out for the little sluices in the middle of the paths.

Otherwise, follow the dirt road straight ahead. About 150 m along this dirt road, at the first legitimate fork, keep going straight ahead **B**, ignoring the fork off to the left.

Skirting a large field to your left, the path then goes

between two hedgerows. Take the narrow branch to your right when the path forks (just before the end of the hedge 'corridor') **C**. This narrow trail climbs steadily uphill, beginning a longish but not too arduous climb, pleasantly shaded much of the way. At the breaks in the hedge, you get a view out to the right of Norcia and the plain.

Soon after **C**, a similar-style path forks off to the left; ignore it.

Keep on uphill, ignoring any downhill digressions to the right (which come near the top).

About 4–5 km outside Norcia, the path comes out on to an asphalt road with the seventeenth-century church of San Filippo Neri to your right, and the signed road to Ospedaletto opposite. Carry on into Ospedaletto.

Passing the bell tower of the Ospedaletto Club on your right, walk round the left side of the house facing you (where the asphalt ends and the dirt track begins again), and bear left out of the village. The track immediately forks: take the left branch **D**. The breezy high mountain pastures here, overlooking the valley to your left, would make a beautiful place for a picnic.

About 5 minutes out of Ospedaletto this track goes slightly uphill for a few minutes and then near the top there is a branch off to the right, just before a newish farm building (probably a hay shed). Take this branch **E**.

Ignore any turns off this path until after about 300 m, when the path forks; take the left fork **F**. Very soon this path dips down and seems to fade out. ATW there is a 'CAI 4' metal marker on a tree to the left. The path is very vague here, but keep going ahead in the same direction along the top edge of the field (among abandoned almond trees), and then curve left around the thicket hedge before a big field. The tracks reappear.

Now comes the scramble: a longish steep descent, overgrown in parts when we were there in lush early summer.

After a long steep descent (close to 1 km) the path hits another big path. Go right.

Almost immediately you'll hit another path. Norcia and the valley are visible from this junction, to your left, and you would think you should go left here, but instead go right for 5 m and then make that left round the boulder, to connect with another downhill left path; (essentially parallel to the path you passed 5 m ago).

This dirt road soon comes out on an asphalt road **G**. Cross over; the gravel road continues on the other side.

Soon the gravel road will intersect with an asphalt road. Follow the asphalt road downhill to the right. This road leads back into town.

30 | PIANO GRANDE AND CASTELLUCCIO RING WALK

The beautiful Piano Grande lying below Castelluccio is unique in Europe, an upland plain of 16 km^2 covered in flowers in early summer. You can walk at will here (avoiding the wild flowers) without danger of getting lost, as this vast alpine plain is almost completely flat and, with Castelluccio sitting snugly on its hill at the far end, it would be difficult to lose one's bearings except in thick fog. (For this reason we have not supplied a map of it.) It's actually more interesting to look down on from the surrounding mountains or from Castelluccio itself – and presumably even more so from one of the myriad hang-gliders and parascenders riding the thermals over it on clear days – than to walk in, as the extreme flatness and deceptive distances can be a little wearying. Mountain bikes or horses, both of which you can rent, might also be more fun. On a cool day though (there's no shade), it's pleasant to wander down along the west side and cross to the east, between the two hills of La Rotonda and Monte Guaidone. If you look back over the plain after you've crossed it, you'll see a clump of trees on the opposite hillside that have been cut in the shape of Italy and Sicily, a bizarre conjunction of forestry and patriotism.

A shifting preponderance of buttercups, poppies and daisies deck the plain in a succession of colours through-out June. In mid-June you can be fairly sure of a fine blaze; the blossoms of the Castelluccio lentil paint the sloped fringes of the plain with broad stripes of pale yellow. Narcissi, fritillaries, wild peonies and tulips, and rarities such as the Apennine alpine star, the Apennine potentilla, and a species exclusive to the region, *Carex buxbauni*, all bloom here over the course of the year. Set off by the ring of mountains rising steeply around it, the plain is an amazing sight; Zeffirelli used it as the setting for *Brother Sun, Sister Moon*.

The Castelluccio ring walk is an exceptionally pretty walk, leading through the rugged, beautiful Valle Canatra adjacent to the Piano Grande, up through woods to high pastures with gorgeous views of distant mountains, and returning along the slopes above the Piano Grande, one of the best ways of viewing it. There are plenty of shady spots for picnics, and if you come in June you'll see wild peonies blooming on the hillsides, along with fields full of wild flowers, and the greenish-yellow lentil flowers. Sheep and a few cows dot the route, and snow was still in the crevices of the nearby mountains in June. The rare Apennine partridge is also said to frequent the Valle Canatra.

As with all walks up here, the weather can change rapidly, so even on a hot day you should bring a water-proof jacket. As always, bring your own water.

Food

There are a couple of bars and small grocers' in Castelluccio, where you can buy sandwiches of the excellent local sheep's cheeses or the alarmingly pink but very tasty local sausage known as *ciaouscolo*. There are also two good restaurants, a large one attached to the Albergo Sibilla, and a smaller one called La Taverna. Both places make good use of the locally grown lentils and spelt, in the form of thick soups (with or without sausage), and the comforting mush called *farro*. Both feature rather tough, plain pieces of grilled pork or lamb by way of main course. La Taverna serves lentil soup with garlic bread, using the local wild greens (*verdure di campagna*) when they're in season, an excellent *tortellini* with butter and sage, and, above all, wonderful pizzas. It also has a better wine list, with a number of bargains including a 1990 Claro/Sagrantino di Montefalco Secco (cantine

Morettoni) for L.15,000, and a 1990 Montefalco Rosso (Arnaldo-Caprai) at L.9,000. Avoid the local screw-top wine.

LOGISTICS

CASTELLUCCIO RING WALK, about 3 hours

🚌 Transport

Ⓜ Maps, guidebooks and trail info

🅨 Eating

⊞ Accommodation

ⓘ Miscellaneous info

🚌

FROM NORCIA

The trip by bus (SSIT; tel. 0743-212211) to Castelluccio is a beautiful one, perhaps an hour in length, but buses are not frequent, and do not even run daily. Check the schedule carefully. The woman who runs Grotta Azzurra in Norcia can arrange rides to Castelluccio with the postman. We gave him L.15,000, but you might ask at Grotta Azzurra what they'd recommend.

Ⓜ

Maps of the area are sold in

Castelluccio at the Sibilla Hotel and the Bar del Capitano.

Routes around here aren't widely marked yet, but CAI Perugia is in the process of doing so. The Universo 'Montevettore' map comes with a supplement that shows the latest stretches that CAI has marked. The CAI 'Monti Sibillini' map has many if not all CAI routes on it, and while it's more expensive than the Sentieri e Rifugi 'Monti Sibillini', it not only has the CAI trail numbers on it but, perhaps even more importantly, it comes with an excellent sew-on wolf decal of the Parco Nazionale Monti Sibillini. (Make sure your map contains one; they are often missing.)

🅨

La Taverna
tel. 0743-870158
Closing day: Wednesday
Book ahead for both lunch and dinner; it's small and it fills up quickly.

Albergo Sibilla
Tel. 0743-870113/870154
We found La Taverna better for
eating, but the Sibilla better for
sleeping.

PICNICS

The sheep cheeses sold at Da
Mauro, the little shop near the
Sibilla Hotel, are very good.

⊞

ALWAYS BOOK AHEAD FOR
CASTELLUCCIO; THERE AREN'T
MANY OPTIONS.
La Taverna
06046 Castelluccio di Norcia
(Pg)
Tel. 0743-870158, or try
0743-870100

Albergo Sibilla
06046 Castelluccio di Norcia
(Pg)
Tel. 0743-870113/870154

**ADDITIONAL
POSSIBILITIES FURTHER
AFIELD**

Canapine, Forca Canapine (tel.
0743-817568/816508)

Da Ilde, Forca Canapine (tel.
0743-808112)
La Fiorite, on the road to Visso
(tel. 0737-98148)
Rifugio degli Alpini, Forca di
Presta (tel. 0736-809278)
Rifugio del CAI, Forca Canapine
(tel. 0736-808186)
Camping Monte Prata, on the
road to Visso (tel. 0737-98124)
Il Collaccio (tel. 0743-99430)

ⓘ

Local CAI: CAI Perugia, Via della
Gabbia, 9, 06100 Perugia; tel.
075-5730334. Open Tuesday
and Friday evenings, 6.30–8.
CAI Ascoli Piceno, Corso
Mazzini, 81, 63100 Ascoli Piceno.
Riding, mountain biking: horses
and mountain bikes can be hired
on the Piano Grande: tel.
0743-817279/817022.
Hang gliding: Fly Castelluccio, tel.
and fax 0743-870209, summer;
0735-632486, winter.

Directions

Passing the Albergo Sibilla on your left, stay on the main
road that bears left out of Castelluccio. After about 50 m,
leave the main road, taking the road that branches up to
the left **A**.

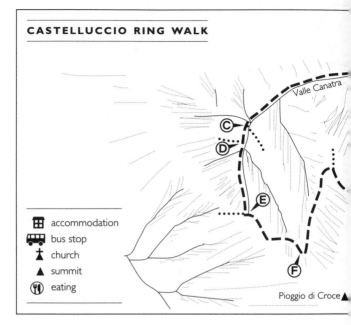

CASTELLUCCIO RING WALK

Valle Canatra

accommodation
bus stop
church
summit
eating

Pioggio di Croce ▲

The Valle Canatra is to your right as you walk. After you've turned into the narrower part of the valley (30–45 minutes from the start) the gravel path gives out and forks into two grassy tracks. Take the right-hand one (which will become slightly more defined) **B**.

The path will soon begin to ascend gently, with a grassy slope to the right and a wooded slope to the left. About ½ hour from the fork at **B**, it climbs up into woods alongside a dry stream bed, and then it curves away from it to the right **C**. About 30 m from here, a track turns off to the right **D**, going steeply up into the woods. Ignore this.

Continue straight on, coming out of the woods along a grassy path flanked by gentle slopes on both sides. At the top of this very gentle ascent you intersect with a deeply rutted track. Take this, leftwards **E**.

This area is a great picnic spot, with shade and lovely

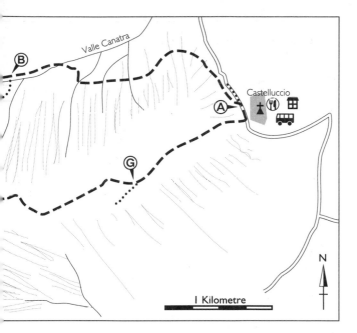

views. If you climb to the crest of the hilltop (Poggio di Croce), you'll get views across a wide valley to snow-capped peaks.

As you walk, you'll see tracks branching off towards the crest of Poggio di Croce, but continue on the main track. In a few minutes the path curves sharply around to the left **F** and you begin the very gradual descent back to Castelluccio. The path is very easy to follow.

About 45 minutes after **F**, the path ends at a T-junction with a dirt road, and a view over the Piano Grande and surrounding mountains. Go left on the dirt road **G**, which leads very soon into Castelluccio.

31 | TWO-DAY SIBILLINI WALK

If you're in good physical shape, and find the prospect of a strenuous but exhilarating two-day walk through some of the wildest scenery in Europe enticing, then this is an adventure you shouldn't miss.

Forca di Presta is about 10 km from Castelluccio, and if you have a car it's worth driving out there just to look round even if you're not doing the walk. The ride there along the Piano Grande, is stunning, and the sheep and the big white Maremma sheep dogs (many of whom appear to be out of work) are a great sight under the colourful wings of the hang-gliders. (If you don't have a car, you should be able to hitch a ride from Castelluccio, or the crossroads 2 km below it, pretty easily.)

The Rifugio degli Alpini in Forca di Presta is a well-run little mountain refuge where you should stay, especially if you don't have a car, as you'll need to start early in the morning. It's a very bare-bones lodging, but it's worth staying the night there for the sound of the howling wind alone.

Rising steeply from the Rifugio degli Alpini, the trail climbs the wind-battered flank of Monte Vettore. Our route veers away a little short of the summit, but on a clear day both the Adriatic and Tyrrhenian seas are visible from it. Descending into the crater-like valley brings you to the curious double pool of the Lago di Pilato (see p. 313) glinting among the barren stones at the bottom. The lake is home to a rare and protected species of shellfish, so swimming is not allowed. Look for the sinister devil-like profile formed by the cliffs on the far side of the lake.

From here the walk is mostly downhill through the

lovely harebell-covered moorland, with beech woods and, towards the end, a rather difficult descent down a steep slope of scree, crossing the border of the Marches to the small village of Foce.

'Mountain resort' seems a grandiose description of this mysterious, rather other-worldly and nearly deserted little village but, judging from the numbers of tents in the meadows approaching it, that seems to be its main function. At any rate, there's a hotel here, with a restaurant,

where you can recoup your energy for the next day's equally arduous (and somewhat longer) hike back across the mountains and down into Castelluccio. This takes you up the steep shingle path known as Il Canale and into thick woods from which you emerge at the high pasture called Il Laghetto, bounded by a terrific, forbidding wall of sheer-looking mountain ridges. The path – reasonably well marked by CAI up here – leads you through a remote, craggy landscape dominated by the triangular rocky peak of Sasso Borghese, and over the ridge, where you'll see Castelluccio in the distance below you. Climbing down, you'll come to the Rifugio Capanna Ghezzi, where you can stay if you've had the foresight to get the key from the CAI office in Perugia. Otherwise it's another 4–5 km back to Castelluccio, primarily on rudimentary dirt roads, but the occasional adventurous car may offer a hitching opportunity if you want it.

This is serious hiking country. The winds can be formidable at the higher elevations and the weather can change rapidly.

Bring a windcheater or sweater on this walk even in high summer; in other seasons wrap accordingly.

Our map tries to take account of the disparity between CAI paths marked on the official hiking maps, and actual paths on the ground, *but you should not embark on this walk without a hiking map*.

Food

If you've got a car you'd be better off eating at La Taverna, but the *rifugio* at Forca di Presta will prepare a simple evening meal and provide you with snacks for breakfast if you're planning to leave at the crack of dawn. The restaurant in Foce serves reasonable pastas and grilled meats. The food is substantial, if not exactly gourmet, and the atmosphere is friendly.

LOGISTICS

**FORCA DI PRESTA TO
FOCE AND FOCE TO
CASTELLUCCIO,** about
5 hours each day

🚌 Transport
Ⓜ Maps, guidebooks and
   trail info
🍽 Eating
🏨 Accommodation
ⓘ Miscellaneous info

🚌

**TO CASTELLUCCIO/FORCA
DI PRESTA**

To Castelluccio: see p. 340.
From Castelluccio to Forca di
Presta: if you haven't got a car,
you can hitch a ride from
Castelluccio (or the crossroads
about 2 km below it). You could
even walk the 10 km or so if you
wanted to, the day before you
begin this walk. Check with SSIT
(tel. 0743-212211) – there may
be a bus.

**RETURN FROM
CASTELLUCCIO**

See p. 340 for transport between
Castelluccio and Norcia

Ⓜ
See p. 340.

🍽
For Castelluccio, see pp. 340–1;
for Foce, see below.

🏨
For Castelluccio, see p. 342

FORCA DI PRESTA
Rifugio degli Alpini
Tel. 0736-809278
Open every day roughly
mid-June to mid-September, and
on Saturday and Sunday at
various other times of the year.
At times when the *rifugio* isn't
open, you can try contacting
them as follows: A. Ruffini,
Pretare, 12, 63043 Arquata del
Tronto (Ascoli Piceno); tel.
0736-809590.

It's also possible to stay further
afield if you have a car. See p. 341.

FOCE
Taverna Rifugio della Montagna
Tel. 0736-856327

ⓘ
Local CAI: CAI Perugia, Via della
Gabbia 9, 06100 Perugia;

tel. 075-5730334. Open Tuesday   CAI Ascoli Piceno, Corso
and Friday evenings, 6.30–8.   Mazzini 81, 63100 Ascoli Piceno

---

FORCA DI PRESTA TO FOCE

From the Rifugio degli Alpini at Forca di Presta, walk down the road north towards the mountains.

Take the path at the base of the mountains, where the road T-junctions with the road from Castelluccio **A**. You can see the path as it crosses the hills from the roads below.

There are old red marks along parts of the trail. The wind can give you quite a battering along here.

After 1½ hours climbing, you'll arrive at Rifugio Tito Zilioli, which is a shelter with a bench, not much more. The shelter is badly littered, having become, as the old CAI plaque posted there warned, a testament to man's stupidity.

From Rifugio Tito Zilioli to the NE the big peak is Monte Vettore and there's a path to it if you want to climb it.

Otherwise, head north over the ridge/hillock (to the left as you stand facing the door of the *rifugio*) and drop down the grassy hillside towards the chasm, facing the big cliffs on the other side. Soon you'll see some red paint marks, an arrow, for the path, which begins again just before you come in sight of Lago di Pilato down in the valley.

When the path forks, about 1½ km (15–30 minutes) after the lake, CAI path 2 will be on the left, and CAI path 3 on the right; bear right on to 3 **B**.

The paths straggle and diverge a bit, but basically you're just following the valley line, staying on paths.

Another 45 minutes or so will bring you to a steeper

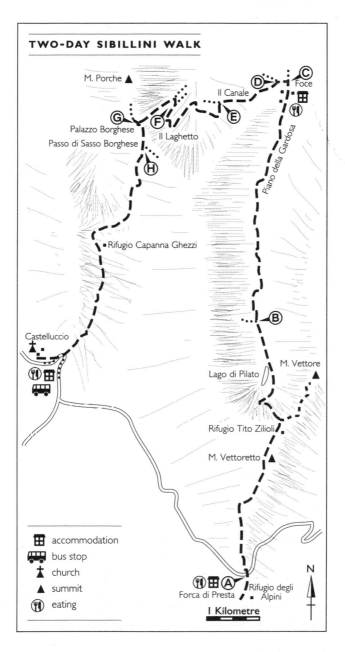

TWO-DAY SIBILLINI WALK

M. Porche ▲

Il Canale

D

C

Foce

G

F

E

Palazzo Borghese

Passo di Sasso Borghese

Il Laghetto

H

Piano della Gardosa

■ Rifugio Capanna Ghezzi

B

M. Vettore ▲

Lago di Pilato

Rifugio Tito Zilioli ■

Castelluccio

M. Vettoretto ▲

accommodation

bus stop

church

▲ summit

eating

A

Rifugio degli Alpini

Forca di Presta

N

I Kilometre

descent into the Piano della Gardosa and Foce. (This descent is rather difficult, and you may want to take it quite slowly.)

Reaching the bottom of this descent, pass a stony area with a picnic table and some wooden-post fences. Keep on until you come to a little stone road, on which you turn left, and so into Foce.

FOCE TO CASTELLUCCIO

Continue on through Foce (i.e., heading north) on the road you entered by yesterday.

After about ½ km you'll come to a little wayside tabernacle on the left; take the path immediately beyond it, also on the left **C**.

At a fork in the path after 5 minutes, take the left fork, climbing steadily **D**. In another 5 minutes the path converges with another path coming from the left.

You are in for quite a long steep climb here, hard work on the soft shingle path. (After 10–15 minutes of steady and more or less straight climbing, another similar-sized track joins you from the right; continue straight on.)

The path enters a wood (about 30–45 minutes after leaving Foce), having been shadeless until now, and soon starts to zigzag.

When the path comes to a clearing, go on through it, ignoring a fork up to the right **E**. About 5–10 minutes later the path comes out at the high pasture of Il Laghetto, and the staggering sight of the mountain wall beyond.

From here the path climbs steeply towards the ridge, and then levels out, passing after a few hundred metres a little corrugated-iron shepherd's hut. Shortly after this you come to some metal drinking troughs **F**. Climb up to the left here, and as you come to the first clump of trees, pick up the red marks signing you up towards the Passo di Sasso Borghese. This is rather a scramble at first, and towards the top you have to keep a careful eye out for the red paint marks, but on the whole it's well signed, and as it flattens, you pick up the red and white CAI marks.

There are extremely high velocity winds up here; be careful.

Marks give out towards the top of the ridge. Simply follow the main path as it zigzags towards the top.

Just before the very top, join the path that goes *left* round the inside of the ridge **G**, towards the triangular rocky peak. You will have seen this path from below as you climbed.

As the path climbs over the ridge, bending round to the right, you'll see Castelluccio below you. Amazing craggy landscape up here; CAI signs resume.

A little below the ridge, on the Castelluccio side, the path divides: the left fork goes along the next ridge, the right, which you take, goes down **H**.

The well-marked path descends towards Castelluccio. After about 40 minutes, where the path makes a fairly marked turn to the right, following around the side of a round hill, you'll see a building below you with a path leading from it to another building with a tin roof. The latter is the Rifugio Capanna Ghezzi, run by CAI Perugia. Go down to this. From here a dirt road takes you into Castelluccio, another 4 km.

Bibliography

Ardito, Stefano, *Backpacking and Walking in Italy*, Bradt
  Publications, 1987
— *A piedi in Umbria*, Roma, Edizioni ITER, 1989
Arrighi, Antonio, and Mancinelli, Andrea, *A piedi nel
  Chianti*, Roma, Edizioni ITER, 1991
Arrighi, Antonio, and Pratesi, Roberto, *A piedi in
  Toscana*, 2 vols., Roma, Edizioni ITER, 1987
Buckley, Jonathan, Ellingham, Mark, and Jepson, Tim,
  Tuscany and Umbria, London, Rough Guides, 1994
Casoli, Curzio, *Trekking and Mountain Bike around Florence
  and Siena*, Firenze, Apice Libri, 1993
Cecconi, Giovanni, and Rensi, Stefano, *Dolce campagna,
  antiche mura*, Firenze, Ed. Libra, 1993
Facaros, Dana, and Pauls, Michael, *Cadogan Guides: Tus-
  cany, Umbria and the Marches*, London, Cadogan Books,
  1992
Guidotti, Simone, *Guida alla natura di Toscana e Umbria*,
  Milano, Mondadori, 1994
Jepson, Tim, *Wild Italy*, San Francisco, Sierra Club
  Books, 1994
Lawrence, D. H., *Etruscan Places* (first published 1932),
  New York, Viking Press; London, Penguin Books
Let's Go, Inc., *Let's Go: The Budget Guide to Italy 1993*,
  St Martin's Press, 1993
Montori, Marco, and Pellegrini, Fabio, *Sulle orme di
  Bacco*, Cortona, Editrice Grafica L'Etruria, 1991

— *Viaggio a piedi dalle Crete Senesi a Montalcino alla Val d'Orcia*, Cortona, Editrice Grafica L'Etruria, 1990

Nabhan, Gary, *Songbirds, Truffles, and Wolves*, New York and San Francisco, Pantheon Books, 1993

Panerai, Marco, *Treno natura.* Firenze, Stampa Nazionale Firenze, 1991

Root, Waverley, *The Food of Italy*, New York, Vintage Books, 1992

Spender, Matthew, *Within Tuscany*, Penguin Books, 1994

Index